DING LING'S FICTION

HARVARD EAST ASIAN SERIES 98

The Council on East Asian Studies at Harvard University, through the Fairbank Center for East Asian Research and the Japan Institute, administers research projects designed to further scholarly understanding of China, Japan, Korea, Vietnam, Inner Asia, and adjacent areas.

Ding Ling in her Peking apartment, summer 1979

DING LING'S FICTION

Ideology and Narrative in Modern Chinese Literature

Yi-tsi Mei Feuerwerker

HARVARD UNIVERSITY PRESS

Cambridge, Massachusetts

London, England

1982

Publication of this book has been aided by a grant from the Andrew W. Mellon Foundation.

Library of Congress Cataloging in Publication Data

Feuerwerker, Yi-tsi Mei,
　　Ding Ling's fiction.

　　(Harvard East Asian series; 98)
　　"Chronological list of Ding Ling's fiction": p.
　　Bibliography: p.
　　Includes index.
　　1. Ting, Ling, 1904–　　　　　 —Criticism and interpre-
tation.　　　 I. Title.　　 II. Series.
PL2747.P5Z65　　　 895.1'35　　 82-3022
ISBN 0-674-20765-3　　　　　 AACR2

To the memory of my father
Mei Kuang-ti (1890–1945)
— a lifetime dedicated to the study and teaching of literature

PREFACE

WHEN I BEGAN MY STUDY of Ding Ling some years ago, there had been no indication for over two decades as to whether she was still alive; I had every reason to believe that my efforts would be solely a matter of examining a number of literary texts. In June 1979, the very same month that I thought I had completed my manuscript, Ding Ling was officially rehabilitated by the Chinese Communist Party. Confronted with this unforeseen but gratifying resurrection, I felt impelled to go to China to meet the living person whose existence for me so far had only been implied by those fixed words on the printed page. A grant from the Committee on Scholarly Communication with the People's Republic of China made this meeting possible.

During my six-month stay in China, from March to August 1981, it was my good fortune not only to have many conversations with Ding Ling, but also to be able to, as she put it, watch her perform ("*kan wo biaoyan*") in a variety of situations. I saw her often at home in the company of her family and husband, Chen Ming, a true comrade whose support has been essential to her continuing survival as a writer. I also had the rare privilege of staying for nine days in a building adjacent to hers, in the Gulangyu Convalescent Home off the coast of Fukien where she was spending the winter. Most unexpected and rewarding of all, I was able to travel with her from July 15 to August 3 to the state farms of the Great Northern Wilderness (*beidahuang*) where she had endured her twelve years of exile and labor reform. In that unique part of China, the northeast frontier that is still being reclaimed, I was able to meet and talk with many who had known and worked with her during that most trying period of her life. On this journey and through my association with her in general I began to understand why Ding Ling is one of China's most beloved and revered authors, and why the writer in that society, so often providing an example of suffering and fortitude, is such a figure of moral authority.

But the details of Ding Ling's personal response to political vicissitudes are matters of history rather than literary analysis; they are another subject and not the one of this book, which focuses on her narrative writings. On this subject she was always gracious in answering my questions, while repeatedly and rightly emphasizing that once a work is written, it is up to others and not to the author to carry out the task of criticizing and interpreting. I have taken into account, when useful, the circumstances of the composition of some of her stories, but have not felt it necessary, as a result of our talks, to revise my analyses. Certainly I can make no claims, merely because I have met the author, to authenticity in my readings of her works.

Most of Ding Ling's fiction is not available in English. Because I could not assume a first-hand acquaintance with her stories among readers and because my approach is to work closely with the texts, I have included sizable quotations from her narratives. This experience of extensive translation has made me all too aware of the impossibility of reproducing the spirit and style of the original in another language; I have tried to be as faithful as possible in my versions even at the risk of sacrificing readability.

All attempts at literary analysis, in light of the richness of the literary works to which they address themselves, are in the end inadequate. Mine would be even poorer were it not for the assistance of many individuals and institutions. I want to thank Patrick Hanan, James Robert Hightower, Harry Levin, Kenneth DeWoskin, and John Berninghausen for patiently reading through the manuscript, and for their encouragement and suggestions. It is a pleasure to acknowledge the generous assistance of Wan Weiying and Ma Weiyi of the University of Michigan's Asia Library. They were tireless in helping me to locate materials in their library and other places.

For my six months in China I am indebted to the Committee on Scholarly Communication with the People's Republic of China and the National Endowment for the Humanities which provides it with funds. I am grateful to my sponsoring units, the Institute of Literature, more specifically the Modern Chinese Literature Research Group, of the Chinese Academy of Social Sciences in Beijing, and the Institute of Literature of the Shanghai Academy of Social Sciences. My colleagues in both places gave me unstinting help in arranging interviews with authors and publishers, introducing me to libraries, supplying me with books and periodicals, and generally easing my problems of shelter and travel.

One of my objectives in China was to read everything that Ding Ling had ever written, including hard-to-find short pieces in ephemeral periodicals or local newspapers. Another was to locate the magazine or newspaper in which each work of fiction had first appeared. Since modern Chinese writers are notorious for revising their literary texts upon republication, I wanted to check each work in its original form against later versions. This and determining the exact date and sequence of Ding Ling's stories seemed necessary in view of my concern to examine the development of her fiction. I am grateful indeed to the staffs of the following libraries for their indispensable assistance in carrying out these tasks: Peking Library, Peking University Library, Qinghua University Library, People's University Library, Shanghai Municipal Library and the Library of the Department of Chinese at Shanghai Teachers' College. This general listing of institutional names cannot convey the reality of the many individuals in the numerous units of each library who might have been mobilized to solve one bibliographic question. Nor can I list individually by name the many scholars and researchers with whom I spent some of the most stimulating hours of my life, discussing everything from the details of a particular passage of Ding Ling's to the larger issues of modern Chinese literature. I must express my gratitude to the central subject of our discussions, whose writings were the occasion of our coming together and have proved so rewarding for those engaged in studying them.

I would like to thank Donald A. Gibbs for providing the photograph of Ding Ling that is the frontispiece of this book.

Parts of Chapter 3 appeared in a different form as "The Uses of Literature: Ding Ling at Yan'an," in *Essays in Modern Chinese Literature and Literary Criticism, Papers of the Berlin Conference 1978*, ed. Wolfgang Kubin and Rudolf G. Wagner (Bochum: Studienverlag Brockmeyer, 1982). Thanks are due to the editors for permission to reprint.

On a more personal level I owe a heartfelt debt to several people without whom this study might never have been undertaken, much less completed. They include my father, Mei Kuang-ti, to whose memory I dedicate this book. Although an uncompromising critic of modern Chinese literature in the 1920s and 1930s, he shared with Ding Ling a profound belief in the bedrock role of literature in society. I am obligated more deeply than words can say to my mother, Ching-ying Lee Mei, my husband, Albert Feuerwerker, and my children, Alison and Paul. All of them, either by voicing support for my work, or perhaps more understandably, impatience at the pace of its progress, enabled me finally to get it done.

Yi-tsi Mei Feuerwerker
Residential College
The University of Michigan
May 1982

CONTENTS

DING LING'S FICTION

INTRODUCTION: THE SURVIVAL
OF A WRITER

FOR OVER TWO DECADES the writings of Ding Ling were banned in China; her name was never mentioned and the outside world had no means of knowing whether she was still alive. Histories of modern Chinese literature produced during those years gave no indication that one of its most prolific and outstanding woman writers had ever written or existed.

Ding Ling had become a nonperson in 1958 when she was expelled from the Communist Party for being a rightist and exiled to labor reform in the Great Northern Wilderness (*beidahuang*). Twenty-one years later, in June 1979, she was named a member of the Chinese People's Political Consultative Conference. Although this is a symbolic body with little actual power, her appointment was the first clear signal of official rehabilitation and a complete reversal of the party's former verdict against her. She was of course by no means the only previously ostracized literary figure to be reinstated under the liberal policies set in motion by the death of Mao Zedong in 1976. But her particular reappearance, all the more dramatic after such a long period of invisibility, seemed uniquely in character and consistent with the pattern of her life, for Ding Ling has been one of the great survivors in modern Chinese literary history. Not only has she survived the dangers of war, exile, hard labor, and imprisonment by the governments of both right and left; she has also endured as a creative and practicing writer. Throughout a lifetime of suffering the full range of persecutions possible amidst the turbulent politics of the past half-century, Ding Ling has remained tenacious in her commitment to the literary enterprise, adapting resourcefully whenever necessary and as long as feasible to the radically changing conditions under which that enterprise has had to be carried out.

Until the time of the antirightist campaign her literary career had spanned three decades. She began writing in the late 1920s as a member of the May Fourth generation and continued after the Communist Party established its power over China and over all literary activities. Although many other May Fourth writers lived on into the 1950s, only a

1

few, very few, continued to be productive. And while some, like Mao Dun, similarly rose to eminence in the cultural hierarchy of the People's Republic, hardly anyone received the kind of acclaim that Ding Ling enjoyed, however short-lived it turned out to be. In 1951 she had been awarded the Stalin prize (second place) in literature for her novel on land reform, *The Sun Shines on the Sanggan River*. Whether or not the Stalin prize is in itself a guarantee of aesthetic excellence, the award was a mark of the high esteem and literary recognition she had attained under China's socialist regime.

Ding Ling's choice of land reform as a subject shows above all what a long ideological road she had traveled from the time she first startled the literary scene with short stories that were almost exclusively concerned with young women undergoing crises of love, sex, and identity. Critics who argue that the changes between the early and later writings are simply so many symptoms of artistic decline often take it for granted that political commitment automatically reduces literary quality. Such an assumption is implied in the introduction to one anthology of modern Chinese fiction, which contains two stories by Ding Ling from "before" and "after": "Compared to 'The Diary of Miss Sophia,' this story [One Certain Night] shows what effect the Communist political conversion could have on the gifts of a creative writer."[1] But before her political conversion Ding Ling was still a young and inexperienced artist. It is not so obvious that her "gifts as a creative writer" reached their highest development in the stories written during that first brief three-to-four-year period.

To say this is not to dismiss the constraints under which her later writing very visibly labors. Both during the early 1930s, when she chose to embrace the Communist cause, and later, as she submitted to the party's increasingly harsh literary policies, politics is a conspicuous defining factor in Ding Ling's writing. It might be tempting to speculate how far Ding Ling would have developed as a writer if her life had not been so fatefully driven by political events, but history did not leave her many alternatives. Indeed, it is precisely her continuous effort to go on writing even as political upheavals and ideological shifts kept narrowing the terms for literary production that makes her such an exemplary object for study. My first concern in studying her fiction will not be with the loaded, perhaps ultimately unresolvable, issue of the relation between aesthetic quality and political control; the place to begin is with the works themselves and, even as politics plays its all-important role, with a close look at her performance as a writer of fiction.

The unique interest of Ding Ling's oeuvre lies in the available record of response — and resistance — to political pressure that is revealed in her works. The many aspects of narrative — selection of theme and subject

matter, concepts of character, notions of causality and plot, use of setting and metaphor, style and language, choice of narrative mode — all reflect changes in the ideological context within which she wrote. As much
as the momentous events of her life, the literary works she produced
dramatize, on all levels of the text, the succession of creative dilemmas
confronting the modern Chinese writer. The main focus of this study,
then, is Ding Ling's fiction as it undergoes distinct phases of development
and exemplifies the ways in which ideology influences narrative practice.

Certain accidents of history and biography, joined to a personality
and temperament that constantly placed her at the dead center of what
was going on, have conspired to make Ding Ling into the writer she is.
We can observe the various operations of ideology on the text as she
moves from one stage to another in her life and work, yet there are large
areas of her experiences about which little definitive information is available. Until the official line toward literature and art in China is stabilized,
any modern Chinese writer (except Lu Xun) is, at least potentially, too
controversial to be the object of sustained scholarly attention. No sub-
stantive critical biography of a modern writer has appeared in China
during the last thirty years. In the case of Ding Ling, the dust over certain
political controversies in which she was involved will have to settle before a satisfactory biography can be constructed. What little we know
about her comes from diverse sources, each with inherent biases and
limitations. The most comprehensive account of her early life is the one
she gave (through an interpreter) to Helen Snow, who visited Yanan in
1937.[2] Reminiscences of Ding Ling as a young writer were written by
grieving friends — who were at the same time not unaware of the sales
value of gossip — after her arrest and presumed execution in 1933.[3] Information about the Yanan years, 1936 to 1946, comes mainly from the reports of visiting foreign journalists. For them she was a celebrity whom it
was mandatory to interview.[4] These reports were followed by the
abusive attacks of the antirightist campaign of 1957, and two subsequent
decades of silence. The interviews with journalists after her rehabilitation
provide but a few tantalizing glimpses of twenty years spent in exile and
prison. Some of her essays since 1979 are reminiscences and laments for
friends whose deaths she learned about upon her release. These occasionally contain information about her own life. The brief biographical
sketch that follows is meant to provide a general framework for the
analysis of Ding Ling's fiction through its successive phases. More detailed references to incidents in her life will be made when necessary as
the works themselves are discussed.

The uncertainty over Ding Ling's biography begins with the date of
her birth, probably in 1904.[5] The place of her birth, however, is

definitely known and significant, for she was from Hunan province, the home of many of China's revolutionary leaders. The child was named Jiang Bingzhi—Ding Ling is only the pseudonym she made up for herself later. Her once wealthy gentry family of Linli county had then entered into a period of precipitous decline, producing, like many such families, its share of degenerate males. Ding Ling's father was one. He had for a time studied law in Japan, but did little with his foreign education after his return. His daughter, who was three when he died, remembers him primarily as a lover of horses and a man of magnanimous spirit. Ding Ling's mother was a more important influence in her life. She must be regarded as an outstanding member of that remarkable generation of prerevolutionary mothers, so prevalent in the biographies of leading Chinese figures in the early decades of the twentieth century. It was the role of these mothers to inspire or conspire with their famous children, even as they were growing up within the traditional family, in the resolute break with the past.

When her husband died, leaving her with a host of debts, a daughter of three, and an infant son, Mrs. Jiang moved back to Changde, her home town, and took the bold step of enrolling in one of the newly founded normal schools for women. She continued her education in Changsha and began teaching, first at an elementary school in Taoyuan and then in Changde. Never in robust health, Ding Ling's younger brother died not long after this move. Ding Ling followed her mother about, pursuing her education at various schools, and for a time stayed in the home of her maternal uncle. There she discovered an attic filled with old books and translations of foreign novels that she read steadily to pass her days of loneliness.[6]

When the "tide of May Fourth splashed against the small town" of Taoyuan, Ding Ling became involved in student demonstrations, speeches, and meetings. Impetuously she followed the example of those who had cut their hair and, conspicuously braidless, became the target of jeers and scorn. She taught in a night school for the poor when she was barely taller than the desk on the platform, acquiring the nickname "little teacher" (zaizai xiansheng).[7]

In 1919 Ding Ling transferred to the progressive Zhounan Girls School in Changsha. Her literature teacher, whom "all considered a saintly person," used articles from the journal Xinqingnian (New Youth), which advocated literary revolution, as teaching material, and introduced his students to modern vernacular literature and to foreign authors. She recalls that Daudet's "The Last Lesson" and Maupassant's "The Two Fishermen" were among her favorite stories.[8] The teacher also encouraged Ding Ling to write. Two of her poems were published in the local paper he edited and she was "tremendously stimulated to see them in print and couldn't sleep at night afterward."[9] When John Dewey and

Bertrand Russell passed through Changsha, she went to their lectures, though they "did not make much of an impression" on her.[10] Young as she was, this precocious activist was leading her school in turbulent demonstrations against the Hunan Provincial Council, demanding equality for women and their right to inherit property.[11]

The following year, together with five other schoolmates, (one of them Yang Kaihui, who later became Mao Zedong's first wife), Ding Ling entered the Yuyun Boys School. This first attempt at coeducation scandalized the provincial capital, but she soon gave it up in favor of the even more drastic step of leaving home and going to Shanghai to study in the Pingmin nüxiao (People's Girls School), founded by Mao Dun, Li Da, Chen Duxiu, Liu Shaoqi, and other leftist intellectuals. Meanwhile, with her mother's support, she had broken off her engagement to a cousin, refusing in a stormy scene to submit to the pressure of her uncle, the head of the family. She published an article without mentioning her uncle by name but denouncing "the whole social stratum to which he belonged." It was her "first taste of the power of the pen." Opposed even more now by the rest of her family, she left for Shanghai, "an exiled insurrectionist,"[12] in the company of her school friend Wang Jianhong. Thus when she was about sixteen, the major themes of Ding Ling's life were already strikingly evident: iconoclasm, feminism, political activism, and a commitment to literature.

Soon Ding Ling became dissatisfied with the school in Shanghai and the two friends decided to educate themselves, sporadically studying literature and painting, hobnobbing with anarchist groups, and generally living an impoverished but emancipated life. After a short stay in Nanking, Ding Ling enrolled in the Literature Department of Shanghai University, enjoying especially the lectures by Mao Dun on the *Odyssey* and the *Iliad*. However her "best teacher was Qu Qiubai," the Marxist literary theorist who had just returned from the Soviet Union, and with whom she had talks on literature and society that ranged over "past and present, east and west." To help her "appreciate quickly the beauty of Pushkin's language" he taught her to read the poems in the original. Wang Jianhong married Qu in early 1924, but died shortly afterward of tuberculosis.[13]

Ding Ling decided to go to Peking University, but arriving too late for the entrance exams, she audited classes under Lu Xun and continued to read a great deal of Western literature. Then she met Hu Yepin, a struggling young poet, a "rare 'person,' . . . one with the most perfect qualities, yet a piece of totally uncut, unpolished jade."[14] Soon they were living together. In his *Ji Ding Ling* (Reminiscences of Ding Ling) Shen Congwen has given us a sensitive, almost idyllic picture of the life of poverty, young love, and literary aspirations led by his two friends in

Xishan (Western Hills) outside Peking. This book by Shen, a dedicated and prolific writer himself, tells us most of what we know about Ding Ling during the years 1924–1930, and particularly about how she decided to become a writer.

While the avowed struggling young writers Shen Congwen and Hu Yepin talked and dreamed of launching their own journal to get out of the clutches of callous publishers, Ding Ling at first saw herself on the sidelines of their enterprise as a future bookkeeper or proofreader. To make a living she tried to find employment as a governess or private secretary, but suddenly she got the strange idea, which was initially taken as a joke, of going to Shanghai to become a movie actress. "It doesn't look as if you'll make it with your writing, Pin . . . by the time there's a book store willing to publish your book, I'll already be a star."[15] But it was Ding Ling's venture into films that failed — a failure, however, which she was able to turn into a literary success: the disillusioning encounter with the film industry became the basis of her first work of fiction. In December 1927 the publication of "Mengke" (Mengke), a story about a sensitive, innocent young girl victimized by a corrupt society as she became a movie star, brilliantly launched the career of this unknown writer. A few months later, with the appearance of "Shafei nüshi de riji" (The Diary of Miss Sophie), an unprecedentedly frank portrayal of the contradictory sexual feelings of a tubercular, high-strung young woman, Ding Ling was well on her way to becoming one of China's most celebrated — and in the eyes of some, notorious — women writers.

But the center of intellectual and literary life was shifting away from Peking and in the spring of 1928, as Ding Ling recalled, "we all went to Shanghai . . . a great many of our hopes still placed in literature."[16] The three friends, Ding Ling, Hu Yepin, and Shen Congwen, published two short-lived journals but these were only "romantic reckless adventures."[17] They also attempted to be their own publishers. In the preface to their first book, a volume of twenty-two poems by Hu Yepin, Ding Ling referred to their publishing venture, the Honghei Congshu (Red and Black Series), as one put together by "several of us, both poor and foolish, who are unwilling to put up with so much humiliation from sordid merchants, and have scrimped on living expenses with the idea of rectifying this profit-obsessed society."[18] Indeed the clever people were already laughing at them for making their first book a volume of poetry. At first it was exciting to ride around the streets just to see their own periodicals displayed in bookstore windows, but reformist indignation and literary idealism were not sufficient to sustain their various publishing enterprises. It took less than a year before they all collapsed, leaving the young people with the worry of how to repay their debts.[19] For a brief period Hu Yepin took a teaching position in Jinan, Shandong, but got into trouble with the authorities because of his radical views and was forced to return quickly to Shanghai. At that time the Kuomintang's persecution of writers and the concomitant radicalization of literature were both intensifying. In Shanghai, because of its foreign settlements and less than totally efficient police force, a political opposition was able to exist with some degree of impunity. Hu Yepin joined the League of Left-Wing Writers when it was formed in March 1930. He became a member of its executive committee and chairman of the committee on worker-peasant-soldier literature. Ding Ling herself was not yet able to "see very well the relation between revolution and literature."[20] Hu Yepin "was progressing, flying ahead; I approved of him, I was also progressing, but I was crawling."[21] While he was away at meetings, she stayed home writing stories on the conflict between love and revolution. Her first child, their son, was born in November 1930.

The day after the birth Hu Yepin informed Ding Ling that he had applied for membership in the Communist Party and had been chosen to attend the First Soviet Representative Congress in Jiangxi, to be held in February. A few days before he was to leave, on January 17, 1931, he was arrested while attending a party meeting at the Eastern hotel. Although a great deal is still obscure about the case, it is probable that infighting between party factions led to the betrayal of this meeting by the rival group to the Kuomintang police.[22] Along with twenty-three or twenty-four alleged Communists, Hu Yepin was executed in Longhua prison on February 7. The brutality of the summary execution aroused wide protest both within China and abroad, and the Five Martyrs (four other young writers were among the victims) soon became one of the most powerful emblems in the history of literary persecution.

In his *Reminiscences of Ding Ling* Shen Congwen gives a detailed account of those harrowing weeks. After absorbing the shock of Hu Yepin's arrest, Ding Ling had to go into hiding with their two-month-old baby, and in that precarious situation engage in frantic maneuvers to gain his release. At first it was almost impossible to obtain reliable information about where he had been taken. She found that out only when Hu Yepin contrived to send Shen Congwen a message, for which they had to pay the carrier handsomely. The same prison messenger later told her how to attempt a visit. On the designated day Shen Congwen accompanied Ding Ling to Longhua prison. She carried a bundle of food and clothing for her husband, and was dressed in a short grey cotton jacket, "looking just like a country girl earning twenty-eight cents a day in a textile mill.[23]

From the early morning they stood in the cold wind among the crowd of six hundred would-be visitors, all waiting anxiously to see who would be allowed to register, who finally would be allowed to go in. By late afternoon they managed to make their way through the series of gates and guards to join the waiting crowd inside. But they did not get a visiting permit. The only thing they could do, a warden told them, was to give him a sum of money "to give to the prisoner"; for that they could be allowed a glimpse of Hu Yepin passing at a distance. From the small iron door at the other end of the room they heard the sound of metal shackles, and as Ding Ling called out his name, Hu Yepin stopped a moment, gave a joyous wave with his two manacled hands, and immediately disappeared behind the door. The news of his death did not leak out until several days after the execution.

What impressed Shen Congwen tremendously throughout that terrible time was Ding Ling's fortitude. When the death of her husband was confirmed, "she did not, before any acquaintance, shed a single tear."[24] "She was a woman full of feeling . . . but during those heartbreaking days, she looked after the child, expended her energy and emotions on various bothersome tasks, never letting anyone see that she was weak."[25]

Ding Ling decided that the only way she could continue to work and make a living in Shanghai was to place the child in the care of her own mother in Hunan. Shen Congwen accompanied her on the three-day trip, and worried constantly that Ding Ling's self-control would break down under the strain of pretending that Hu Yepin was still alive in Shanghai so as to conceal from the old grandmother what had actually happened.

The effect of her husband's martyrdom was to reinforce Ding Ling's commitment to the socialist cause. Back in Shanghai she became more active in the League of Left-Wing Writers and assumed the editorship of its literary periodical, *Beidou* (Big Dipper). In the first issue, published in September 1931, began the serialization of her long story "Shui" (Flood), which depicts the suffering that drove the peasants to rebellion during the widespread floods in China in 1931. It was hailed by Communist critics as a landmark example of a new proletarian fiction, and represented for Ding Ling a radically new departure in both subject matter and technique. She became a member of the Communist Party in 1932.

Beidou, outstanding among the many ephemeral leftist periodicals of the time, was subject to much harassment by the Kuomintang authorities and peremptorily closed down in July 1932 after seven issues. Ding Ling continued to write while living in hiding in the International Settlement. She began a novel based on her mother's life but had completed just about one-third of it when she was suddenly kidnapped by Kuomintang agents at her home on May 4, 1933. She has spoken of her suspicions that Feng Da, the man she was then living with, may have betrayed her, but his role in the kidnapping as well as the whole story of her detention is still quite unclear.[26] Rumors of her execution inspired reminiscences, memoirs, and eulogies as well as new collections of her works, and added to her fame. She was moved by her jailers to Nanking and confined in various houses for a period of three years. A second child, a daughter, was born during this time, and her mother came to stay with her, while Feng Da became very ill with tuberculosis. The main purpose of her house arrest apparently was to persuade her to renounce the Communist Party and place her talents at the service of the Kuomintang.[27] Although she refused, the conditions of detention seem to have ameliorated somewhat over time. She first managed a short trip to Peking, and then in September 1936 she escaped to Shanghai, whence she proceeded to Xian. At the end of October she set out for Baoan in Shaanxi province, which at that time was the headquarters of the Communist Party. For the last stage of her journey she disguised herself as a soldier from the Northeast and traveled through treacherous territory for nine days, on foot and, for the first time in her life, on horseback. Upon arrival she was welcomed as a heroine, Mao Zedong honoring her with a reception and later with two poems written especially for her.[28]

Ding Ling soon immersed herself in the activities of the Communist-controlled Border Regions. She visited the front, traveled with the troops, served as vice-director of the Political Department of the Red Army Guard Unit, and became active in the Women's League and in the Literature and Art Association. When the War of Resistance against Japan broke out in 1937, she organized and directed the Northwest Front Service Corps, spending several months with her troupe on the road from Yanan to Taiyuan performing plays and songs in the small villages of Shanxi and Shaanxi to spread the message of uniting to fight Japan. One important member of the troupe was the young writer Chen Ming; he and Ding Ling were married in 1942.

Ding Ling's experience of taking art directly to the people, a public that contrasted sharply with the sophisticated urban readers of her earlier fiction, demonstrated new possibilities about the uses of art. It was an issue that was becoming urgent in Yanan. This poor, isolated ancient town, which became the capital of Chinese communism after January 1937, was the unlikely base where the party worked out the revolutionary techniques that were to carry it to power some twelve years later. The controversy in Yanan, which directly involved Ding Ling, was over the proper role of art and literature within this extraordinary total effort. While Ding Ling's fiction at the time emphasized heroism and the positive outcome of struggle, she did not believe that a generally affirmative stance toward collective goals need preclude all possibility of criticism. On this issue (the "bright versus the dark side" controversy) she came into conflict with the Communist Party during the 1942 rectification movement. As editor of the literary page of the party's newspaper, *Jiefang ribao* (Liberation Daily), Ding Ling had called for critical essays (*zawen*). Her own contribution, 'Sanbajie you gan" (Thoughts on March Eight), published in 1942, discussed the special plight of women even in the liberated areas. An earlier story, "Zai yiyuanzhong" (In the Hospital), had portrayed the contradictory feelings of the main character as she finds that the new revolutionary situation fails to live up to her expectations. Other writers who had, like Ding Ling, been drawn to Yanan for ideological reasons likewise undertook to criticize in their writings the dark side of the Yanan reality: the social inequities and the restrictions on expression. These writers argued that literature had special responsibilities. Mao Zedong's answer to these critics was given in his historic "Talks at the Yanan Forum on Literature and Art" on May 2 and May 23, 1942. By explicitly stating that literature and art were subordinate to revolutionary needs, he not only rebutted their criticism but also clearly asserted the party's control over all cultural activities. While the principles enunciated in the "Talks at the Yanan Forum" were interpreted with varying degrees of stringency over the years, the limits within which the writer could practice his vocation had been defined.

The 1942 Yanan rectification movement, a prototype of the thought-remolding campaigns that were to punctuate the history of the Chinese Communist Party for the next thirty-five years, was relatively mild. Its public example and target of focused attack, an essential feature of all subsequent campaigns, was limited to only one person, the relatively unknown writer Wang Shiwei, even though all the authors who had written critically of the Yanan situation were reprimanded and led to admit their mistakes. Ding Ling's self-criticism, particularly of the negative bias in her article on women, was published as part of her denunciation of Wang Shiwei. Removed from her position as literary editor of *Jiefang ribao*, she spent the next two years in study and reform work at the party school and in the countryside. In early 1944 she was assigned to work in the Border Regions Cultural Association. After this two-year hiatus she returned to writing under the new guidelines, producing a series of reportage sketches based on model characters and uplifting real-life incidents.

In July 1946 Ding Ling took part in the land reform movement the radical phase of which had been initiated by the party after the end of the Sino-Japanese War, in Huailai and Zhuolu (in southern Chahar). Her experiences there and elsewhere later provided the basis for her major novel, *The Sun Shines on the Sanggan River*. Published in 1948, this work on land reform explored the genuine fictional possibilities of an ideologically circumscribed form. It won for her considerable acclaim (including the Stalin prize in 1951), but was to be her last published work of fiction for almost three decades.

When the People's Republic of China was established, Ding Ling was one of the most prominent members in its cultural hierarchy. At the inauguration ceremonies in July 1949 of the All-China Federation of Literature and Art Circles, she gave a special address and was appointed a member of the standing committee. She became vice-chairman of the All-China Union of Literary Workers. More important in terms of influence was her editorship of *Wenyi bao* (Literary Gazette), the journal of the Federation of Literature and Art, and later her deputy chief editorship of *Renmin wenxue* (People's Literature), the journal of the Union of Literary Workers. Under the sponsorship of the party she organized and headed the Central Literary Institute in Peking, a training school for writers. Ding Ling also held other positions in the party, at one time heading the Literature Bureau of the party's Propaganda Department. For the first time in her life she traveled abroad, as a member or leader of official delegations to various congresses in Hungary, Czechoslovakia, and the Soviet Union.[29]

Her writings from 1949 to 1957 include little fiction and consist mainly of essays, addresses, travel reports—generally pieces written in connection with official functions or produced for public occasions.[30] On the whole they follow the party line of the given moment, yet one detects a continuing sense of concern, even of urgency, in her statements about literature. Repeatedly she addresses the question of how one can produce a good piece of literary work. Although she certainly did not consider literature an autonomous, self-contained activity and accepted the auxiliary role assigned to it in the overall revolutionary scheme, she did maintain the dedicated writer's belief in literature's distinct nature and value, which under the political circumstances were becoming increasingly difficult to define. During the antirightist campaign her downfall came when she was accused of setting up literature against the party leadership.

The history of political campaigns against writers in the People's Republic of China is complex and painful to contemplate. Factional struggles and feuds, some of which can be traced back to the 1930s in Shanghai—when the habit of vituperative debate and adroit quoting out of context seems to have established itself—gave the main continuing impetus to the campaigns. Such campaigns provided chances for rivals to take over editorships of important periodicals and became the means for relative unknowns to propel themselves into high positions in the cultural bureaucracy. Of course there were also genuine ideological disagreements or uncertainties over the place of such refractory and extravagant things as literature and art under conditions of scarcity. When the margin between starvation and economic viability is as narrow as it is in China, how much latitude should be given to any literature that cannot clearly demonstrate its usefulness for the achievement of collective goals? Utilitarianism and philistine moralism, which historically have been the enemies of art everywhere, could now find in revolutionary China a powerful ally in fundamentalist political ideology. In the case of Ding Ling, the particular mix of motives was reinforced by the opportunity to make an example of a prestigious writer.

Ding Ling herself played an active role in certain of the tamer early literary campaigns. In 1951 she led the criticism of Xiao Yemu's story "Women fufu zhi jian" (Between Husband and Wife),[31] and charged literary journals with lacking clear political and ideological direction.[32] But her position in the cultural hierarchy had begun to weaken; the decline became evident in 1953 with the reorganization of the Central Literary Institute and her replacement as deputy chief editor of *Renmin wenxue*. Next year a long investigation of *Wenyi bao* began. Even though she had resigned as editor in 1952, the journal had been in the hands of her close colleagues Feng Xuefeng and Chen Qixia. In 1955 and 1956 the Writers' Union convened meetings and passed resolutions to condemn her, but these were not made public.[33]

Her fall was brought about by the antirightist drive launched abruptly in 1957, during the relatively relaxed period of the Hundred Flowers. Beginning rather mildly with criticism of the Chinese Democratic League, the campaign moved on with ferocity toward its real targets—the veteran revolutionary writers Ding Ling and her colleagues Feng Xuefeng, Chen Qixia, and Ai Qing. The intense period of the campaign lasted for three and a half months, from June to September of 1957. Meetings were convened by the party committee of the Writers' Union to denounce Ding Ling, but as the campaign moved into high gear the meetings were enlarged to include people from the Propaganda Department, the Ministry of Culture, and other groups; the final meeting was attended by 1,350 people. In August news of the struggle against the "Ding-Chen antiparty clique" was made public, the signal for the onset of nationwide reports and accusations in newspapers and magazines. Ding Ling was criticized for sexual immorality, professional failings, her superiority complex, and ideological shortcomings; for maligning the peasant masses in her fiction; and for traitorous conspiracy against the party. The records of the criticism meetings against her, during which a total of 140 people spoke out, have not been made public, but from fragmentary revelations the impression is that she refused to admit to the charges against her, and that the self-criticisms she offered were not considered acceptable. Perhaps because Ding Ling held out more stubbornly than the other "rightists" and did not seem to be sufficiently penitent, her punishment was relatively severe. She was expelled from the party and removed from her positions; her works were prohibited and her rights as a writer and citizen taken away. In 1958 she went to do labor reform in the Great Northern Wilderness where she remained for twelve years. The scanty facts about her life in and since exile have emerged piecemeal mainly in interviews with various journalists; much less has been revealed about what it was like to live through that unimaginable time.[34]

In the Great Northern Wilderness she was sent to work on a large state farm in the Tangyuan district of Heilongjiang province, and acquired much expertise in raising poultry. A year later she was appointed cultural teacher, responsible for culture, recreation, and political study in the livestock brigade. She produced *yangge ju* (plays based on folk songs and dances), set up story-telling sessions, and put out wall newspapers, which she enlivened with her newly developed skills in calligraphy and illustration. In 1960 she went to Peking to attend the Third National Writers' Congress, which she was permitted to address in a written statement.

With the onset of the Cultural Revolution her "days of fear" began. By then she had been moved to Baoquanling State Farm for over a year. Having been labeled a rightist, she was open to attack by anyone carried away by ideological fanaticism during this period of near anarchy. Starting in late 1966 her home, a thatched hut seven meters square to which she had been moved, was raided dozens of times by groups of Red Guards; all her "long and short manuscripts, diaries, notes, materials, any scrap of paper with a single word"[35] were taken away and irretrievably lost. Her attempts to save her writings by burying them or caching them with friends, even by sending them to the Public Security Office as "criminal evidence" against herself, were all unsuccessful. She also suffered much physical abuse during struggle-and-criticism sessions, and was injured by kickings and beatings. In 1968 she was shut in the "cow shed" (*niupeng*), the place of detention that each unit set aside for any of the members whom the collective — or rather, those momentarily in power — wished to punish. She was released ten months later and sent to perform menial labor under the "supervision of the revolutionary masses." Taken to Peking in 1970, she was held in solitary confinement for five years in the notorious Qincheng prison for political prisoners. For fear of losing her power of speech in her isolation she often recited or sang to herself. After a period she was allowed reading material and thus read through the works of Marx, Lenin, and Stalin. Only upon her release in 1975 did she learn where her husband Chen Ming had been all this time — in the same prison, one cell away. The two were then sent to a mountain village outside Changzhi, in Shaanxi. There she was given a monthly allowance and freedom to move within the commune. After three years she was allowed to return to Peking.

Official rehabilitation in 1979 finally permitted Ding Ling to resume her career as a writer. The ban on her books was lifted, and both new and old works could be made available to the public. But despite prolonged periods of enforced abstention she had continued to write all along when she could, even under the most trying conditions, even when utterly without hope of publication. One long piece of reportage on a model heroine of the Northeast reclamation area, "Du Wanxiang" (Du Wanxiang), which she had written in 1966, was destroyed in the course of a raid during the Cultural Revolution. The rewritten version, published in July 1979, was her first literary work to appear since 1956. After a writer has lost over twenty years of her creative life, the poignant but inevitable question must be, how much time is there left? Labor in the harsh climate of the Northern Wilderness, physical maltreatment, and the five years of solitary imprisonment have exacted their toll, exacerbating the problems of ill health and old age.

During an interview in June 1979, a reporter for the *Guangming ribao* (Guangming Daily) found Ding Ling preparing an edition of her selected works for republication. She talked about her plans for writing; there was a great deal she wanted to write but "age might not let me." Having finished "Du Wanxiang", a twenty-thousand-word piece, she was writing a longer work, *Zai yanhan de rizili* (During the Coldest Days) — a sequel, some thirty years later, to *The Sun Shines on the Sanggan River*.[36] Meticulous with numbers, she estimated that she had already written over 100,000 words — concern over her health led her to compress the originally projected eighty chapters into fifty — and expected the book to be about 500,000 words long. "If I can finish this long work, and write a few short pieces, that will probably be just about it." A physical ailment required her to stand up and walk around after an hour or two of sitting, but she would not allow it to hinder the writing. The interview concludes with a portrait of the incorrigible writer at work:

> She is, after all, over seventy. To avoid interruption of her literary ideas and to keep on with the writing, Chen Ming [her husband] thought of a device: a five-ply board suspended from the neck to form a writing board. Thus she can write while seated in a chair, she can write also while standing up. Such was the image this reporter saw of Ding Ling at work — she was sitting in a wicker chair, leaning against that specially devised writing board, writing, writing . . .[37]

This compelling image of undaunted persistence occurs in the reports of several journalists who interviewed Ding Ling shortly after her reemergence. Her intense commitment to the literary vocation confirms, in a sense, just what her critics charged her with during the antirightist drive. At the time, of course, she was accused of innumerable errors. As such a campaign gathers momentum, the crescendo of accusations can attain a kind of savage totality, so that the target is stripped of all redeeming features and all his acts fall within the range of crimes or misdeeds. To the core charge of "one-bookism" (*yibenshu zhuyi*) against Ding Ling, however, one may have to concede a certain "justification." (Campaigns tend to spawn neologisms, and if this one suggests the belittlement of books and literature, that was, after all, a main purpose of the campaign.)

Ding Ling was reputed to have said, "If you've written a book, nobody can knock you down," and, "If you have a book, that is something of your own."[38] These statements were taken as boasts about her prize-winning book, *The Sun Shines on the Sanggan River*, and also as evidence of her "bourgeois" view that literature was an individual creation for securing personal profit and fame.[39] What had earlier been regarded as her greatest success was now turned against her and defined as her most unforgivable failing. She was attempting, in the eyes of her critics, to set up "one book" — the achieved literary work — in opposition to party leadership. Thus the antirightist campaign against Ding Ling was waged as a "struggle to protect the socialist line in art and literature,"[40] or, as the headline of one editorial forcefully proclaimed, "Smash the Antiparty Clique of Ding Ling, Chen Qixia, Feng Xuefeng: Protect the Leadership of the Party in Literary Matters."[41]

Ironically, such an assumption on the part of her critics — that there was a necessary and irreconcilable opposition between literature and the party's socialist line — was just what Ding Ling throughout her career had tried to deny. With all her dedication to the literary vocation, she also considered herself, even during the period of her expulsion, a true member of the Communist Party. She did not see the issue, as an outsider observing from the vantage point of a Western democracy might see it, in terms of a clear-cut conflict between artistic freedom and political control. That is why easy partisan labels based on preconceived notions about socialist realism will not fit her case. Ding Ling took as seriously as possible the party's policy on literary matters, while attempting to continue the conscientious practice of literature. As the party line hardened, reconciling her allegiance to literature with her loyalty to the party became ever more difficult. But she went on experimenting to see what could be done, or possibly to discover what new things could be done, within more and more narrowly defined boundaries. Her record of exploring the limits of revolutionary literature, of writing creatively under political restraints, may be seen as a series of partial successes until she was forced to give up the effort altogether. Because she persisted in writing, the sequence of narratives she produced demonstrates not only what was happening to fiction as the political situation changed, but also what, as a result, was happening *in* fiction. Her work shows how narrative procedures respond to shifts in ideology.

As a term, ideology has itself become "thoroughly ideologized."[42] For the purpose of analyzing Ding Ling's fiction however, I will use ideology as a neutral term, divested of its political, and perhaps pejorative connotations. Rendered nonevaluative, it becomes a useful conceptual tool for objectively examining and explicating the narrative text and discovering the interrelation of its various elements. Ideology may be broadly defined as "a body of maxims and prejudices which constitute both a vision of the world and a system of values,"[43] and thus may be either implicitly assumed or explicitly stated in any work of narrative. This vision of the world and its corollary values, beliefs, or prejudices guide the writer in selecting, classifying, interpreting, and patterning the welter of experience around him. Put another way, out of the almost limitless range of human possibilities the writer restricts himself to what can be covered and organized from a particular perspective. Ideology, then, is this perspective. It is that which imposes order on chaos and confers significance on contingency; it establishes the canons of relevance and makes narrative coherence possible. In this broad and neutral sense, ideology will naturally, if at times only implicitly, be present in all narrative texts, including what may be regarded as Ding Ling's apolitical fiction.

The ideology of the Chinese revolution, insofar as it informs and shapes a particular literary work, operates in distinct ways on the text because of its prescriptive as well as explicit character: the Maoist vision of the world and system of values includes specific theories about the goals and function of literature. Therefore in committing themselves to the revolution writers are also consciously submitting to the dominance of these theories and accepting all the consequences that will have on their literary practice. The writer must thus evaluate each element of his or her work to see if it will further the goals of China's socialist revolution. His text will be expected to provide clear and demonstrable evidence of ideological compliance.

In spite of such restrictive conditions, the relation between ideology and narrative, especially in the hands of a writer committed to his craft, remains complex and unpredictable. No matter how rigidly defined, ideology cannot absolutely cover all that will happen in any given work. The short story or novel written according to Maoist ideology is still not completely predetermined. Indeed, throughout Ding Ling's career Maoist ideology itself and what it might require of literature was only gradually emerging through such historical events as the rectification movement and the Yanan Forum on Literature and Art. At the time when Ding Ling was producing her fiction it was still to a certain extent up to narrative practice to disclose the concrete and precise ways in which characterization, plot structure, narrative mode, or the use of setting would be affected by ideological demands.

Ideology and narrative practice were both subject to change, and in any case there is no one-to-one, totally formularized relationship between them. Within Ding Ling's fiction there are instances of harmonious solution but also of compromise and resistance. It is the tensions generated between ideological pressure and narrative response, and the different kinds of successes or failures in the writer's management of them that give rise to the interest and complexity of her literary works.

Ding Ling produced a few negligible plays, some scattered poems, and not a few essays, but she was primarily a writer of fiction. Up to the time of the antirightist campaign she had written two long novels (one remained unfinished), two novelettes, and some sixty short stories and sketches. Her fiction (until that long break in her career), falls into four quite distinctive phases; they show the increasing commitment to the revolution resulting in a deeper implication of politicized ideology in narrative practice.

In discussing each phase I will emphasize a different aspect of fictional technique: the one which seems most useful for approaching that stage of her development. In the first chapter, on Ding Ling's subjective phase, the emphasis is on the interplay of points of view between narrator and character; in the second chapter, as she turns outward towards a revolutionary literature, it is on milieu and its use as political metaphor. After she arrives in Yanan and becomes involved in the controversies over the uses of literature, characterization is stressed as the area in which the issue of "bright versus dark" representation of reality can best be examined. The fourth and final chapter, on her fictional treatment of the historical experience of land reform, focuses on problems of plot.

Since one of my points is that ideologies, whether explicit or not, inscribe themselves on microlevels of the text, each of the first three chapters is followed by a close analysis of one representative story, to show in greater detail how the issues particular to each period of her work manifest themselves within the created product. Besides, any individual piece, even the slightest of stories, when taken aside and looked at by itself (and why should we deny ourselves this main pleasure of criticism?) becomes a richer work, a complex and distinct entity, transcending in part whatever generalizations we might make about the group or phase to which it belongs.

The first of the three narratives is a diary in which the diarist, telling her own story, ends up questioning the process; the second recounts the problems encountered during one day in the life of a writer who has just joined the revolution; and the third is a biographical sketch of an old opera singer who undergoes reform and becomes an artist of the people. All three works comment in diverse ways on the situation of the writer or artist and on his role in society, each pointing to a different phase of an abiding preoccupation of Ding Ling the writer.

Running like a dark thread through her fiction and thus through this study is what may be called the "fate of literature" motif; the story of what has been happening to literature in modern Chinese history. For Ding Ling's works are intensely concerned with the meaning and writing of literature itself. In approximately one-fourth of her stories writers appear as major, if not central, characters. It is significant that they dominate only the early stories. Once she arrives at Yanan, the claims of writers, when they appear in her fiction at all, are targets of satire or other forms of devaluation. As her writing expands in scope and moves away from the introspective, self-absorbed diary to the sweeping vision in her last novel of China in revolution, the writer's figure diminishes in size and importance. Yet in spite of this progressive depreciation of the writer, it was on charges of literary arrogance that Ding Ling was sent into exile and forced to renounce a writing career. Her reinstatement is indeed evidence of the writer's survival, but coming after those twenty perilous years, it also underscores the extreme precariousness of that vocation. Her life, as well as the succession of writers portrayed in her work, raise pressing questions about the writer's role, about the validity of literature, and its hopes for survival in a world of radical political change.

1

SUBJECTIVISM AND LITERATURE

WITH A FEW EXCEPTIONS, the thirteen or fourteen stories Ding Ling wrote in 1927–1929 are about lone young women.[1] Away from home, living unconventional lives in the amorphous semimodern city, they appeared to share certain superficial characteristics with their author. Because of this, many of her readers assumed that Ding Ling's stories mirrored in diverse ways the story of her own life — an assumption that was reinforced by the confessional mode of her writing. During this first phase Ding Ling was hardly alone in such literary introspection; indeed, she could easily qualify as a female member of what Leo Lee has called the "romantic generation of modern Chinese writers."[2] The themes of love and sex in her stories, the frequency of patent autobiographical allusions, the focus on the alienated sensitive individual — all would seem to link her to the writers so vividly portrayed in Lee's book.

Yet in some important ways Ding Ling stands apart. Being a woman is not the least of them, particularly since her own critical attitude toward the image of the suffering female restrained her from the kind of sentimental indulgence found in the writings of suffering *male* romantic authors. In her stories the love experience is not so much an excuse for subjective effusions as an occasion for tough moral self-questioning. Characters are, to be sure, in confrontation with the world, but they must also face up to who they are themselves. Her manipulation of fictional points of view allows an interplay of complex and ironic perspectives on personal experiences even when they are drawn from real life. Furthermore her intense exploration of subjectivism in literature during this period soon led her to an exposure of its limits, so that by early 1930 she was moving away from romantic concerns and toward revolutionary commitment, ready to begin the search for a broader arena for literature.

Autobiography into Fiction

In the three years that Ding Ling concentrated on subjective themes, she succeeded in extending the range of Chinese literature to areas of experience it had never encompassed before. She succeeded, paradoxically, because she was extremely self-centered in her early writing, recording and revealing many aspects of the sensibilities of her own young emergent generation. Our interest in that record, our recognition of its precious quality, is due to its having been, in the long perspective of Chinese literary history, a record that was possible for only a fleeting moment. Before and after the late 1920s confessional writings on the preoccupations of youth were rarely produced in China.[3] Ding Ling's early works seem obsessed with the uncertainties and search for self-definition that characterize youth's first encounters with experience. These stories bear the unmistakable hallmarks of a young writer and are in this respect characteristic of the literature of the early May Fourth era.[4]

Ding Ling's distinction came from the particular revelations she was making about young women. There were a few other women writers, but none achieved her reputation or popularity.[5] A contemporary critic considered Ding Ling's first collection of short stories, *Zai heianzhong* (In the Darkness), "the best among works by women," because "in style it is different from that of women writers up till now, it points to the actual life and pain of women today, it contains delicate analyses of women's psychology, it creates bold and outspoken descriptions."[6] It was typical of literary criticism of that time to comment on the unprecedented audacity (*dadan*) with which Ding Ling depicted the conditions and emotional states of women; her fame — or perhaps her notoriety — was based on what she was perceived to have dramatically disclosed.

As the transformation of Chinese society began to accelerate in the first decades of the twentieth century, there was a rapid and dramatic shift in the roles of youth and women.[7] Both were becoming the vanguard of revolution in a society that had traditionally been dominated by men and those who were old. Women and youth had less to lose by turning against the world as it was. But rebelling against authority and convention in unprecedented ways, they also had to bear the brunt of violent change. It was not only the novelty of their emergence that attracted new literary attention; the particular social and psychological strains they labored under made them especially interesting subjects.

In comparison with youth, women had been relatively visible in traditional literature, but they had been presented less as subjects in their own right than as objects or images catering to the needs, desires, and projections of a preponderantly male authorship.[8] But now both youth and women were discovered as serious subjects and were achieving sudden prominence in literary works. Among the writers, those who were young, or female, or both, were confronted with two emerging realities, that of the external world, and that of themselves within it. Their writings were a response to the struggle to define this new self-awareness.

Literature assumed an unusually personal meaning for writer and public, and that was the major reason for the extraordinary phenomenon of author-character-reader identification during the romantic generation. In a story Ding Ling wrote in 1930, a writer looking back on his career is ready to give up writing. His readers are

> students of the petty bourgeois class above high school level. They feel that the writing suits their tastes . . . perhaps the events reflect their ideals, the characters seem so lovable, partly resemble themselves. They further believe them to be reincarnations of their author, so they fall in love with the author.[9]

There were authors who encouraged the reader to identify with their characters and thus with the author himself. Ba Jin repeatedly presented himself as one of the main characters in many of his novels and short stories.[10] Yu Dafu's unabashed belief that "all literary works are autobiographies of their authors . . . because art is life, life is art, why should we separate the two?"[11] was shared by many of his readers, and the way he exemplified this belief in his living and writing was a source of his popularity. The public responded to fiction writers and their protagonists as Western youth responded to movie stars. "The emotional life of this 'reading generation' centered on May Fourth literature to an extraordinary degree . . . no one came closer to giving voice to their inner feelings."[12]

Even though Ding Ling, in referring to the "May Fourth phase" of her work, always denied that she had been writing about herself,[13] it was the ability to "give voice to the inner feelings" of her readers that seemed to make these repeated denials necessary. Author-character identification may have been proof of the effect she had on her readers, but it also became a burden she was condemned to bear. Almost thirty years later, after Ding Ling's writings had undergone several radical transformations, these early stories were brought back as "evidence" in the campaign against her; her own character was attacked through the characters she created. Throughout the antirightist drive of 1957, the running refrain was that Ding Ling was the incarnation (*huashen*) of her own characters, or, which is of course the same thing, that the characters were incarnations of their author.[14] Even more damning, the image of Ding Ling as a writer/character was fixed by the productions of these first three years— if later characters were negative it was because they were found to exhibit traces of the bad prototypes.[15] Such critically naive or politically calculated blurring of the distinction between life and literature, between autobiography and fiction, plagued Ding Ling throughout much of her literary life.

The tendency to read Ding Ling into her characters extended to anticipating her looks. One critic in the early 1930s confessed to forming an image of the author as a "Lin Daiyu type, or someone in the first stage of tuberculosis" because the psychology of her women characters was so "sensitive and morbid," but in meeting her found out what an egregious error that had been: "Ding Ling turns out to be plump and short, serious in demeanor, profound in expression; in her external appearance, she is absolutely different in character type from the women she writes about."[16] This must have been unsettling news indeed to many of her readers.

A closer look at the actual stories themselves will similarly reveal discrepancies between the materials drawn from real life and the transformations of art. Two works based on autobiographical experiences illustrate particularly well the complex relation between autobiography and fiction, and the different kinds of critical issues this relation can generate.

Paradoxically the first one, "Qian laile ke de yueye" (A Secret Visitor on a Moonlit Night), is mistakenly attributed by Shen Congwen not to Ding Ling but to Hu Yepin. When Shen visited his two friends in Hangchow, they invited him to see the locale where the incidents described in the story had "taken place." Shen writes that the "naval student" (his appellation for Hu Yepin throughout his *Reminiscences of Ding Ling*) showed him how "the clever thief in the story 'Laile ke de hei ye' [A Visitor on a Dark Night] [*sic*], which Hu wrote, really (*dangzhen*) climbed in here and escaped through there."[17] Shen Congwen's garbled version of the title casts doubt on the reliability of his memory concerning other aspects of the story. If he had reread the text he would have found an unequivocal statement on its authorship in the opening paragraph:

> Ping thought up this title for me. I'm so dull, my idea was just to write out the story straightforwardly and send it back to Hunan for mother to read . . . I wanted to tell Ma about this incident which had so unsettled yet amused me, so that Ma would know that although it has been another couple of years since her Zhezhe has been away, that particular timidity and fearfulness she inherited from father remains as it was when she was small.[18]

The couple had been living in a friend's house on a quiet hillside by West Lake. One moonlit night, barking dogs, the moving shadows of banana leaves, sounds of footsteps in the kitchen, convince them that a thief has broken in. They see the beam of a flashlight, the backs of retreating figures, but wait in fear until daylight before daring to enter the kitchen, certain that all their things have been taken.

> The door was tightly closed, we softly pushed it open. Everything was as it had been, not even a tiny trace there of anything. The kettle that I suspected had been used to boil water during the night was in its old place; it had not been moved at all.

Looking at each other we smiled incredulously. We still think we must have been dreaming, and can't help but laugh at ourselves whenever we recall the way we had acted.[19]

In addition to bungling the title and the attribution of the story, Shen Congwen seems to have missed its point. If the story teases with questions about how one can tell the difference between what one fearfully imagines and what actually happens, then Shen's on-the-spot testimony further confounds the issue. This treatment of a "real life" incident that ends by asking whether one can know how much of it was real is one of Ding Ling's slighter efforts. A more significant instance of turning autobiographical fact into fiction and an illuminating example of the writer at work is "Guonian" (New Year's).

It is winter vacation for eight-year-old Xiaohan,[20] a time of New Year festivities in her uncle's large household where she lives and time any moment now for her mother's arrival. Her mother teaches school in another city and lives there with her little brother. As with "A Secret Visitor on a Moonlit Night," contemporary accounts attest to both the biographical truth of this story and the authenticity of its setting. The editor of one anthology of Ding Ling's writings justifies his inclusion of "New Year's" despite its lack of historical significance (shidai yiyi), meaning presumably that it does not address itself to any timely issue, because Ding Ling had once told him that

> her mother had written her daughter that after reading this story, she could not stop her tears from flowing. The circumstances of herself in those years struggling to bring up the children rose before her eyes again in her lonely old age. Thus "New Year's" can be said to form a segment of the autobiography of Ding Ling's childhood, and can help the reader understand her early environment and her life as a child.[21]

This anthology appeared in 1933, when Ding Ling had been abducted and people feared she was dead. The rumor thus conferred a poignant value on all scraps of information about her life, especially one corroborated by the mother's reported response.

The story was further anchored to the reality of Ding Ling's life by verifiable details. As one critic wrote,

> The customs of celebrating lunar New Year in Western Hunan are described very much as they are. I remember this was the first work of the author I had read, and from reading it I knew that the place she described was my home town, guessing correctly that she and I were from the same place.[22]

But valuable though "New Year's" may be as a document on customs in western Hunan or as a "segment of autobiography," our interest is in what Ding Ling achieves as she puts this recollection of the past into narrative form.

By focusing on this particular season, which allows her to juxtapose its festivities with the return and impending departure of the mother, Ding Ling captures and counterpoints the many moods of childhood, ranging from almost magical happiness to desolate loneliness. As the story progresses Xiaohan fluctuates between anxiety and joyful reassurance in her mother's presence, yet feeling always the need to exercise self-restraint. Vacation passes too quickly. "As soon as it is the 16th all the lanterns and decorations are taken down . . . There will be no more gay evenings with burning braziers, bright lanterns, the sound of laughter and talk . . . she will be sitting by herself before the lamp, everything silent, the nursemaid nodding on the chair, the mice making noises [in the mother's empty room]."[23] The end of the story is a moment of release and conciliation, when Xiaohan is held by her mother, crying hard, yet feeling, under her mother's gentle patting, "as if she had never experienced such happiness."[24]

The center of consciousness in the story is the child, not quite eight years old, who experiences extreme emotions but is agonizingly anxious about expressing them. The spectator-narrator is actually a fusion of child and adult, imposing a double vision on the events of the past, achieving a subtle balance between what the child self-consciously perceives but is unable to articulate fully, and what the knowing, empathizing adult sees, looking back twenty years later. At the dinner table, Xiaohan's uncle has just said something about sending a servant to see if her mother was about to come, suddenly putting into words the question nagging at the child's mind but which she had been afraid to ask:

> She sensed that the cousins, brothers Qiang and Mao, and even the maids standing by the table were all looking right at her. She felt sad, but also very happy, and with grateful eyes she looked at her uncle and aunt. She felt only that Uncle was still very stern, very big, too high up to reach, even in breathing he seemed to reveal an authority different from ordinary people. Aunt was, as usual, pretty, smiling, capable, kind, but never able to conceal that cold expression which so scared Xiaohan. Xiaohan did not understand this; from the time she was born, her environment had made her different from other children. Her nerves were very delicate, things that others felt she could not understand were already on her mind and caused her unhappiness. From the time she was little she had been treated courteously by her aunt, but she always felt it was hard to be close to her. Many people liked her, praised her for being clever, cute, wise, good-tempered . . . but she could never get her aunt to like her . . . she quickly lowered her eyelids.[25]

This hypersensitive, self-conscious child, lonely and ill-at-ease in a cold world, is the typical Ding Ling heroine in embryo. In the telling of the story Xiaohan becomes more than the self remembered from childhood; she also joins the gallery of fictional characters Ding Ling created during this period, sharing with them recognizable traits. Autobiography is thus rendered into fiction and fundamentally transformed through the purposeful structuring of feelings, the play of dual narrative perspective, and the typecasting of character.

Negotiating the hairline boundary, invisible as it may have been to some observers, between experience and fiction, life and literature, would throughout Ding Ling's career be the constant challenge to her narrative art. In her first group of stories, art results from recording the encounters of the self with the world in the course of the search for identity. For the young women who figure in these early works, love and sexuality make up the field where the battle of the self is won or lost. The same kind of intensive soul-searching of youth engenders the activity of writing, but the questions "Why does one write? What does it mean to write?" continue to be asked even after Ding Ling outgrows the youthful preoccupations with self-identity.

The Self in the World

Ding Ling's first published story, issued in 1927, is about Mengke, a young woman from the provinces who comes to Shanghai and becomes a movie actress. The story takes off from an actual experience, but the heroine succeeds where her author in real life had failed. Although Ding Ling's purpose in trying out for the movies was to improve a precarious livelihood that depended on uncertain family subsidies and Hu Yepin's pitiful income as a writer, the notion was also inspired by her reading of literature.

According to Shen Congwen, the examples of three women in *La Dame aux Camélias*, *Madame Bovary*, and *Notre Coeur*, "before helping her write, encouraged her to go to Shanghai." Their stories led her to think, "Wouldn't it be worth it for her to go into that vast, expansive human sea to seek a brand new life in which laughter and tears were mixed together, and take a chance on testing her own destiny?" The venture failed and left Ding Ling filled with contempt for the film industry, but it did bring her for the first time "into serious contact with the realities of life."[26] As Shen puts it:

> A film studio is not unlike a miniature society. Although she was only a spectator, from her spectator position she could learn to know the faces of various social types and their relationships. The loneliness of her position intensified the attention she paid to the conduct and behavior of other kinds of people. While the film company could not make this woman writer into a star of the silver screen, it did teach her a meaningful lesson about life.[27]

The lesson about life becomes material for a story that centers on the struggle of the self against a harsh world, as the unworldly Mengke gradually learns what the world is like. The world humiliates and degrades; more particularly it exploits the innocence and vulnerability of the young, attractive woman, making her into an object, a commodity to satisfy its own lewd desires. The story begins and concludes with thematically parallel episodes. At the start Mengke leaves art school in indignation after trying to protect a model who had been "insulted" by a teacher. In the end she herself can make a living only as a movie star, a career that makes her feel she is "selling not just her body but even her soul."[28]

What demoralizes her and leads eventually to such a capitulation is her stay in the modern, fashionable, affluent household of her aunt and cousins. The fatal lure of this environment, which will compromise her integrity and undermine her trust in the world, is embodied in her cousin Xiaosong, twenty-five years old. Back from France just half a year, he is a translator of foreign fiction in magazines. Fascinating as this Western connection is, it also, as often in Ding Ling's stories, signals something suspect, inauthentic, possibly corrupting. The cousin charms Mengke with talk about the museums, theaters, and restaurants of Paris, and takes her to the Ka-er-deng (Carlton?) cinema to see *Chahuanü* (Camille). There is much submerged sentimental eroticism in this scene (her identification with the actress also presages Mengke's own future) so that later when she finds the cousin in a hotel with a "whore-like woman" she feels betrayed. This shocking evidence of male treachery, as well as the shallowness of her cousins' lives underneath all that Western veneer precipitates Mengke's decision to flee her aunt's house. Then, without making very explicit the logic of the outcome, the story has her fall straight into the "deep pit of hell."[29]

"Amao guniang" (Miss Amao) likewise has as its central character a young girl who begins in innocence and is defeated by the world. While Mengke discovers the world as it is, a place where sacrifice of integrity and self-respect are the conditions of survival, Amao destroys herself because she desires to escape from the confines of her environment and then learns that escape is impossible.

When Amao leaves behind the remote, isolated valley village of her childhood, and is sent forth as a bride to live at her husband's home on a hillside by West Lake, she becomes aware of hitherto unsuspected possibilities in life. Initially these are represented by the distant but visible city of Hangchow. "As soon as it was night, from far away across the Lake, where sky and water met," the city would "shine like densely clustered stars, a large golden light reflected on the water."[30] In the company of some neighbors she finally gets her wish to visit Hangchow, but at one point during the long walk the city seems to be much farther away than she had realized, "a mysterious place, a place which perhaps one could not reach."[31] This pattern of expectations aroused and then thwarted is repeated throughout the story; each new experience and discovery becomes a new source of despair.

In part it is Amao's own particularly innocent outlook on the world that entraps her in this pattern of frustrated expectations. The story is told primarily through her as the center of consciousness, but the narrator constantly steps outside to place the character's "romantic" view of things into realistic perspective. When Amao and her neighbors return from the city by boat, she sighs as the lake water carries her farther and farther away,

> but as they approached home, she became very happy again; it was due to a kind of vanity. When Third Sister and Yuying pointed out their houses to her, she could see them nestling deeply in the mountain valley, which was better than all those nearby. In the valley there were also many elegant houses half hidden from view. From the lake it looked as if their houses were right on top of a Western-style storied red house. Fortunately she had forgotten that theirs were the only crude small tiled huts in the valley, built of old boards and patched everywhere with old and rusty metal plates.[32].

Such movement in and out of the protagonist's consciousness is reminiscent of the ironic method in *Madame Bovary*, which Ding Ling is reputed to have read in translation at least ten times. More than one of her friends have testified to her fondness for the novel,[33] but unlike Flaubert, Ding Ling is sympathetic toward the plight of her heroine. Her juxtaposition of the dual points of view is less artful but also less calculatingly cruel.[34]

Amao's exposure to the glitter of the city and her intermittent contacts with the fashionable people who occupy the elegant houses around hers create a desire for a better life, and when, despite all her efforts, this life turns out to be beyond reach, she sinks into a deep depression, into the "sorrow of hoping without hope." Her health fails, she swallows a bunch of matches and dies in horrible pain. There is the sound of a violin from a nearby mansion. When Amao first heard this music—unseen, foreign, suggesting the unattainable, like her glimpses of the city, her dreams for a different life—she had been filled with an inexplicable sadness. After the screams of her final agony, the violin too falls silent.

Amao is the young Chinese peasant girl from the village who discovers the material wealth and mysterious culture of the city's semi-Westernized sector and is destroyed by her passionate longing for them. In another story Ding Ling writes about a lower-class victim of the modernized city who is a survivor. The prostitute Aying in "Qingyünli zhong de yijian xiaofang li" (A Small Room in Qingyün Lane), falling asleep on the wet splotchy bed after her customer leaves, dreams of being again in the arms of the lover she left in the village, but unlike Amao she knows her dreams are useless, are in fact "stupid and laughable."[35] With the nonchalant resilience that has enabled her to survive for three years in her sordid Shanghai environment, she gets on with the preparations for the evening's work and stands on the street waiting for the two or three dollars she hopes the night will bring.

In "Shafei nüshi de riji" (The Diary of Miss Sophie), Ding Ling's best-known story, the threat of destruction comes not so much from the outside world's violation of the innocent individual as from what she finally learns about herself in her confrontation with the world. The diary form is employed to carry out a kind of intense self-examination that would not have been possible for the less sophisticated, less self-conscious peasant bride or prostitute. Miss Sophie, about twenty, away from home, and living by herself in Peking, not enrolled in the university though most of her friends are, is much more typical of the heroines in Ding Ling's early fiction. With few or attenuated family connections, these young women rarely have family or given names, but take unconventional Westernized ones like Sophie, Isa, and Lia, or poetic ones like Yecao (Wildgrass). Very often they are impoverished or in ill health, living in rented shabby back rooms (tingzijian) of dreary apartment buildings, surviving anonymously and precariously in the interstices of the huge city. Their insecurity and isolation come from their having broken away from the traditional social structure and conventional codes of behavior: economically perhaps, but even more morally and spiritually, they are totally on their own. They live on the fringes, away from the institutionalized restrictions of marriage, a regular job, or school. But what they often discover in their free-wheeling, anarchistic existence is that in facing the world they must also encounter themselves.

Among these early women characters Miss Sophie emerges as the most representative, or rather as the most extreme, because she receives the most extended treatment. Her emancipated way of life is carried further than most because her advanced state of tuberculosis prevents her from engaging in any regular occupation and encourages reckless behavior. She finds herself strongly attracted to Ling Jishi, a man who has the "handsome air of a medieval knight" but a despicable soul. Her diary centers on this perverse passion: while she indulges in feverish fantasies of longing for him she realizes at the same time that he is unworthy of them.

Like other objects of temptation in Ding Ling's stories—Mengke's cousin, Amao's city—Ling Jishi is both enhanced and tainted by Western connotations. (In fact, being from Singapore, he is only ambiguously Chinese.) Tall and slim, he has a white complexion, bright red and temptingly soft lips—an important focus for Sophie's fantasies—and hopelessly "Western" values.

> What does he want? Money, to entertain in his living room the young wives of his business associates, and several white and plump sons, exquisitely dressed. What is his love? To squander money in the brothel for some momentary sexual gratification, and to sit on the soft sofa clasping a scented body, a cigarette in his mouth, laughing unrestrainedly with friends, left legs over right knees . . . an enthusiast of debates, tennis matches, studying abroad at Harvard, becoming a foreign service officer or ambassador, or inheriting his father's occupation, going into the rubber business, becoming a capitalist. [She sees through him, but is hopelessly infatuated anyway]: He has so insanely stirred up my emotions . . . I know for sure, that if he would tightly hold me, let me kiss him all over, and then cast me into the ocean, into fire, I would happily close my eyes and await that death which would forever preserve this love of mine. Alas, to think that I am in love with him, all I want is for him to let me have a good death.[36]

The see-saw battle of contradictory impulses that the story traces in detail rises to a hysterical pitch and finally climaxes in a kiss, representing for Sophie both victory and degradation. After that she sends her lover away and castigates herself in despair: "All in all, I have wreaked havoc on myself. If a person's enemy is himself, how, oh heavens, can he seek vengeance and indemnity for all his losses?"[37]

Even as Sophie records in her diary the hysterical course of self-destruction, she is quite fully aware, on one level at least, of what she is doing. Going to hell with both eyes open is—precisely because one does see where one is going—a journey worth documenting. The author's claim here is that no matter how deserving of condemnation, she merits our attention in spite of, or even because of, what she is. This unapologetic dwelling on the self is one of the most characteristic themes of May Fourth literature, and a radically new departure in Chinese fiction.

Discussing the important effects of the "autobiographical attitude" in European narrative, Robert Scholes and Robert Kellogg note that it is "one of the main distinctions between novelistic characterization and the kinds of characterization presented in all earlier narrative." When novelists put themselves into their characters, they conversely "find in themselves an extraordinary range of dramatic possibilities, made up of aspirations, suppressed desires, masks and antimasks, nobility and depravity."[38] The discovery of "suppressed desires" and "depravity" did not begin of course with the great novelists: they had been anticipated in this by the confessions of St. Augustine and St. Theresa. Since there is no tradition of Christian writing in China, it is striking to note the similar avowedly confessional motivation of the single great example of the autobiographical attitude in past Chinese fiction: the eighteenth-century novel *The Dream of the Red Chamber*. In the preface the author speaks of having made an utter failure of his life.[39] It is the subjective projection of the author that permits the book's "great leap forward" in expanding the range of psychological representation of the inner life to include its seamy side.

The autobiographical attitude appears in certain other genres of classical writing: the diaries, letters, informal essays, poetry, and notes or jottings (*biji*) of the literati. As Jaroslav Průšek has pointed out, there are important similarities between some of these traditional forms and the subjectivist writings of the May Fourth period.[40] But these personal, informal compositions with their many observations about personal experience, and marked as they often were by self-irony or the playful idiosyncrasies of the writer, were not occasions for the profound explorations of human personality, much less of its negative aspects. The more immediate models for the twentieth-century autobiographical attitude in Chinese fiction are works imported from the West. The translation of *The Sorrows of Young Werther* in 1921 seemed to call forth the same kind of emotional response the original did in Europe almost a century and a half earlier,[41] in part because of the confessional nature of the story. Autobiographies, writings openly incorporating autobiographical material, or fiction assuming autobiographical forms, letters, and diaries abound in the writings of the 1920s. In all these efforts there is the "same determination to lay bare the naked truth."[42]

The new frankness, the readiness to speak about one's weaknesses, passions, and humiliating or shameful experiences precipitated a veritable explosion of possibilities in characterization and subject matter in Chinese fiction. Suddenly dominating the literary consciousness was the dark side of human experience, which had simply not found expression in previous literature. In particular the examination of hitherto unmentioned, perhaps unmentionable facets of the inner life of women, who had hardly been visible as serious subjects in the classical literary tradition, yielded unprecedented revelations. Against this background we can understand why Ding Ling's works, especially "The Diary of Miss Sophie," which may appear rather tame by today's standards, had the effect of "a bomb shell thrown on the deadly quiet literary scene."[43]

The subjectivist and individualistic tendencies in modern Chinese thought and art were both a cause and a consequence of the revolt against tradition.[44] The moral and social conventions of the past, which had for centuries provided the standards for behavior and judgment, were losing their validity in the general atmosphere of political upheaval and cultural iconoclasm. For the young readers and the young writers, the battle was to be fought in the arena of love and marriage. Whereas in traditional Western fiction love and marriage signified the conclusion to the apprenticeship of youth and passage into settled adulthood, in early twentieth-century Chinese fiction they often merely triggered the beginning of action, since the rebellion against arranged marriages was precisely where the stand had to be taken against traditional authority. The generational conflict, the break with the past, and the assertion of the self were concretely and repeatedly dramatized in the tragic outcomes of arranged marriages or in the struggles against them.

In most cases the lines of conflict were clearly drawn. The central issue was the easily defined one of true love against oppression; the individual, with his claims to genuine, demonstrable feelings and integrity, against the evil system. But this is not the case with Sophie. At large in the amorphous big city, she is a free agent, she is not backed into any corner by outside powers. The broader context of her predicament, the larger social forces operating upon her—the critical cliché that Sophie represents the despair of the petit bourgeois individual caught in the transition from a feudal to a capitalist society—are not considered by the narrator. Sophie sees herself, and not an identifiable institution, as setting the terms of her life. This becomes the source of her final despair: her recognition that she has no one to blame but herself.

It is therefore this self, the self on which everything hinges, that she seeks to analyze and understand through the diary. Her infatuation is proof that the self does not act in its own interests, much less morally or rationally, but can she even make sense of it? While she endlessly dissects her own behavior, she is also anxiously asking, can I really be known to myself as a subject? As an individual "beyond rebellion," broken loose from the confining structures of tradition and society, adrift in the world, Sophie finds that what she is forced to fall back on is the chaos within— the questionable, perhaps inexplicable self.

Love and Sexuality

In "The Diary of Miss Sophie" the onset of love uncovers the contradictory and perverse aspects of personality. Although in the great love stories of the past (Dream of the Red Chamber, The Peony Pavilion, The Western Chamber) sexual passion always contained the potential for undermining rationality and the social order, it was not until the literature of the May Fourth period that love and sexual feelings became intensely problematic and capable of totally subverting the individual's sense of self. Miss Sophie is an extended example of this, but there are other stories in which moral predicaments and crises of identity and relationships are revealed through the tangles of love. While Ding Ling's bold, outspoken exploration of women's sexual feelings made her notorious among her contemporaries, she often was able to seek access through such feelings to other aspects of the human condition.

The very early story "Shujia zhong" (Summer Vacation) concerns the love affairs of a group of young women school teachers, but on another level is about the sense of malaise among "progressive" individuals who feel out of time and place. It was too easy in school to "pick up knowledge outside books, forgetting what one came to school for, from morning till night to be head-over-heels involved in kissing, embracing, stealthily placing letters by pillows, in bitterness, tears."[45] But the carefully specified time-space context of these apparently trivial activities invest them with further meaning.

The ironically named Self-Reliance Girls School (Zili nüxiao) is located in the town of Wuling, a provincial backwater. The school has been made over from a tiny dilapidated temple, its main hall appointed like an auditorium, its side rooms serving as classrooms and teachers' bedrooms. The teachers' modern way of life and occupation, like the school itself, must make their way in makeshift, uncertain fashion among the most uncongenial surroundings. After several years in town, the bobbed hair of the teachers, the light-colored blouses and short skirts they have adopted still attract "the eyes of the entire street" whenever they appear. Furthermore it is summer vacation, and whenever it is hot, "there is nothing one can do; there are few trees, few wide spaces, just densely packed houses enclosing narrow streets."[46] These young women, idle between terms, oppressed by heat, are trapped in boredom and frustration.

Two public occasions momentarily interrupt the tedium: a variety show at a school and a "new style" wedding, each a modern event staged against the incongruous backdrop of the provincial town, each inviting leers and scandalous gossip about the teachers among the townspeople. The young women's vaunted *dushen zhuyi*, a self-sufficient but not necessarily celibate "bachelorism," sounds brave but does not enable them to rise above the tearful bickerings of futile, petty love affairs. Homosexual love may have been a salacious subject for that time; in the story it also becomes a kind of metaphor for the semiliberated, the would-be avant-garde who lack the resources to transcend the restrictive conditions of their existence.

A more sympathetic view of the hazards of sexual passion in an unforgiving environment is presented in the story "Xiaohuolun shang" (On a Small Steamboat). A teacher who unwisely falls in love with a married man is dismissed by the school for her conduct, only to find her lover betraying her with someone else. The story begins with Jie Dajie boarding the small steamboat and is told in flashback as she travels into an uncertain future, "gazing at the endless ranges of green mountains, the turbulent flowing water, feeling lost and adrift with no place to go."[47]

Both stories portray women as victims—of men, institutions, conventional mores, but also of their own feelings. The dark mood of suffering and self-destruction in the writings of many other contemporary women writers like Lu Yin, Feng Yuanjun, and Xie Bingying [48] came from the sense of oppression that women suffered and was reinforced by a concept of woman as a being imbued with extraordinary sensitivity, fragility, and capacity for pain. This image of the suffering woman was a carry-over from traditional literature. Women rarely spoke in their own voices in the past—the number of women writers in China's four-thousand-year tradition is minuscule—but male writers did often assume the personae of women in voicing complaints about rejection by their lords, separation from home, and similar painful situations. The sensitive and suffering female also existed in the Western tradition and, along with other themes of Romanticism, turned out to be one of the more congenial imports during the May Fourth period. Certainly the importance of love and marriage as *the* subject among the young writers of that time provided endless occasions for describing women crushed by marriage, or dying from blighted love. Traditional culture and Western influence both contributed the notion of the passively suffering female, one that seems to have been accepted by women as part of their self-conception when they began to write about themselves.

While focusing also on the female condition Ding Ling nevertheless struggled to counter this idea of women in many of her stories:

> In my stories of the past, the main characters were often women. This is natural because I myself am a woman and understand better the weaknesses (*ruodian*) of women. But because of this there has been much misunderstanding. Actually I strongly dislike the weaknesses in women, but this is like Fadayev's writing about Mechik in *Huimie* (The Nineteen); although he does his utmost to expose Mechik's faults we can see where he takes his part. I may not feel sympathetic towards the women in my writings, but what I write is not always in accordance with my own opinion. At the beginning the two may not be very far apart, but as I write the gap becomes wider, and at times what I write turns out to be the opposite of my intention. [49]

This seemingly uncontrollable ambivalence, this conflict between intention and practice, sympathy and censure, stems from Ding Ling's view that women suffer not only as victims of society but also from self-defeating female weaknesses. The two stories just discussed present women in this light, but Ding Ling also wrote many more stories in which women try to be strong and hard (*qiangying*), and fight to counteract their weaknesses. For them, being in love may also be an occasion to test their strength. The young woman faced with love is therefore a variation on, or one important aspect of, the theme of the self confronting the world.

However, there are no easy victories for the strong and hard woman. Very often she fails in another way: having asserted herself, her own conscience and self-consciousness rob her of satisfaction. Miss Sophie's "victory," as she terms it, when she finally gains a kiss from the object of her infatuation, is also immediately seen as degradation.

The "Salome-type" flirt in "Yige nüren he yige nanren" (A Woman and a Man) takes the initiative in arranging a rendezvous with a poet—a modern one who affects the Japanese-style name Ou Waiou—because she "wanted to see herself victorious," she could not rest until she "could see another's soul acupunctured by her and vibrating in her palm." It was like an addiction: "if she could not under conditions of danger and secrecy play with (wan wei) a heart she had roused, she apparently would not be able to go on living." When they are together, she does not find in her poet the satisfaction she had envisioned. But even in the middle of the "hot prickly proceedings" the heroine exhibits a certain self-awareness:

> Weidi understood also in her own heart that it was like acting in a play, but she could not bear to laugh at herself: she was very sympathetic towards her own predicament. She sighed gently, assuming a mysterious mien just recently learned from the movies, haughty, deeply expressive, and doleful.[50]

There is a double point of view at work here: the self-consciousness of the main character and the narrator's gently ironic tone both serve to distance the reader from the action. The battle of the sexes is transformed into a comedy of play-acting and miscalculations. At the end, Weidi can't wait to get back to her husband.

"Ta zou hou" (After He Left) focuses on the moral qualms of a girl who capriciously exercises her power over her lover by sending him home at 2:00 A.M. in the rain. The story begins after he leaves and is told entirely in flashback through the recollecting and evaluating consciousness of Lia. The process leads her to conclude that in acting as she did she has used her attractions like a prostitute. The progression of her reflections is meticulously plotted as it moves from smugness to self-criticism to self-pity: "Why was she like this? She did not understand, she wanted to know what made her this way, but was afraid that after understanding she would feel worse."[51]

The "narrated monologue" permits the "merging of the point of view of the author and the point of view of the character":[52]

> But in a flash, everything in her universe changed. Alas! How terrible are thoughts when given free rein: Lia had been happy; but she did not want to wallow in happiness, she wanted to coolly perceive her own good fortune, to prolong it and engrave it in her heart. Who could know that this is how misfortune is built? She thought about everything, she was happy about everything,

then suddenly she began to reflect on her true feelings. And she refused to be slipshod, she was so mistrustful that she finally landed herself in misery . . . Timidly she began to analyze herself.[53]

This sort of "collaborative," constantly evaluating self-consciousness will not allow characters to let go of their love experiences until they have complicated them into occasions for close questioning of themselves as human beings. Such self-questioning is all the more insistent when the assertive woman, striving to counteract the image of the passively suffering weak female, finds herself caught in a moral dilemma brought on by the exercise of power. In Ding Ling's works of this period there are many lovers, many variations of the same theme, but the relentless examination of the self that each situation demands shows her to be a writer of high moral seriousness, in spite of the scandalous nature of what is going on within most of the stories.

Yet it was this focus on love and sexuality in her early writings that made her vulnerable to accusations of "immorality" later on, when she became a target of the established Chinese revolution. During the anti-rightist campaign of 1957 she was attacked for her preoccupation with sex; indulgence in the kind of sexual fantasy found in "The Diary of Miss Sophie," for example, was called "a sort of opiate for youth . . . they will want to find the 'happiness' Sophie had from Ling Jishi's person and completely forget the class struggle of real life."[54] This criticism implies that puritanism is necessary in a revolutionary society because sexual fantasies can be expected to divert or distract one from working stead-fastly for collective goals. Although such literary censorship may be seen as another example of obscurantist party intervention in aesthetic matters, there is indeed the risk, as Ding Ling's stories themselves suggest, that persistent exploration of the love experience may leave the individual unsure of where he stands in relation to the external world, and this uncertainty could interfere with his ability to assume an effective social role.

The outpouring of puritanical outrage during the 1957 campaign was directed against Ding Ling's personal life as much as against her works. As an author she was held personally responsible for the sins of her characters. The gossip mills had ground out more than sufficient material concerning her own early love relationships to intimate that the "immorality" of her fictional creations mirrored her own. Such criticism, both naive and deliberate in its refusal to recognize the distinction between life and art, also points to the particular hazards of being a female writer.

The feminist concerns in Ding Ling's own life and writings belong to those of the "second generation." She did not involve herself in the pri-

mary battles against the flagrant, institutionalized forms of female oppression, such as arranged marriages, foot-binding, concubinage, female
infanticide. These were largely left behind when she moved from Hunan
to live the life of an emancipated woman in the semi-Westernized cities of
Peking and Shanghai. She did write about women imprisoned in stultify-
ing marriages, seduced and betrayed by faithless lovers, or forced into
prostitution to survive in a society which regarded them as commodities,
but more often she presented women who were no less victimized even
while apparently free of such external forms of oppression. Her "liberated" women who engage in love relationships outside the pale of conventional structures give us new insight into the basic, internal contradictions of the female condition. Such women are subject, paradoxically, to
the consequences both of their emotional vulnerability and of their self-
conscious assertiveness. This is a source of their harsh self-criticism and
despair. Ding Ling was able to achieve such insights into women's experience only because she unflinchingly dared to explore largely uncharted
psychological and moral territory. Her audacity contributed much to her
early literary success but also made her an easy target for attack later.

There was no doubt a parallel between her liberated lifestyle and her
literary avant-gardism; both stemmed from a resolute break with convention. Iconoclasm was common to the generation of May Fourth writers, but for a woman, given the greater social and literary obstacles that
she had to overcome, it was necessary to be even more of a self-assertive
rebel. For Ding Ling to undertake literary and political work, a certain
kind of pride was useful and even indispensable. According to Shen
Congwen in his *Reminiscences of Ding Ling*, she required "just this bit of
pride, and the disgust and contempt roused by the commonplace reason-
ing but swaggering behaviour of males (*nanzi*) in general before she
could perceive her own vocation and responsibility."[55]

But once she had begun the pursuit of her vocation there were other
handicaps resulting from her female identity. In Shen Congwen's view
the relationship with Hu Yepin, a "hothouse and cradle of this woman
writer's soul,"[56] was supportive yet restrictive. While it nurtured her tal-
ent, it also circumscribed her experience. Even more insidious, the relationship made it difficult for Ding Ling to accept and capitalize on her
own success while Hu was still struggling as an unrecognized poet. "In
her victory, she felt she had to say smilingly to old friends, 'This is all
Pin's achievement, without the naval cadet there would have been no
book.' " Success seemed equally difficult to accept, whether it came *in
spite of* her being a woman, or *because* of being a woman. She was indig-
nant over the rejection of Hu's manuscripts and left many of her own unfinished in the belief that hers had won acceptance over his "just because

she was a woman."[57] Otherwise, according to Shen, she would have produced twice as many works between 1927 and 1930.

Whether Shen Congwen's estimate of the extent to which Ding Ling's creative output was thwarted is accurate or not, he did perceive what an extraordinary effort it took for a woman not only to launch herself but to continue as a creative writer. The effort required may explain why of all the women who began as writers in the 1920s — Bing Xin, Lu Yin, Ling Shuhua, Su Xuelin, Feng Yuanjun, and others[58], Ding Ling has almost alone sustained an actively productive career for over twenty years. And in extending the self-questioning she so often portrayed in her characters into the realm of creative writing itself, she found one of her most constant themes.

The Meaning of Writing

Writers figure in many of Ding Ling's short stories. Some are characters whose work is to write, others are "writing" the story itself as diarists or letter-writers. In several stories, writing is the actual outcome of the action, the final event, the resolution of the plot. Writing, the act of composition, may in fact be one way to handle sexual dilemmas and overcome the weaknesses inherent in being a woman. The very brief story "Yecao" (Yecao) is about a woman in the process of writing a story while working her way out of an emotional entanglement:

> Today, she was feeling terribly vexed because she had projected some very fervent feelings onto a very cool and rational woman, and had, moreover, introduced a light layer of melancholy. This was really not the character in her imagination, but this was precisely a weakness of women that she could understand best. She didn't know what to do, to tear up the manuscript and rewrite it or to go on but without being sympathetic to this woman. She could not stop thinking about this vexing matter, gradually she thought of the social environment that caused women to overstress emotions, she thought how pitiable women were; then as she reflected, she began to loathe herself.[59]

In "real life," however, she is able to overcome such feelings and when she meets her supplicating lover that evening, he accuses her of "having a heart that is harder (*ying*) than that of any woman, you are not to be shaken, you love only yourself and your work."[60] In essence, she agrees with him and turns away, though not without some lingering regret, and walks home to her writing, "as if very happy, singing some new-formed phrases."

There is a mirroring or doubling effect in the relationship between Yecao and her story, and between Ding Ling and *her* story about Yecao. We are not told how Yecao eventually deals with the fictional character who turns out to be weak and emotional; her own emotional difficulties are solved through the commitment to writing. By thus depicting Yecao's success in life if not in literature, Ding Ling is expressing her confidence in the efficacy of writing as a means for handling the problems of living. But this kind of optimism and faith in the function of literature does not represent the whole of Ding Ling's attitude; she explored the problem from different angles, dramatizing in two diary stories of this period a fundamental doubt and anguish on the matter.

The implied questions of each diarist: Why am I writing this? What is the relation of writing about me to what is happening to me? are prominently raised in Miss Sophie's case. Because she is involved in an impossible love, and is perversely irrational, she writes out of the need to understand what is happening to her, and to understand herself. In the end she concludes the diary disillusioned both with its subject — herself — and its capacity as a form for managing that subject.

The existential nature of writing is viewed from a different and more practical angle in the story "Zisha riji" (A Suicide's Diary). Lacking the dense psychological detail and the sexual histrionics of Miss Sophie's diary, this slighter journal covers a mere nine-day period, beginning with the central character, Isa, deciding to commit suicide. The diary is a record of her attempts "to talk herself into" the act and of her failure to carry it out. As the story opens, "A fine-point pen moves with a scratchy noise down a brand new pad of manuscript paper, words appear that are even more sprawling than usual"; thus begins the diary that will "continue to be written till the day I die."[61]

The interdependence between writing and dying is further underscored when Isa writes on page three of the manuscript pad, "This is the day I go to death, . . . So the diary is now finished . . ." "But events often turn out in unexpected ways."[62] Although Isa hopes for death she is afraid to embrace it; when riding the trolley towards the ocean ("without the ocean, she would not consider suicide") she becomes terrified at the sight of the water and instead of getting off the trolley, she stays on it to the last stop on the line.

As a character she is not contained within her own writing, because in contrast to "The Diary of Miss Sophie" this story does not consist of the diary entries only. The entries are embedded within a narrative that describes Isa's appearance and behavior from the outside. This narrative consciousness, although extrinsic to the diarist's dialogue with the self, does not always speak in the voice of a totally detached or objective observer but often serves as a supplementary register of the character's inner state, in language similar to the diary:

> She did not get anything ready, she couldn't bear to put those things in order, she thought it probably better to let them stay in the same place. She wrote a

letter to her father, did not finish it and tore it up . . . She waited all morning in her room, not knowing what she was thinking, just feeling dazed. She wanted to go on the boat right away, but it was taking so long to get dark; she began to be impatient with all the bother there was even in dying. Actually at this time, in her subconsciousness (qianyishi) she was probably also very worried that the sun was setting too quickly. Could she really just like that cut herself off from the world?[63]

The narrator's omniscience can bring out contradictory or subconsious feelings the diarist is not aware of; the narrator can also extend the story beyond the diary and place it in an entirely new light. There is a sudden change of tone in the last section as we find ourselves moved from the inner state of the character to her external situation. The old landlady comes in with a tearful countenance, grumbling about the overdue rent. Isa has only a dollar (yuan) and some thirty odd pennies (tongban) in her drawer. In desperation she hands the landlady the nine-page diary attaching a note to it: "For help in an emergency, in exchange of this for a little money, please give any sum, large or small, to the bearer!"[64]

The story ends on this plea for help. Ironically, the diary that began as a record of the progression toward death turns into the means for a kind of survival; the pittance it can be sold for provides a temporary livelihood. Thus the story can be read as an emblem of the writer's condition as perceived by Ding Ling at that time. It is at the edge of privation that the writer must struggle to survive, while wresting from it both the impetus and material for her writing. The suicide's despair is turned into a source of life and literary creativity.

This martyr's pose and the self-pity it implies grew out of the harsh conditions of the writer's existence in the 1920s and 1930s. One measure of his hardship was that everything—his ability to fend off the landlord, his standard of living, his survival—depended on the quantity he could produce. Writers were paid by the number of words th rote, easily calculable on the standard manuscript paper that was premarked with vertical rows of small rectangles where individual characters and punctuation marks would fit. The convertibility of each word, each page into money was immediately manifest; a source of unremitting pressure.

In his Reminiscences of Hu Yepin, Shen Congwen includes some vividly detailed accounts about the life together of his two friends. In 1926 to 1927 (the first draft of "Mengke" was appearing "a page or two at a time on top of the tiny desk"), "because of his unceasing efforts at writing, and certain opportunities to become better acquainted with those editors who had some power to control our manuscripts," Hu Yepin was able to bring in about twenty-five yuan each month, but their life was still "really awkward and ridiculous." In December they might have a coal stove but no coal to put in it, and when the cold air became oppressive they would sit in bed and read. At the end of the month when rent was due, when dawdling and excuses no longer sufficed, they would "seek a pretext to go out, walking in the snow along the river, not daring to return until deep into the night."[65]

Shen Congwen wrote his two books on Ding Ling and Hu Yepin after their arrests and presumed executions, intending to recall them as young idealists, innocent victims of harsh political facts they may not have fully understood. Thus his reminiscences of the couple at times seem to confer on their shabby surroundings, their walks to the pawn shop, their wrangling over thirty or fifty cents, an almost idyllic, insouciant charm, "although they were that poor, poverty to them was not a hardship."[66]

But a passage Ding Ling interjects into the story "Miss Amao" (a "slice of life" that appears irrelevant to the rest of the text), speaks directly of the writer's existence in rather more bitter terms. To "rustic, ignorant Amao" all women were just like herself, with the same vanity and desires:

> She did not know . . . there were also those women who did their own cooking, their own washing, who spewed out their own heart and blood to write, submitting to someone to count up the words and pay them out a little money to live on, who labor under a great many pressures yet still want to learn something—those women who write to tell the world that which in their loneliness (*gudu*) they see but have no friend to share with, who yet receive nothing more than deathlike cold indifference, who still patiently walk the path of literature, already beneath the notice of this materialistic petty profit-craving age.[67]

The physical hardships entailed in doing her own washing and cooking—squatting by a low small stove set on the floor—represented, to a woman of Ding Ling's wealthy gentry background, a real and unwonted burden. But the real source of bitterness was the "deathlike cold indifference" of the "petty profit-craving age," the loneliness of the writer's profession.

What was happening in China as it entered the modern world was in many respects similar to the passing of the patronage system that began toward the end of the eighteenth century in England (and elsewhere), causing the writer, in Raymond Williams's words, to become a "fully-fledged 'professional man'" and bringing a major change in the nature of the relationship between him and his readers. His work then became subject to the "laws of the market," which were largely impersonal and seemingly capricious.[68] The loss of patronage meant the loss of a well-defined and clearly understood relation to at least some part of society. In traditional China the writer of classical literature had the security of knowing that he was writing for his fellow scholar-officials, both those who were

his contemporaries and — thanks to the deathlessness of the classical language — those of the infinite future. Although there were also writers who
earned their living through their work, they were almost without exception practitioners of certain types of drama, fiction, popular songs — genres which had not been recognized as serious literature. They probably
did not entertain a sufficiently elevated notion of their profession to
suffer from a sense of alienation from their public. In traditional China
both classical and popular writers felt that they "belonged" or at least did
not consciously sense that they did not.

By contrast, in early twentieth-century China the writer was struggling to create a new literature for an audience that had yet to be established. Even more threatening to his sense of relevance, the serious writer
discovered that in the market he was in losing competition with another
more or less new literature, the "Mandarin Duck and Butterfly" type of
popular urban fiction whose only purpose was to provide escape.[69] The
mass appeal and blatant commercial success of this popular fiction were
doubly bitter to the May Fourth writers since one of the important argu-
ments in their fight against traditional literature had been its elitist nature. In creating a new literature *they* were supposed to be carrying out
their self-appointed mission of reaching the people. But what they
"spewed out their own heart and blood to write" remained "beneath the
notice" of their age.

In the passage from "Miss Amao" the writer's activity is described by
Ding Ling as both issuing from and ending in loneliness. This sense of
loneliness (*gudu* or *jimo*) occurs like a refrain in references she makes to
her writings of this period:

Why did I write stories at that time? I think it was out of loneliness (*jimo*): dissatisfied with the impasse (*wu chulu*) in my life, a lot of things I needed to say,
but no one to listen to them, very anxious to do some work, but no opportunity. So for convenience I took up my pen, to analyze for myself this society.[70]

These thoughts, written in 1933, are echoed in 1950:

Apart from my stories I could not find a single friend, so I wrote stories. My
stories could not help but be filled with contempt for society and with the stub-
bornness of the individual's lonely (*gudu*) soul. My suffering, and the great
desire to break out of the old, narrow circle, also affected Yepin.[71]

Although there is a marginal acknowledgment of the broader context within which the lonely enterprise of literature must be carried out,
"society" referred in part to the difficult conditions of artistic production.
The insecurity of writing for an impersonal, amorphous public, the elu-
siveness of proper recognition or recompense, and the sheer hardships of
a life devoted to art reinforced the writer's sense of alienation and continually tormented her (or him) with questions about the purpose of writ-

ing. The personal loneliness and pain that Ding Ling identified again and again as the impulse and consequence of literary practice determined to a great extent the subject matter of her early fiction: its intense concentration on the "individual's lonely soul," the self alone against the world. The implications this subjectivism had for writing are pursued to their furthest limits in "The Diary of Miss Sophie."

"The Diary of Miss Sophie"

The diary covers the brief period of December 24 to March 28, the harsh winter months dangerous for people suffering from tuberculosis. Immediately in the opening sentences the protagonist conveys her feeling that the world, including the very elements, is set against her.

> Today it's blowing hard again! Before it was dawn I was awakened by the wind. The servant came in to light the fiire; I knew that no matter what there would be no going back to sleep then.

A misfortune, particularly as it is no easy matter to get to sleep:

> I also knew that if I did not get up, my head would feel dizzy. When under the covers I am too fond of thinking about all kinds of strange things. The doctor said the best thing is to sleep a lot, eat a lot, not to read, not to think, but this is precisely what is impossible for me; every night it is always two or three before I can fall asleep. Then before dawn I'm awake again.

The winter wind victimizes in other pervasive ways:

> On a day blowing like this, one cannot help thinking of all kinds of irritating things. Moreover once it blows I cannot go out for amusement, and, shut up inside with nothing to read, what else is there to do? Am I to sit idly by myself, waiting for time to pass? Every day I wait, dragging on, wishing only for winter to go by quickly; as soon as it is warm my cough is bound to get better. Then I can go back south if I choose, or go to school if I choose; but the winter is really much too long.[72]

So ends the first paragraph, establishing not only the adverse nature of Sophie's environment, but suggesting also a kind of conspiracy between it and certain aspects of her personality to undermine her well-being. The cold winter, the blowing wind, the ill-timed actions of the servant stimulate Sophie's hypersensitivity, her perverse inclination to think, her persistent insomnia; together they make constructive action or positive choice — to get well, to go south, or return to school — difficult.

Throughout the diary Sophie feels caught in contradictory situations. The state of perpetual conflict and wavering is reflected in the frequency of such words as *dan, you, sui, qishi, jing, fan, pian, pianpian,* (but, furthermore, although, actually, nevertheless, on the contrary, perversely) to indicate the relations between clauses or sentences, a verbal pattern microcosmically reflecting her basic condition. Sophie is constantly fluctuating between the many opposites set up in the story: wholesome milk and ruinous wine, health and illness, laughter and tears, life and death, truth and deception, friendship and loneliness, regard and disgust for herself. The diary follows the shifts and turns in her experiences; nothing is settled, nothing is clarified before leading immediately to its opposite. The restless turmoil is intensified by the dominant contradiction of being in love with a man she despises; in the end the self-scrutiny this experience provokes drives her into the impasse of near-suicidal despair.

This, in summary, is the main "action" of Ding Ling's most famous short story — a portrait of the "modern girl" (the English phrase was often resorted to, the phenomenon being as yet too new for the Chinese language) that "stunned a literary generation."[73] A common contemporary observation was the story's historical "truth"; just a few passages of "The Diary" can "make us understand the greater part of the new modern woman."[74] Mao Dun, whose own novel *Eclipse* contained a gallery of portraits of young women and was being serialized in the same issue of the *Xiaoshuo yuebao* (Fiction Monthly) in which "The Diary" was published, later referred to Sophie as "representative of the contradictory psychology regarding sexual love found in young women liberated since May Fourth."[75] Implicit in the notion of contradictory psychology was a recognition of the pathological aspects of her personality: the *fin de siècle* (*shijimo*) female temperament produced by sickness (*bingtai*).[76] Much of the work's impact on its contemporary readers came from their perception of the disorder raging within the central character as being truly symptomatic of their own time.

Illness, in the particular form of tuberculosis, is not only the physical condition of the protagonist but also an indispensable part of her personality, a powerful source of much of the story's "romantic agony."[77] Illness is more "interesting" than health. It sets Sophie apart from the others; it frees her from regular occupation, reinforcing her restlessness. The tubercular person is supposed to be more sensitive, more fragile, more open to pain and suffering. Miss Sophie is thus qualified to be a member of the line of *duochouduobing* women (laden with sorrow and illness), the most famous example being of course Lin Daiyu in *Dream of the Red Chamber*. A nineteenth-century Western counterpart could be found in Marguerite of *La Dame aux Camélias*, which was a particularly popular import during the May Fourth period.[78] The rise in temperature that is a symptom of tuberculosis also contributes towards the febrile, somewhat hysterical tone of "The Diary," but on a metaphorical level life itself becomes heightened; the awareness that death could be imminent — at one time Sophie coughs blood and has to be taken to the hospital, causing a gap in her diary from January 19 to March 4 — makes her infatuation both more urgent and more hopeless. The disease intensifies her oscillating and contradictory attitude toward the object of her passion.

Sophie's ambivalence toward sexuality is also characteristic of the particular limbo in which the quasi-liberated young woman found herself during the 1920s and 1930s, when she was only partially freed from the traditional institutionalized modes of womanly behavior. While critical of her friends who "suppress the expression" of their love out of fear of pregnancy (p. 208), implying that she herself would not be held back by similar considerations, Sophie also worries that her own actions are not what a "respectable woman (*zhengjing nüren*) would do" (p. 207). Her heart leaps up, she is "ashamed and afraid" when she is alone with Ling Jishi (p. 212), she indulges in fantasies of "dissolving" under his kiss, yet when she sees the "fires of lust" burning in his eyes, she rejects him for "his contemptible and shallow needs" (p. 222). The first time she meets him and sees those "bright red, tender, finely curved lips" — they will become an obsession of hers — she is like a child longing for candy, "but I know that in this society, I am not permitted to take that which will satisfy my stirrings, my desires, even if this will not injure anyone" (p. 205).

Sophie defiantly proclaims her passionate desires, yet does not feel free to indulge them. Her predicament, as has been pointed out, is due to particular sociohistorical conditions. Thus Mao Dun refers to Sophie as "an individualist, a rebel against traditional morality . . . the despairing cry of rebellion by a young woman whose soul bears the wounds of bitterness and melancholy of its time."[79] From the perspective of 1957 and a presumably less repressive society, another critic writes that the characters in Ding Ling's works were "filled with the ardor of youth's freedom to love (*ziyou lianai*) aroused by the May Fourth Movement, but which at the time could only bring a sense of disillusionment and emptiness; it remained the froth of an ideal that could not be satisfied or realized."[80] The stylistic as well as psychological agitations throughout the story are the manifestation of a sexuality that had been liberated and aroused but had no socially legitimate means of fulfillment.

Yet in the extremely subjective world of "The Diary" external reality, like the blowing wind reduced to a noisy disturbance intruding upon Sophie's overwrought nerve endings, scarcely exists in its own substantial right. Restrictive social obstacles become internalized restraints, so that what one sees is not so much a woman pitted against a repressive society, but one continually at war with herself. Sexuality, like tuberculosis, becomes a personal affliction, and in many ways the two are seen as analogous. Both are powerfully destructive forces, deeply subversive of physical and mental well-being, and both can lead to annihilation. Sophie's fantasies of dying are either in the form of the "death bed scene"

(p. 206), surrounded by "sisters kneeling and weeping on the bearskin rug," or as the culmination of passionate kisses and embraces (pp. 219–220). Finding herself in double jeopardy, Sophie must struggle to define and preserve intact some sense of self. The writing of the diary is the externalized form of the struggle.

Ding Ling's chosen mode of narration has profound implications for the development of her theme. Miss Sophie is one of the few first-person narrators in her fiction, the diary one of the very few times when Ding Ling rigidly confined herself to narrating a story exclusively from within the internal point of view of a main character. Sophie is never seen objectively from the outside. All her relationships with the other characters in the story constantly confirm in her mind their utter inability to understand her; thus the reader has no other corrective focus, albeit indirect, with which to compare her view of herself. Sophie says that to her friends she appears "aloof, haughty, eccentric," and her characteristic plaintive cry is, "Why doesn't he understand me a little better?" She wants to be understood, not merely loved, but Wei, the man pathetically in love with her, and Ling Jishi, the man she is desperately in love with, seem to understand her least of all. The pain she feels because Ling does not understand her is driven home when she realizes that his comment, "Sophie, you are really a strange girl," reflects merely his observations of some things about her that he is unaccustomed to seeing, like her torn gloves, perfumeless dresser drawer, her old toys; it is not made because he is impressed in any way with her as a different kind of person. Yet in the same paragraph she admits, "I have never said anything to him that really comes from myself . . . I am very sad; I am unable to make myself understood and respected by him" (p. 219).

There is always the question, hovering at the edge of Sophie's consciousness but not directly confronted, as to whether the world's failure to understand her is due to her unique complexities or to her own willful mystification. She is aware that she is often playing a part, deliberately creating the opposite impression of what she thinks. "I deceived Yunlin, as if telling lies were my instinctive faculty and today I exercised it effortlessly" (p. 206). She tells the man whose love she wants that she has a child. "I was really able to fool him; I was proud of my dishonesty" (p. 209). She fluctuates between her worried search for understanding and her own deceptive efforts that repeatedly sabotage it. This duality also characterizes her performance of the narrator's role.

Although the distinction between first- and third-person narration is a much overworked one,[81] since the narrator's pronominal reference to himself as narrator does not necessarily in itself tell us anything, the I-narration does permit certain forms of self-conscious dramatization to be built into the narrative process. To be "both chief actor and exqui-

sitely appreciative spectator" of one's personal drama will always raise
the question of in what sense one is "acting,"[82] with all the attendant ambiguities of that word. The ambiguous role of the "acting" narrator is dramatized in one of the few fully developed *scenes* in the diary:

> March 21: Just as I finished my milk and eggs, a familiar knock sounded on the
> door and a tall shadow appeared against the paper window pane. What I
> wanted to do was jump over there to open the door but held back by some
> strange feeling, I held my breath, and lowered my head.
>
> "Are you up, Sophie?" The voice was so soft and tender, it made me want to
> weep.
>
> Was it because he knew I was already in a chair? or because he knew I was
> incapable of getting angry and refusing him? He gently opened the door and
> entered. I was afraid to raise my wet eyelids.
>
> "Are you better, did you just get up?"
>
> I couldn't answer a word.
>
> "You're really angry with me, Sophie. You don't want to be bothered with
> me. I'd better leave, Sophie!"
>
> For him to leave would of course be just right with me, but I suddenly raised
> my head and with my glance stopped his hand as it reached for the door.
>
> Who can say he is not a cad? He understood. He dared to grasp my two
> hands tightly.
>
> "You're playing with me, Sophie. Every day I've walked by your door afraid
> to come in. If Yunlin had not said you were not cross with me I wouldn't have
> dared to come today. Sophie, are you annoyed with me?"
>
> Anyone could have seen that if at this moment he had dared to hold me and
> wildly kiss me, I would have fallen into his arms weeping and saying, "I love
> you! I love you!" But he was so cool (*lengdan*), so cool that it made me hate
> him again. But inside I was thinking, "Do embrace me, I so want to kiss you on
> the face!" (pp. 216–217)

Since actions are shown to belie the state of one's inner feelings, as
the self-conscious witness of her own unpredictable shifts of behavior,
the narrator (and the reader also) is not able to say with any degree of as-
surance which speech, which gesture, represents a true self even at a
given moment. Throughout the diary Miss Sophie is struggling to evolve
an intelligible and authentic image of the self, a self that could manage
the crises of love, of ill-health, of isolation; but the self-portrait as it
emerges is so baffling and unsettling that she is soon caught in an additional, all-subsuming crisis, one of self-knowledge, or rather, the crisis of
determining whether the self is ultimately knowable.

Behind the questions of what to do and how to act is the question
which the mode of narration itself simultaneously propounds and dram-
atizes: Do I make sense even to myself? Sophie's neurotic self-dramatiza-
tions and her ambivalent attitude towards the world work together in

powerful ways with the functioning of the diarist as narrator. The diary form must postulate an innocent narrator, one of restricted omniscience, in whom "the suppression, delay, and distribution of exposition is not only perfectly natural but almost inescapable in the very nature of the case."[83] The diarist can only know at the end of each day or at the moment of writing what has transpired so far, but has no foreknowledge of what the next day will bring. Each entry's conclusion opens up the questions "What will happen tomorrow? How is all this going to end?" By such means the diarist creates and sustains for herself and the reader a state of suspense and uncertainty as she moves from entry to entry, drawing the reader deeply into the journey of discovery she has embarked upon. There is, first of all, the tantalizing uncertainty that accompanies falling in love. Does he or doesn't he love me? Do I or don't I love him? If he doesn't, and I do, and know I shouldn't, what does this predicament tell me about myself? The first question leads to the others. But the point at issue is not so much the outcome of the love affair, which seems doomed from the start, but the self-probing that it sets in motion and what it will reveal to Sophie about herself. However, given the contrary behavior of the protagonist as she herself sees it unfold, anything can happen.

Endlessly she interrogates herself in the pages of the diary. "Can I say what it is that I really want?" (p. 206). And later, "But then what is my point after all? This is really hard to say" (p. 214). Although apparently written only from one point of view, that of the main character, at times the diary resembles a series of dialogues between multiple selves. "What do I want? Nothing will help me" (p. 210). At one point, however, the internal conflicts, the split between observer-critic and actor-agent create in the writer a state of near paralysis:

> I haven't written anything again for several days. Whether it's due to my sour mood or some nameless feeling, I don't know. All I know is that since yesterday I have just wanted to cry. When others see me cry they imagine I am thinking of home, thinking of my illness; when they see me laugh, they think I am happy and congratulate me on the radiance of my health . . . But all so-called friends are the same; to whom can I confide my fond heart, which disdains tears yet is incapable of laughter? Furthermore, since I understand so well the various desires in the world that I am unwilling to relinquish, and the distress that results from every effort to pursue them, even I am no longer willing to be sympathetic toward this sorrow that comes on unrepentantly. How then can I take up a pen and express in detail all my self-accusation and self-hatred? p. 214)

We hear again the complaint that her friends fail her by always misunderstanding what lies behind her tears and her laughter, yet the causes of her moods and behavior are inexplicable also to herself. Moreover, she is losing patience with the contradictory self she is coming to perceive. The language in this passage, characteristic of the style of the diary in general, reflects her frame of mind. There is an extraordinary number of sentences and clauses that emphatically revolve around first person or reflexive pronouns: I, my, self. This points to Sophie's self-absorption and in itself represents a departure from Chinese linguistic practice, but the long convoluted clauses would also be recognized as European (*ouhua*). Each of these modifying clauses, apparently struggling to delineate with precision her real state of mind, and strung together with such connectives as again, whether . . . or, but, yet, even (*you, haishi . . . huoshi, dan, er, lian, geng*) leads only to clauses that seem to contradict or gainsay what has gone on immediately before. Together they mirror the tortuous backwards and forwards movement of the character's internal situation. The accumulation of words, instead of progressing toward the possibility of clarity or understanding, serves only to undermine it and reveal a state of impasse. Sophie feels she can no longer take up her pen; she has almost written herself, so to speak, into the impossibility of further writing.

In recording the encounter between this individual self and the world, the diary has therefore also been investigating the process and limits of writing itself: the encounter between the individual and literature. Much of the diary is about the writing of the diary. Miss Sophie examines her motives for undertaking it, questions its purpose, its effectiveness, and in the end, thoroughly disillusioned, renounces it. Very late in the story, she discloses that the diary had been initiated at the request of her most intimate friend, Sisten Yun, "a high-strung, ardently emotional person" (p. 210), who seems in certain ways an extension or alter ego of Sophie herself. Also a victim of love—through an apparent prank of the gods she fell in love with "the man with the pale white face" (p. 217)—she is destroyed by a ruinous marriage and dies (instead of Sophie) during Sophie's stay in the hospital. The *raison d'être* of the diary is thus removed with the death of the one person for whom it was first undertaken and whom the writer trusted to understand it.

The most important "implied reader" of the diary is of course the writer herself, whose purpose is to "assess and analyze her developing situation,"[84] and through the process to assess and analyze herself as a person. She is aware that the evolving impression is not one that would meet with general approval. The "morality or rationality" of others would probably censure her for the diary and "might cause me to feel just as badly as if I had been guilty of some crime" (p. 218). Yet on one critical occasion she acts against her earlier resolutions by showing the diary to her suitor Wei, in the hopes that he will not continue to misunderstand her. "If Brother Wei could know me, I would regard him as the only friend to whom I could open my heart"; but although he reads the diary over and over again, all he understands is that Sophie is in love with "him," the other man, that he himself is not good enough for her. The diary thus fails completely to "explain" her to Wei:

So who can understand me then? Even if he could have understood this diary which merely expresses one ten-thousandth of myself, it would only pain me to sense that limitation. And isn't it painful enough already, in my longing for another's understanding, to have to resort to showing a diary where every means through words is tried over and over again in explanations?   (p. 219)

She feels that she has wasted (*zaota*) the diary (a phrase she will repeat regarding her own person after Ling Jishi's last visit to her), and in extreme vexation wants to rip it up.

Although it is suggested that the diary's inefficacy is tied to the inadequacy of words, "Tonight I really went mad. How at such a time do language and writing show themselves to be useless!" (p. 221), the diary also casts grave doubts on the intelligibility of the self, on the self as a source of meaning and authenticity. But then is there anything else? All actions, facts, people, the external world, shed their independent substantiality as they are filtered through the subjective consciousness of the diarist. Her environment is barely sensed except as it causes annoyance, her friends are not people in their own right but merely shadows, memories, or sources of occasional support and much irritation. The only physical presence in the story, the only object described in specific detail is Ling Jishi. References to his tall stature, his white, delicate face, soft hair, and bright red lips run through the story like a refrain. But this seductive presence is merely the facade that hides a "low and ugly soul." Even after she grasps the despicable truth about this man, the initial attraction, deceptive as it had been, continues to exercise a fatal power over her. Ling Jishi is therefore also not a "real" person, or rather whatever is "real" about him is denied as he is made over into an image through her sexual fantasies and self-deception.

This disconcerting infatuation leaves the self, the presumed seat of knowledge, integrity, and coherence in the fictive world of the diary, in a shambles. Sophie is appalled to find that she is ready to give up her rational understanding, moral will, even the instinct for self-preservation for a passion that is based on nothing but a recognized delusion. "How should I explain it? The psychology of a woman gone completely mad over the looks of a man!" (p. 222), as she writes in the last day's entry. When on the last night she receives "as if in a dream, the miracle in her fantasies," the kiss she had thought she would be willing to "sacrifice everything for," she does not feel the "soul-intoxicating happiness" she had imagined (p. 222). As the "soft and moist warm thing" is put to her face she thinks "I have won! I have won!" but at the same time she is filled with self-contempt; she pushes him forcibly away and weeps (p. 223). The disillusion with the self and its passions is complete.

The pace of the story quickens as it moves towards the end. The last six days take up about one-fourth of the diary, with Sophie looking back at the diary's motivation and its demonstrated inadequacies (March 22), reflecting on the impending move to Xishan, which brings out premonitions of loneliness and dying (March 26), and indulging in sexual fantasies that reach a feverish pitch and culminate in death (March 24, 27, 28). All the strands of action in the story are thus brought together rapidly before the denouement. The diary must be concluded, not just because we have come to the end of the story, but because the writing of the diary itself has also been a plot line interwoven with the fabric of events. The diary entries had been Sophie's tears, each drop falling on her heart,

> but now Sophie no longer needs this—tears to vent anger or to console, because everything seems senseless, and shedding tears is the deepest expression of this senselessness (*wuyishi*).   (p. 222)

All that is left for her to do is to "go south where no one knows me and squander the remainder of my life." The passion expended into nothing, the self-scrutiny leading to self-condemnation, the diary that is given up as "senseless" converge in a conclusion of despair and self-pity.

Far from being a transparent medium, a mere window through which to see the action of the story, the diary is self-reflexive, not just a means for self-investigation by the main character, but itself a subject of investigation. Sophie's struggles toward affirmation and understanding of the self through writing turn out to be self-defeating, in part because the diary form, as she employs it, is revealed to be uniquely adapted for such defeat. The self coming into view, emerging through the pages of the diary, seems inexplicable to Sophie, because the diary-writing process fails to explicate. This solipsistic exercise in self-negating circularity is Ding Ling's most extreme statement on the relationship between subjectivism and literature.

The particular narrative form of "The Diary of Miss Sophie" was especially effective for an instructive interweaving of the central themes of Ding Ling's first period, the themes of the isolated self in the world and the meaning of writing. By exploring their implications to the farthest limits, the story offers an example of what the Marxist critic Georg Lukács, in reference to twentieth-century Western bourgeois literature, has called the "ideology of modernism."[85] Lukács' thesis is that the strict confinement of the protagonist within the limits of his own experience and the exclusion of pre-existent and objective reality beyond the self lead ultimately to the negation of literature. But one can argue that modernist ideology, rather than resulting in the destruction of literature, has broadened its boundaries to encompass the possibilities of its self-negation. Indeed the "modern" writing experience, while perhaps denying outward reality, powerfully affirms the existence of literature by showing that it can come into being even in the process of subverting itself. Such an expanded view of literature, however, was impossible in Ding Ling's fictional practice as it was in Lukács' critical theories. What he asserts to be essential in literature, a commitment to realism and a sense of history as seen from a specific perspective, point to the new direction Ding Ling's writing took soon after "The Diary." Within two years political developments in China, an introduction to Marxist ideology (though not necessarily as interpreted by Lukács), and the particular circumstances of her personal life led to a crisis of confidence in the kind of literature she had been writing. But the impasse reached in "Miss Sophie's Diary," the consequence of both theme and the operation of narrative form upon theme, may be seen as a prediction of that crisis, as a signal that the writer was prepared to move out of the self-confinement of subjectivism.

2

TOWARD A REVOLUTIONARY
LITERATURE

HAVING PUBLISHED some fourteen short stories in three years, Ding Ling seemed well on her way to a promising career as a major writer, but she had also been typed as one who specialized in the introspective modern young woman suffering the predicaments of love. During the next three years, from 1930 to 1933, the writer and her fiction went through a radical change — in fact, became politically radicalized. Ding Ling might have turned away from her early themes in any case, sensing perhaps that their fictional possibilities were nearing exhaustion; as it was, her writing was thrust onto a new course by external events. Indeed, for a few anguished years her life seemed to be a heightened, concentrated enactment of the tragic predicament of the Chinese writer during the first half of the 1930s. For many writers literary choices were increasingly dictated by revolutionary commitment and made against the threat of possible or actual martyrdom. In Ding Ling's case, the involvement of Hu Yepin in the politics of the Chinese Communist Party and his brutal execution by the Kuomintang inevitably had a fateful effect not just on her life, but on her notions of literature, the writer's role, and the kind of literature she was engaging to write.

Even before Hu's death, Ding Ling's own exposure to Marxist ideology was already extending the range of her fiction and turning her attention away from the subjective lives of her characters to the milieu in which they lived. As she took the first steps in this new direction, her stories portrayed characters who were themselves struggling to develop in a similar way.

A Year of Transition

Three of the fictional works Ding Ling wrote in 1930 — the short novel *Wei Hu* and the twin stories "Shanghai, Spring 1930" (I and II) — at first glance seem to be merely more treatments of a subject so prevalent and predictable at the time that it was referred to as the "love and revolution formula." During a talk given in May 1931 she admitted that the tangle of revolution and love had been a "shortcoming, and was no longer appropriate. But these stories were written last year; now circumstances have changed greatly."[1] While she was acknowledging the defects of these works and stressing their transitory nature, we can see the significant ways in which for her they were also transitional. Seen together the three stories are not just more variations on a contemporary hackneyed theme; in the light of her subsequent development, they show Ding Ling negotiating a passage *from* love *to* revolution, from the focus on internal experience to the outer world of political reality.

Even while defending *Wei Hu* against certain critics, Ding Ling apparently accepted its classification as a "love and revolution" work:

> Many people see the date of publication and insist on judging it as proletarian literature (*puluo wenxue*); I feel this is really unfair. My attitude in writing was different; what I demanded of the work was therefore also different. I did not plan to make Wei Hu into a hero, nor did I plan to write about revolution. I merely wanted to write about a few pre-May 30th characters.
>
> So for some days I wrote five thousand words a day. I was very excited, very happy. But when it was published in *Xiaoshuo yuebao* and I read it again I was terribly distressed. I discovered myself that it was only a very vulgar story fallen into the trap of the love and revolution conflict in the Guangchi manner.[2]

How much of this is genuine repentance — a trace of defiance is detectable behind the self-deprecation — is hard to say. In any case Ding Ling was clearly accepting the distinction between "proletarian" literature and "love and revolution" literature and quite prepared to make a blanket dismissal of the latter.

The love and revolution formula was characteristic of the "romantic generation," since both ingredients were linked by the "same emotional denominator." According to Leo Lee, here closely paraphrasing the language of those of whom he writes, "This revolutionary passion sprang from the very volcano of subjectivism which had emitted earlier the lava of love and sex in the early twenties."[3] The fact that the two ingredients were always so linked tells us something about the way revolution was perceived and experienced by the young intellectual writers of the time. The leftist writers of formulaic fiction in the 1930s, romantic, subjective, and passionate as they were, did to some extent capture the historical realities about those who made the revolution. Tsi-an Hsia discusses Ding Ling's two "Shanghai, Spring" stories in terms of their "interesting view of history," which he concedes contained certain elements of truth:

> These sketchy studies of ennui, eroticism, and revolutionary zeal, these little episodes about discontented intellectuals who do not actually suffer from material want, these vignettes filled with self-pity — do they contain some of the most significant events at the time and place referred to? Only in the eyes of a

few of her contemporaries; but these few were not entirely wrong. If the importance of an event is to be judged by its consequences, then the handful of young people, who broke away from their families and lovers to participate in street demonstrations foredoomed to failure, were harbingers of bigger events to come. It was young intellectuals not unlike the characters in Ding Ling's stories who kept replenishing the ranks of revolutionaries. It was they who carried on and spread the revolution in its most difficult time.[4]

But even if partially authentic, these attempts at literary self-portraiture by the revolutionary generation did not continue for long. Although the young intellectuals may have persisted in the romanticized view of themselves, they were beginning to lose confidence in literature: as it was conceived and practiced, it did not seem adequate for the portrayal of revolutionary reality. Ding Ling's stories in particular show that literature itself had become the issue.

In her fiction of 1930 about "love and revolution" conflicts literature enters the fray through the lovers, at least one of whom is always a writer. It could turn out to be an ally of either side but it is always present as the indispensable third ingredient in the formula. What happens to literature is one of the questions asked within each story as the conflict develops, and the answer is by no means uniform, reflecting Ding Ling's interest in exploring the complexities of the subject.

Wei Hu could be subtitled a "portrait of the revolutionary as an artist." The hero, who appears first in the coarse blue cotton clothes of a worker, is addressed from the beginning as "Tovarisch Wei" (*Dehualisi Wei*), his dual role as revolutionary/artist endowed with the romance of a recent sojourn in the Soviet Union. Recognized as the author of *My Diary*, (a characteristic title), he dazzles the girls with his talk of Chopin, Beethoven, Tolstoy, Turgenev, Sholokov, and his criticism of Russian women (he is experienced). There is only one thing about him that Lijia does not like; "he is a communist," but then, "he understands art, and he understands life."[5]

Lijia and her very liberated women friends, student-artists between schools, who have shed their family names, are independent, loud, unrestrained in their behavior, vaguely anarchistic, "too worshipful of freedom, everywhere scornful of men, and they thoroughly misunderstand Marxism." But the heroine has an "innocent, ardent, and child-like soul." It takes about two-thirds of the book for Lijia finally to declare her love for Wei Hu, because she needs to become disillusioned first with her anarchist friends who "merely in a state of bewilderment enjoyed what they themselves considered a free life."[6]

The last third of the novel is given over to an idyllic description of three months spent in rather bourgeois surroundings, time devoted to ⁎

passionate embraces and kisses interspersed with the reading of poetry, Wei Hu's own or Western poetry in translation. Hovering at the edges of the book is a textile factory strike, but love causes Wei Hu to neglect his revolutionary tasks as well as his job—teaching in a progressive school in Shanghai. Finally he faces up to the realization that Lijia and work are incompatible and accepts a party assignment to go to Guangdong, making the decision to break irrevocably with her: "He stood awhile downstairs . . . then with broad strides walked out, unaware that tears had covered his face. Ah! This sweetness of life, never to be had again!"[7]

Wei Hu is of course saying farewell to a dream, to the adolescent's last fling before facing the harsh realities and mature responsibilities of a politicized life. In the portrayal of this love affair and its principals Ding Ling seems to be at her most self-indulgent. Both lovers are greatly sentimentalized: Lijia is compared to fire, to the wild wind, her hair in disarray, her dress blown about, a free spirit, "in whose veins ran the heavy melancholy of Shelley, Byron, and Goethe." Wei Hu is the dream lover of such a young girl, older, mature, with an exotic past that includes a foreign mistress, and a present weighty with heavy political responsibilities, though these remain vague. Moreover he has at his fingertips a wide range of literature to enhance his ardent love-making. In his final letter he leaves his love Lijia his Western books that he will never read again, his love poems, his diary, all for her to deal with as she likes, "burning them would be a good thing."[8]

The conflict, as Wei Hu himself recognizes, is not between Lijia and his work, but deep within himself, between two aspects of his character. Alone one winter afternoon in a deserted park he realizes that "it is already the last moment," and that he must choose:

> After a long fierce battle, all that belonged to beauty, love, soft dreams and hopes and pleasure was broken and destroyed. And what he had had before, a kind of endurance and hardening of the will, again seethed in his whole body. He saw the future shining more dazzlingly bright even than blood.[9]

Thus the novel is not so much about the conflict between love and revolution, since the revolution hardly exists in the work as a tangible reality, as about the renunciation of what the committed individual comes to see as inimical to revolution. The obstacles include love, anarchic freedom, self-indulgence, and also, it would seem, the literature that nourishes love and makes possible one's deepest expressions and experiences of personal happiness. By weighting its descriptive interest on the side of love, *Wei Hu* is a nostalgic lingering on what has already been or will soon be lost and past, rather than a positive affirmation of the revolutionary future.

In the two "Shanghai" stories the two main characters must likewise renounce love in favor of revolution, but they need not give up literature. Instead, they seek a new kind of literature, not the kind that will enhance or is even relevant to love, but one that will serve the revolution. The entanglement between love, revolution, and literature has been stripped in these stories of some of the trappings of the fantasy and romance so marked in *Wei Hu*. In "Shanghai, Spring 1930, I," the triangular conflict gains substance by being placed within the context of a carefully delineated deteriorating relationship. Parallel to the successful writer Zibin's growing lack of self-confidence is the transformation of the heroine, Meilin, from his complacent mistress into active revolutionary. Her awakening to the truth of her own situation and to the need to reach out for other means of self-fulfillment provide the prime motivating force in the story's development. Literature had brought them together:

> She had read his novels, had worshiped him; later when he fell in love with her, she accordingly loved him too. When he asked her to live with him, she of course agreed. But she should have known that once she lived with him she would lose all social standing . . . She realized that apart from him, she had nothing. In the past she had read many classical and romantic novels; her ideal was that if there was love, then everything else could be given up. From the time she had been in love with him, she had truly left everything to throw herself into his embrace. And stupidly she had gone on thinking she was fortunate, was happy all this time. But now it was no longer so. She had to have more! . . . She could not just be shut up in a room to be the after-work entertainment of one person. Even if they did love each other! True she still loved him, she affirmed that there would not come a day when she would turn her back on him, but she seemed to feel that invisibly he everywhere oppressed her. He did not permit her any freedom; it was worse than in a traditional family. He coddled her, humoured her, provided her with all types of material satisfactions. But in his thinking there was only the one idea that she should love him and love that which he loved. She continued to muse. Why was it? He was so gentle, yet so tyrannical.[10]

Like Ding Ling's earlier heroines Meilin is also living beyond the pale of convention, but unlike them she is not searching for independence and identity through or within a love experience. Instead she recognizes the necessity of breaking away from love, since despite the comfort and even happiness it offered, it could not but be confining and oppressive to the self. The love relationship she feels trapped in was shaped by romantic notions of literature as much as by anything else. Yet her personal liberation is not the uppermost concern now. What she will need is to become aware of a radically different kind of literature and to seek self-fulfillment through commitment to a larger collective cause.

The two lovers grow farther apart. While Zibin is absorbed in plans to astonish the world with a hundred-thousand-word novel, a satire on a Chinese Don Quixote, Meilin attends meetings of leftist literature study groups. There she meets workers, young writers, students. A woman textile-mill worker "wants revolution, but also to learn some literature that we can understand."[11] She is just beginning to write and would like help with a factory newsletter (*tongxin*). At the end of the story Meilin is taking part in a street demonstration, and Zibin, informed of this in the note she leaves for him, shuts his manuscript pad with a slam and flings it into the drawer. He has been in despair over his writings, which to his friends show him to be "a person who totally belonged to a different age."[12]

Times were changing, as the date in the title of the story indicates. For Ding Ling literature had reached a turning point in 1930. The story includes a passage that is much quoted because it summarizes the disillusionment with literature in words that go straight to the heart of the matter:

As for writing, I sometimes feel that it would not be much of a loss if we gave it up entirely. We write, some people read, time passes, and there is no effect whatsoever. What is the meaning of it then except we've gotten paid for it? Even if some readers are moved by some part of the plot or certain passages — but who are these readers? Students of the petty bourgeois class above high school level who have just reached adolescence and are most subject to melancholy. They feel that these writings fit their temper perfectly, expressing some melancholy that they can feel but not really experience . . . But in the end? Now I understand we have dragged these young people down our old paths. The sort of sentimentalism, individualism, grumblings, and sorrows with no way out! . . . Where is the way out for them? They can only sink deeper and deeper day by day into their own gloom, not seeing the connection between society and their sufferings. Even if they could improve their language and produce some essays and poems that may win praise from some old writers, what good, I ask you, is it to them? And what good to society? Therefore with regard to writing, personally I am ready to give it up.[13]

Significantly this critical statement is made not by either main character in the story but by their friend Ruoquan, a type of minor character who was beginning to appear frequently in Ding Ling's fiction. This figure may be called the "mentor," and is usually a party member or a more progressive or experienced comrade. While the main characters struggle for enlightenment or to overcome self-doubts and weaknesses, the mentor with his superior insight comes up immediately with the right answer. He is the person the struggling main character can turn to at the moment of crisis or decision, as Meilin does; the one who will "listen to her, understand her, and help her."[14] Often the mentor is a vague and shadowy figure, he may even be nameless, but his presence is necessary as a standard against which the protagonists can measure their aspirations. He does not directly participate in the action, nor interact in any complex, intimate way with the other characters; Ruoquan does not, for example, fall in love with Meilin. This noninvolvement protects the mentor from the uncertainty and vulnerability suffered by the more "human" characters.

With a mentor figure available, the characters need not feel, as did Sophie, Amao, and Mengke of the earlier stories, that they are tragically alone in facing the outside world. Indeed the presence of the mentor guarantees a positive outcome in the story, or rather he only appears in the positive stories. He is inevitably an abstract character, because he is not an individual but the representative of the collective, or of an idealized, optimistic image of the collective.

A similar embodiment of the ideal is found in the relationship between the secondary pair of lovers in "Shanghai, Spring 1930, II." They exist on a plane of reality different from that of the major characters; their relationship is an ideal, a goal to which the major characters can only aspire. The central character, Wangwei, works in a proletarian literary organization. His lover-opponent in the love and revolution collision is a seductively beautiful woman totally unsympathetic to his work. The story lingers on Mali's physical attractions and the love-making that tempts Wangwei to neglect his political responsibilities. She leaves him and he has a last glimpse of her, dazzling and elegant as ever, with another man, as he himself is being pushed into a black iron van, arrested for making a speech at a demonstration. During these closing moments of the story, Wangwei also sees his colleague Feng Fei arm-in-arm with a bus conductor. The dream he himself once had of union with "a revolutionary woman"[15] is now realized, as evidenced by Feng Fei's happy face, in this secondary pair of lovers.

In *Wei Hu* literature had seemed incompatible with revolution, but the "Shanghai Spring" stories specify that only subjective, individualistic, melancholy literature needs to be set aside; a new literature that will serve the cause of political revolution will somehow emerge through contact with textile-mill workers and bus conductors. In all three works the outside world of revolutionary activity, whose urgent demands are threatening the beautiful dreams of love, youth, freedom, and romance, remains rather indistinct. There is no real sense of pressing external reality. The meetings with workers, the street demonstrations, the work assignment in faraway Guangdong lack the concrete specificity of the changing emotional relationships or the inner turmoil of the torn-apart characters.

Ding Ling published one more work in the transitional year of 1930, in which she combined the love-revolution-literature ingredients in a radically different way. "Nianqian de yitian" (The Day before New Year's) is further set apart from the other stories because its matter-of-fact depiction of everyday details suggests a close connection with actual personal experience. There is little glamorization of the lovers:

> She was an apparently ordinary woman, named Xin, around twenty-four. Somewhat rough and stubborn. Thick, dark, strong and long eyebrows, a determined look in her eyes, showed something of her character. No job or family, but she often wrote fiction and the like for magazines to make some money. She lived with a young man of about the same age who also depended on selling his writings.[16]

They fret over the lack of coal and rice, worry about the rent money, quarrel over her habit of reading in bed. Revolutionary activity is relegated to her nightmares (she is high-strung):

> This morning she was having another such dream again . . . She was pushing her way through a wildly shouting crowd; she wanted to get up front. She was panting, an irrepressible excitement, general confusion, everything around was becoming madder. She heard the sound of bayonets, the hooves of horses, the grating wheels of the fire engines. Then she saw many soldiers, a lot of blood, a lot of faces of those who had been chopped down and killed. Just as she was going to cry out, she woke up.[17]

More revolutionary violence is expressed in this nightmare than appears in the other stories Ding Ling wrote in that year, where the characters are supposedly already engaged in actual struggle. But the fact that horror and ugliness are still "only a dream" in this story may account for its containing one of the warmest and most tender love relationships Ding Ling ever presented in her fiction. In spite of the dire poverty and the petty spats, this love, in contrast to all the others, nevertheless supports and sustains the literary enterprise.

The young man goes out to look for some money to tide them over till the new year. In a long narrated monologue Xin reviews the exhausting effort, the economic precariousness, the almost paralyzing self-doubts that beset the writer's existence and repeats to herself, "no matter what, I am going to abandon this business of writing, and before I am dead, do some more practical work." Yet the story ends with a strong affirmation of the literary commitment. After being refused at several places, her lover returns laughing and clutching a twenty-yuan advance from an editor, "now we can get through New Year's!"

> But what about all the debts, all the interest . . . A big black shadow came over her heart, but she purposely evaded it . . .
> The lover was too young, his whole body brimming with that healthy and brave force of life. All the dark shadows of existence, like the cloudy drizzling

weather, left her mind. At night while they sat across from each other at both sides of the table munching oranges, she began the piece she had been planning to write.[18]

In the following year Ding Ling wrote another story, "Yitian" (One Day), which also concludes with the writer physically engaged in the act of writing, taking up his pen because of, or in spite of, what has happened. But the nature of literary commitment had changed. By then the young lover had become a martyr, and violent death, once only a nightmare, turned into reality in her personal life. There were new tensions now between the outside world and the practice of literature and the need to accommodate both in new ways became imperative.

Milieu and Metaphor

In response to political exigencies, Ding Ling attempted in her "love and revolution" fiction of 1930 to turn away from excessive concern with the individual's subjective life. But the external reality for which her characters suffered the pangs of renunciation was but vaguely delineated. After 1930 the outside world is closely observed and represented more concretely. The range of character and subject matter is greatly expanded. The stories are no longer dominated by young, mostly female, displaced intellectuals, but include old women, factory workers, the urban poor, vagrant beggars, peasants in the countryside. Narrative interest shifts from the internal mental and emotional states of her characters to their physical and social environment.

In the earlier stories physical surroundings, when taken into account at all, often acted as an irritant to the individual's sensitive nerves, reinforcing his sense of opposition to his world, and reminding him of his rootless, alienated condition.[19] Now the stories become explicitly grounded in material reality, characters *belong* to a particular place; they cannot be detached and perceived apart from their spatial context. Yet the ways in which the world out there is brought into the story and related to the story's theme vary markedly from work to work.

"Tianjiachong" (Tian Family Village), written in 1931, is one of the first to utilize a detailed setting to express a political theme. From its opening scene the story glows with the beauty of the countryside and with the hopes for a better life for those who live in a state of happy intimacy with it:

The sun had just gone down behind the mountain opposite the door; the sky was colored with rosy clouds. Groves of trees on the mountain had already turned dark, thickly and sharply etched against the transparent pink sky. Yaomei [Little sister]—she was just fourteen this year—was standing under a peach tree on the threshing floor, her face shining, rosy, a little like the flower petals. She looked at the whole scene that was soon to fade away, her heart, as it so often was, filled with happiness.[20]

This happy contemplation is broken by an anxious sigh from her mother, an ominous note leading up to the main event of the story — the visit of Third Miss, the landlord's daughter — an event that will disrupt the peasant family's settled country life and give it new direction by introducing its members to the necessity and possibility of revolutionary change. The meeting of an enlightened member of the landlord-gentry class, a carrier of revolutionary vision, with the peasants, for whom and by whom (once they are mobilized) the revolution is to be carried out, is of course historically correct as well as ideologically proper. The meeting receives here one of its most idealized literary treatments. Third Miss is almost a fairy-tale figure, a fantasy self-image of the upper-class intellectual among the peasants, whose political consciousness she intends to raise:

> They were much merrier. They had found a person to listen to their everyday affairs, to listen to the hardships of their lives, to listen to their pathetic enjoyments. This person not only listened, she responded, she asked questions, she explained to them the reasons for their unrewarded labor. And she gave them ideals and hope, and the possibility of realizing them. She taught them, encouraged them, but they still thought of her as a lovable child, because she did not forget to be deliberately mischievous, to make them laugh, to make them forget her own position, so that they just felt like poking her, touching her, or even embracing her.[21]

Ding Ling herself admitted that the figure of Third Miss was romantic (*luomantike*) but insisted that "the material was true." She also accepted the criticism that her description of the countryside had made it "too beautiful."[22] "How happy you are!" exclaims Third Miss the morning after she arrives:

> She turned around to look, feeling that the house was somewhat older now. Of course, from another point of view (*kanfa*), this was the best foil to the scene: that tranquil-looking ancient black tile and wall, that beautiful thatched shed, that low section of mud fence; yellow earth of such a clean dazzling color. Large tree groves embraced the house, hills that were not precipitous extended soft limbs to hold it gently. And beautiful fields stretched out before it like a painting. What a lovely fairyland![23]

The passage is of course written from the point of view (*kanfa*) of Third Miss, happy to find herself again in the country and recalling her previous visit of six or seven years ago. But her enthusiasm for the rustic landscape and enjoyment of such chores as feeding the ducks and chickens, taking out the cow, fertilizing the vegetables or picking the bugs off them, are in seeming contradiction to the message of revolution that she brings. When Ding Ling was criticized for this, she responded that she "loved the countryside," and that she had written about the "relatively tranquil countryside of the past." But she admitted also that her feelings for the countryside had issued from a kind of "middle peasant consciousness" which she "should be able to overcome."[24]

Point of view, then, was a matter of class consciousness, and ideology should determine the perception and presentation of the world. Ding Ling's description of the countryside in this story and in her later novel *Mother*, in which she appears as a three- or four-year-old girl, abound in passages that find wonder and charm in the rustic scene, as if it were seen fresh through the eyes of a child. Although the ambience of the "Tian Family Village" may have derived from happy childhood memories, the idealized treatment of the peasantry had its political base: one is buoyed by the company of peasants because they are the reservoirs of revolutionary virtue and energy. The problem was how to balance this animating image of the peasants with the idea that revolution was imperative because they were bowed down by misery and exploitation.

It is not the objective world — whatever that may be — that should be the object of representation, but the world seen as ripe for, or in the process of, revolution. The portrayal of reality, the specificity of the setting, will in large measure depend on where the story's events fall on this revolutionary time-scale. While the prerevolutionary world is pervaded by darkness and suffering, the world well on the road to revolutionary progress is buoyant and hopeful. One difficulty was where to place the story of "Tian Family Village." The fleeting though wondrous presence of Third Miss, presumed killed at the end of the story, is not sufficient to move her friends forward out of the stage of prerevolutionary darkness. The beautiful descriptions of the countryside were therefore ideologically incorrect because chronologically misplaced.

The problematic handling of the countryside in "Tian Family Village" and Ding Ling's subsequent apologies show how fraught with difficulties the representation of milieu could be. In his study of realism and the rise of the novel, Ian Watt speaks of the significance of a novelist like Defoe who would seem to be the first who "visualized the whole of his narrative as though it occurred in an actual physical environment."[25] In her new concern for external realism, the visualization of the narrative within an actual physical environment will indeed become one of the main characteristics of Ding Ling's fiction, but the visualization, unlike that of Watt's early realists, will always be from a distinctly political point of view.

Indeed, her very emphasis on the environment, far from being merely a technique that enhances narrative realism, has important political implications in itself. The material world into which a character is born, the physical circumstances of his field of action, are seen as almost totally determining his being. The fact of being a peasant from a drought-stricken village or a cigarette factory worker in a depressed city takes precedence over any other kind of information that can be known about an individual.

Miss Amao of Ding Ling's earlier fiction was, to be sure, a poor trapped peasant, but she was even more an innocent young girl given to romantic longings. Although she was a victim of her social environment, the detailed description of her prolonged process of disintegration, into which the reader is deeply drawn, conveys a sense of an individual self who suffers but who nonetheless is also to a certain extent *actively* involved in her own fate. Amao cannot escape her surroundings, but her tragedy is on one level self-willed; she has grasped at the freedom to indulge in thoughts at least of rebellion against her condition. This is not the case with Acui in Ding Ling's 1932 story "Fawang" (The Net of the Law). Acui has a miscarriage, which indirectly causes her husband to lose his job as a blacksmith in a cigarette factory. He turns into an alcoholic and under his abuse her suffering is totally passive and hopeless:

> He did not go home till it was dark. Seeing his wife there without any sign of life, he would fly into a temper, thinking that if she had not had her miscarriage he would not have lost his means of livelihood. Moreover, he had to support her. All day long she lay spread out on the bed, yet she would not die. At first he cursed her, then he beat her; once he got used to using his hands, he would at times beat her very severely.
>
> Acui had no strength to resist at all. She could only cry, but crying infuriated him further, so she had to restrain herself. She was feverish and sore all over but forced herself to get up and do the work. Her husband had turned into a tyrant, and she did not know what had become of her own family. Getting their daily food had become a problem, but she had no way of finding work. Each thought was like a whip, lashing day and night on her already withered skin and flesh.[26]

Eventually Acui's husband murders his wife's best friend, whose husband he believes to be responsible for his job loss. Acui is detained as a hostage until the criminal is caught; in the end she dies in jail and he is executed. But as the story makes clear, he has been driven to that ghastly crime because of social injustice. Like his wife, and all the other characters in the story, he is also a helpless victim, trapped within the "net of the law"; none can escape the total system of corruption and oppression.

There is little elaboration from within of the subjective suffering of the characters; we merely observe the external events of their lives taking place in a solidly specified social and physical world. In such a world, a shaky staircase, coal fumes in the alley, the noises of children crying and women cursing in the neighborhood, all the details of a highly particular-ized setting reveal the awfulness of the characters' situations. But we learn little else about them. What is essential about a character is not his unique and complex subjective consciousness but the material and social world that defines and simultaneously simplifies him. The selection and treatment of details from the milieu create the mood of the story; the bleakness of "The Net of the Law" sets it obviously in prerevolutionary time.

In realistic fiction, according to Jonathan Culler, there will be at least some elements whose function it is to assert its "representational or mimetic orientation." At the most elementary level they are the "descrip-tive residue": objects, gestures, that tell us nothing about any character and have no function in the plot, whose sole function is to be there, to anchor the story in the real by signifying "we are the real," "this is reality."[27] However, in a politically committed work, any item in the text that denotes a concrete reality could also signify "this is reality that has to be changed, or is in the process of being changed."

Whatever realism, or the depiction of reality as it is, may be, there is no comfortable place for it in the Marxist lexicon. Depending on its placement in the historical timetable of revolution, realism will always be preceded by a specified modifier. It will either be "critical," in works depicting prerevolutionary reality, or it will be "socialist," in works de-picting reality in its revolutionary development. But if realism, as Harry Levin defines it, "is nothing if not critical,"[28] critical realism is a tautol-ogy, while socialist realism, because of its tendency to idealize, is self-contradictory. The qualifiers are necessary only because of the Marxist assumption that no reference to reality can be neutral or value-free. The "pure representation of reality" is not possible for a politically engaged writer, such as Ding Ling had become; every object or item, no matter how trivial or insignificant, must carry some kind of negative or positive political meaning. In this way all objects in the milieu acquire a meta-phorical dimension.

The 1933 story "Ben" (Flight) is filled with such loaded realistic de-tails. The sun rises on a group of old peasants who have been waiting over half the night in the cold windy station for the morning train to Shanghai. They line up at the ticket booth; the clink of the (borrowed) silver dollar thrown onto the counter "strikes the heart" as they anxiously try to suppress their unease about their fearful and costly journey. They are going to the big city, about which they know nothing, because their crops have failed and they can no longer come up with the rent; the fami-lies that were left behind are living on rice husks. All their hopes lie in the help they expect from relatives who are supposedly working as laborers in Shanghai. "No matter what, a brother-in-law is a brother-in-law, he's not going to just watch me starve to death," they console themselves, after they arrive and begin wandering about the strange bewildering city, asking for directions. But the descriptions of every object and scene along their path suggest the futility of their pursuit:

Here was also an old dog which had lost its fur; it looked homeless, its stomach hanging down as it feebly sidled, looking at the passersby with strange eyes.[29]

The exposition unfolds on two levels that ironically comment on each other; the purpose and hope of the trip that is revealed in the peasants' dialogue is everywhere cruelly belied by the world of objects about them. When they finally arrive at one brother-in-law's neighborhood, with its puddles of stagnant water and smells of garbage piled up in the courtyards, the reader already knows, although the characters do not yet, what to expect:

The face of a twelve- or thirteen-year old girl looked out beside the diapers hanging on the bamboo pole. She gazed at them stupidly with large startled eyes, her wispy yellow hair making her face even uglier. From the front side room appeared a dishevelled head; something or other was hanging next to it in the window. Piled in confusion on both sides of the house were broken bottles, broken earthen jars, rags. Footsteps could be heard inside the room but no one paid them any attention.[30]

When the brother-in-law appears, his "ruddy strong peasant's chest withered, his sunken profile" unrecognizable, the laughing and greetings die away on both sides as mutual despair suddenly sinks in. The description of the physical milieu in cumulative detail, while not directly contributing to the action, has prepared us for this moment: the recognition of hope deluded.

The peasants find their city relatives to be near death with illness and hunger; they learn about brutal conditions in the factories, about strikes and killings, and the hundreds of thousands who are out of work. Some in the group stay and become lost in the city. After burying his sister, Zhang Dahanzi returns home with one of his country neighbors. Without any money for their fare the two men begin the long walk home along the railroad tracks. They see again that monstrous train, which had once symbolized all their hopes of flight from doom:

But from far away came the grating sound of the train, then they saw the great lights of the engine, the thick black smoke, the tar-colored sky. Then the train rushed toward them flying, brushed past their bodies, and rolled forward again. This was the train to Shanghai, and in that train, in the fourth-class carriage lit up with electric lights, there were again the crowds of people from the

country, those who were fleeing to Shanghai because they could no longer survive back home; they were in there sleeping now, their mouths hanging open,
saliva dribbling, dreaming their pitiable and absurd dreams.[31]

The train in "Flight" is a physical object developed into a complex
vehicle of meaning; used as a device to set in motion the story's action, it
is shown to be an illusory mode of escape that does not take one any-
where. By reappearing to mock the former passengers who had once
boarded it with such expectations, it symbolizes also the hopelessness of
flight from doom and conveys the political message that only a total
transformation of the world will provide a real way out.

In "Flight" Ding Ling achieves a fine balance between the presentation of physical objects to establish the story's milieu, and their use as
political metaphor. Meir Sternberg has discussed how the "elaborately
established metaphorical relationships" between different factors or elements in a novel contribute towards the "internal universalization of the
theme that gives the main action its credibility."[32] Through linkage and
analogous relationships, objects in the environment help establish a credible coherent fictional world — this is the kind of world in which things
happen this way. But in "Shui" (Flood), regarded as a landmark story by
Communist critics, the elaborate metaphorical relationships striven for
are not adequate for the establishment of credible action.

The first two of the story's four sections take place at night, so that
the actual physical environment is "visualized" in a rather special way.
Contributing to the atmosphere of fear and horror is the fact that it is
night and there is only a tiny bit of pale blue light from a crescent moon.
The members of the family, later joined by refugees fleeing from neighboring villages, are sitting huddled in the dark house, while at some distance the rising water threatens the dikes. In the dark, terrors are magni-
fied, the sound of the wind, of barking dogs heard from time to time, and
then the clanging gongs and calls for help from those manning the dikes
all portend that disaster will soon strike.

The peasants cannot be seen either but are merely heard as anonymous, disembodied voices in the dark. In the midst of general panic individual characteristics do not matter; people remain nameless, faceless,
their identities are never fully established — they are soon to be wiped out
anyway by the onrushing waters. The old grandmother, "teeth gone,
deaf in the ears, her head all bald, who speaks to herself in a dry tremu-
lous voice," is recalling the famines and plagues of the past. She tells how
the fortune teller had predicted the year would be a crisis for her, and
here it is. Hers is the voice of doom and the voice of memory, her monologue ("generation after generation it's still the same") expressing the fatalistic attitude of peasants towards the suffering that has gone on since

time immemorial. The young children who do not understand what is going on reinforce the general sense of fear and helplessness.

Instead of a precisely delineated situation, Ding Ling presents a feeling, an atmosphere. Similarly, the flood is not realistically described but shown through a series of metaphors as a menacing force with a living will: "The water swiftly stretching its terrifying long legs, whose color could not be seen clearly in the night, became a bottomless black torrent, roaring a thunderous cry, fiercely rushing about." Elsewhere it is "that terrifying water which had swallowed up everything, still acting on its wild nature (*yexing*)."[33] Such animistic metaphors are reminiscent of Zola, whose "scientific objectivity" and protest against social injustice had long made him one of the most discussed Western writers in China.[34] Coincidentally, the same issue of *Beidou* in which the second installment of "Flood" appeared contained a translated article on his writings.[35]

Also suggestive of Zola are the big crowd scenes in "Flood," the explosive movements of masses of people animated by the same overriding emotions, the mob behavior that in the face of panic and despair becomes a form of madness. There is a similar reducing of human beings to the level of animals, "voices roared like the huge, hoarse cry of wild animals," or "Those who remained, dragging their leftover lives, feebly crawled and crawled about."[36] Yet toward the end of the story this same exhausted, starving crowd of wretched subhuman beings is galvanized into a fighting force that will march into town to seize the granaries that the authorities have refused to open for them. Apart from a speech by an unknown man up in a tree there is no attempt to explain this transformation; it is simply forced through by a "transposition" of the flood metaphor:

> So when dawn was about to break, this troop of people, this troop of hungry slaves, the men in front, the women running behind, roaring with the exuberance (*benfang*) of life, threw themselves onto the town even more furiously than did the flood.[37]

The story suggests that the flood of overwhelming terror and suffering can somehow be changed into an overpowering force of revolution — another unstoppable flood. But the story fails to make this transformation convincing. One problem is that objects and people are not clearly perceived or concretely realized; they exist as charged images or anonymous emotional states. Perhaps such a technique should discourage us from applying the usual canons of plausibility. Yet the question remains as to whether the story has managed to establish through a pattern of thematic reiteration, or the development of metaphorical or analogous relationships, a coherent fictional world, credible on its own terms.

When "Flood" first appeared in 1931, its apparently innovative techniques were hailed as providing the appropriate form of expression for a new political consciousness, the "burgeoning of the new fiction that we should have." It was seen as an example of the "author's correct and resolute understanding of the class struggle" and by taking as "its protagonist not one or two persons but a large mass of people," its focus was not "individual psychology but the unfolding of collective action."[38] For similar reasons, it was praised, even if retrospectively in 1955, as marking a breakthrough both in the new literature and in Ding Ling's own development. The story was

> truly the beginning of Ding Ling's great leap forward . . . It took as its background the great floods in 1931 that spread over 16 provinces, and described the infinite disasters and the earliest awakening, uniting and rebellion of the traditional Chinese peasant. From writing about the life of petty bourgeois intellectual youth to writing about the life of struggle among the broad worker-peasant masses, this interval signals the remarkable change and progress in the writer's creative thought. And even more important, this difference and progress represented precisely an important tendency in the development of our new literature: from being for the petty bourgeois class to being for the worker, peasant, soldier; from writing about the petty bourgeois to writing about the worker, peasant, soldier. The appearance of "Shui" indicates that the creative path of its author was developing along such a correct course.[39]

However, in spite of the writer's "remarkable change and progress," the work still did not go far enough. Its main defect in the view of both contemporary and later critics was that it merely emphasized the self-awakening of the peasants without paying due attention to the teaching and leadership role of the party. Instead, this role is given in the last few pages of the story to the "dark-faced, half-naked peasant on the branches of a big tree"—he is one of the few characters endowed with a physical appearance and location from which to speak, but is still presented only as one voice among many others, appearing suddenly in their midst to articulate what turns out to be on everyone's mind. To introduce the party, perhaps in the guise of a "mentor figure" who by definition could not simply be "one of them," would have meant a drastic overhauling of the entire structure of the story. He would be an intrusive figure hard to accommodate among characters conceived as equal and anonymous members of a collective. The story, admittedly an experiment that does not quite come off as it stands, would nevertheless be altered out of existence by ideological tailoring.

But such were the extraliterary criteria to which Ding Ling was increasingly submitting her work in committing herself to the party. Her fiction was not turning outward to the world as it was, or as it might be apprehended by the random workings of a singular artistic intelligence, but to a world explicitly defined a priori by an ideology that she was earnestly acquiring. What remained for her to do was to test the limits superimposed by political guidance and explore ways of working within them. For this chosen literary path the conception of the writer's role had to be adjusted accordingly.

The Writer as Martyr

Ding Ling's fiction between 1930 and 1933 is particularly preoccupied with the figure of the writer. Six writers were portrayed in the four "love and revolution" stories, four more followed in the next two years in a continuous effort to examine the writer's role under specific political conditions.[40]

"Shiren Ya-luo-fu" (The Poet Alov), a rather malicious portrayal of impoverished White Russian émigrés in Shanghai hiring themselves out as strikebreakers, is not a serious treatment of the subject. Alov represents the image of the poet at its counterrevolutionary worst; his pathetic bragging about the days when he was a student in St. Petersburg and, in elegant attire, recited his poems at the Countess' soirées[41] only emphasizes his present downfallen state and the irrelevance of his kind.

In "Mouye" (A Certain Night), Ding Ling's fictional account of Hu Yepin's execution, the unnamed central figure's identification as a "warmhearted poet, faithful and hardworking"[42] is essential. Although twenty-three or twenty-four alleged communists were executed on February 7, 1931, in the Longhua garrison headquarters, only the writers among them, in spite of their negligible positions in the party, became apotheosized as the Five Martyrs.[43] Why it is that writing particularly qualifies people for the legends of martyrdom is an intriguing question that lies at the core of the complex relationship between literature and politics in modern China. This relationship was intensely dramatized in the heartbreaking events of Ding Ling's personal life during these few years and in her struggle to continue and justify literary production in the face of them.

It is this same relationship that makes it difficult to evaluate "A Certain Night" as an autonomous story or an aesthetic entity. Although the story, which was published sixteen months after Hu's death, no doubt incorporates unverifiable details, some of which could only have been pieced together much later, Ding Ling said that the content was "probably all facts" (zhe dayue dou shi zhenshi).[44] She describes the main character briefly losing consciousness from the initial shock of the summary death sentence announced only minutes before it was carried out, his subsequent uncontrolled fury and defiance, and then his calm acceptance and feeling of solidarity with his comrades as they face the machine guns. The description has a distant and impersonal tone, however, as does the entire narrative. Here, for example, is the group of prisoners walking to their death:

The sky was black, black without end. From that blackness came raindrops and lumps of snow, from that blackness came the wild roaring of the north wind. The earth was gray, like fog, the accumulated snow in the night reflecting a deathlike gray. Guards, prisoners, the sound of shackles, the sound of bayonets, no one spoke, no one moaned, no one sighed or wept; toward the yard, that deep corner of the yard, the temporary execution ground, they moved without stopping.[45]

In view of this air of general idealization, much of the story's emotional impact on its contemporary readers could only have resulted from feelings evoked by the events themselves.

The response of the reader far removed in time, place, and political climate from the facts described must, however, be based on something very different. How do we react, for example, to the account of the prisoners' breaking out into the "Internationale" at the moment of being killed? The question is not one of plausibility; there is historical evidence that people have on occasion done just that.[46] The question is rather whether *any* aesthetic treatment, even one more subtle than Ding Ling's, of such an occurence can be made to seem persuasive to a reader not already committed to what the "Internationale" stands for. On the other hand, can the noncommitted reader be relied upon for a more proper or "objective" response? Or is there not a possible blind side to a stance of detachment as well? To be cynically suspicious of all forms of heroism may be just as much an impediment to objective perception as to be sentimentally engaged.

Another difficulty the readers have in trying to see the story in itself arises because they detect a conscious, prior intent of the author to utilize the story as a means toward an end. Our own preconceptions come into play once we feel under pressure to respond first, in Keats's phrase, to the "palpable designs" the work has on us and this interferes with our ability to respond to it as a self-contained entity.

Ding Ling's harrowing situation during the days of Hu Yepin's arrest and later execution has been movingly and vividly described by Shen Congwen in his *Further Reminiscences of Ding Ling*.[47] Reading "A Certain Night" with that material in mind makes us even more aware of opportunities lost; an intense, personal experience has been turned merely into the occasion of yet another story about haloed revolutionary martyrdom. But perhaps for Ding Ling this rather abstract, distant, formularized literary exercise provided a kind of supportive and healing effect. Contributing her own experience into the common fund of revolutionary legends may have served as a consoling reminder that one neither dies nor survives alone. Such speculations will not take us very far. What we do see is that "A Certain Night," as a *generalized* treatment of one particular individual instance of martyrdom, is the result of a kind of depersonalizing self-surrendering process; the writing itself signifies a symbolic martyrdom on the part of the writer. Both the writer within the story and the writer producing the story sacrifice or efface their own private selves in the service of a greater cause.

There is one story that breaks Ding Ling's tendency during this period to treat the situation of the writer always in relation to broad political and public issues. In spite of the many references to Hu Yepin's execution, the uniquely intimate self-portrait, if that is what it is, given in "Cong yewan dao tianliang" (From Night till Daybreak) may well be the exception that proves the rule. The main character is an unidentified third person, but the narrative is replete with references to specific names and events in Ding Ling's life.

A lone woman is walking to her "so-called home" one evening, the sights and sounds of the city filling her with rambling and affecting thoughts. It is the anniversary of her younger brother's death many years ago. She thinks of her grieving mother, now taking care of her own young son Xiaoping born after his father's death. When she arrives at her rented upstairs room, a line of *his* poetry comes to mind. She recalls that from the trolley window she had seen a profile looking so familiar that she had almost joyously called out to him, "Hey, Pin," before she had remembered and had to check her tears. Earlier, a chance encounter with Mrs. F in a department store had brought back memories of her frantic behavior and despair on that fateful night when her man had failed to return. She noticed that Mrs. F had been fondling a child's pretty outfit but did not buy it. Feeling much sympathy for the F's impoverished condition but also envy for their present happiness ("they are now as we once were") she now impulsively goes to a pawn shop and with the five dollars given her, buys a pink silk dress for their baby girl. In the morning this irrational behavior born of self-pity is seen for what it is. She tears up the note to the F's, lets the pink dress drop to the floor, and goes over to the manuscript laid out on the table to resume writing a story. (From the description, it can be identified as "Tian Family Village.")[48]

The story thus ends with the act of writing as a restorative to counter life's pain, and a reaffirmation of her commitment to go on. It is the kind of positive role that literature can perform for the writer herself. What is unusual for Ding Ling's fiction in that period is how the entire story remains on the level of the apparently random and the intensely personal. Indeed this account of the happenings of one night, with its many allusions to actual names and places, its sequence of chance encounters, rambling thoughts, fluctuating moods and inconsequential behavior, reads like a straight and fresh transcript of immediate experience. Her grief and the struggle to confront it are profoundly private matters; there is no reference either to the political meaning of Hu's execution, or the public context of her own literary activity. This relatively unknown story and the much anthologized "A Certain Night" were both triggered by the same traumatic event, yet there is a marked contrast in their narrative approaches — one so immediate, the other so impersonal — and correspondingly in their respective notions concerning the relationship between literature and the writer.

After Ding Ling's "love and revolution" fiction of 1930, with the one exception of "From Night till Daybreak" in which writing was still seen as ministering primarily to a personal need, there was no literature for her without its political motivation. This imperative to turn personal material to public account through writing was anticipated in two stories that Hu Yepin wrote shortly before his own death bcame a political event. The two stories — fictionalized versions of the birth of their child — were prophetically entitled "Xisheng" (Sacrifice) and "Yigeren de dansheng" (The Birth of a Person). In the first, the young wife aborts the fetus (female), which nearly costs her her life. In the second, the baby (a son) is allowed to be born in a hard delivery described in minute-by-minute excruciating detail.

The events of both stories take place within a context of economic privation and urgent political meetings, the pressure of manuscript deadlines competing with the progress of the mother's labor pains: "But he had just written half, when the moans of his lover suddenly became piercingly severe. He had to put down his pen and rush to her bedside."[49] In each case, the baby — actual or potential — is seen as disrupting or threatening important work that has to be done. Yet his new identity as a father was something that Hu Yepin also took pride in; in his last letter to Ding Ling from prison, written on the day when, unbeknownst to him, he was to die, he signed himself the Young Papa.[50]

That day was February 7, three months after the birth of his child whom he had once killed in fictional imagination.[51] Another three months later Ding Ling published Hu's two stories and her own two "Shanghai, Spring 1930" stories together in one volume. In the preface she states that other works had been started, but they "died in infancy" (yaoshang), making her quite sad, for "although these are a few short pieces, they should be seen as one whole, each piece only allows one to see one section, one corner, and is not representative."[52] She thus points to the underlying link between the whole cluster of themes in this collection: sacrifice, death, birth, the relinquishing of life, love, the old literature, and the beginning of a new literature and a new life. By taking its title from Hu's story, "The Birth of a Person," the volume looks toward the future. Her preface ends with the date "May 15, three months and eight days into the new era."

The preface was not the place for the indulging of private grief: "I need not now speak about my own thoughts in order to move people to compassion,"[53] but grief and the need for some form of sublimation could have been one impulse behind the emotional gesture of the surrender of self she makes to her readers. They are asked not to default on their responsibility to express their opinions, to give her severe criticism, to encourage, push, and guide her, "because I only belong (shuyu) to all of you. Believe this statement!" Her plea is to be accepted as "a small but diligent and faithful worker in literature (wenzishang de gongzuozhe), who is willing to belong to you."[54]

This notion of the writer as owned by the public is carried further a few months later, in the January 1932 issue of Beidou (Big Dipper). As editor of the journal, Ding Ling had solicited comments from twenty-two writers, including Lu Xun, Mao Dun, Yu Dafu, Ye Shengtao, and others, on the topic "Reasons and Solutions for the Depressed State of Creative Writing" (Chuangzuo buzhen zhi yuanyin ji qi chulu) Her own "concrete" but somewhat "fragmentary" opinions included:

Item: Regard the people (dazhong) as master;

Item: Do not separate yourself from the people, do not consider yourself a writer (zuojia). Remember that you yourself are one of the people; you are speaking for the people, speaking for yourself.[55].

Two different terms are used by Ding Ling in the above passages to refer to the writer, reflecting changing notions about writing. While such terms were not used with any clear consistency during this period, zuojia is a closer equivalent to "author," "creative writer," with connotations of individual autonomy, as well as of "professional," "specialist."[56] On the other hand, wenzi shang de gongzuozhe, "a worker in the language," or the more common wenyi gongzuozhe, "literature and art worker", merely designates the writer as one kind of worker among others. Such a leveling of the special notion of literature was implicit in the wenxue dazhonghua (popularization of literature) debates during the early 1930s.

The final issue of Beidou, which, during its brief existence from September 1931 to July 1932, was outstanding among the many short-lived journals sponsored by the League of Left-Wing Writers, included many articles on the dazhonghua question. Ding Ling called it the "main problem in the present stage of the literary movement."[57] The League's executive committee had concurred, in its resolution of November 1931 on "The Task of China's Proletarian Revolutionary Literature" (Zhongguo wuchan jieji geming wenxue de xinrenwu).[58] Dazhonghua, a concept of utopian dimensions that are lost in its translation as "popularization," envisions a tremendous enlargement of the possibilities for literature, a transformation of it into something for, of, and by all the people, but the process begins by diminishing the importance of the individual writer.

The denial of literature as an exclusive craft practiced by the individual is implied in the discussion of the proper language for literature. A cause of much frustration was the recognition that the vernacular, the medium of the new literature since May Fourth, had become, in the words of Qu Qiubai, "a new classical language" (*xinshi wenyan*),[59] just as elitist and inaccessible to the masses as the classical language had been. The stricture that "writers must eliminate the sentence structure (*yufa*) of intellectuals and study the ways of expression in the language of the worker peasant masses"[60] was directed against the "Europeanized" and obscure style of much contemporary writing, but it also sought to place literature beyond the exclusiveness of a specialist activity. *Dazhonghua* precluded the conception of literature as a distinctive way of using language, and reduced the individual author to a representative of a specific class consciousness.

The debates on the popularization of literature during the early 1930s constitute only a brief episode in the continuing efforts to develop a mass literature for a revolutionary society. Some of the discussants at the time appeared to be innocently unaware of the enormous complexity of a program that would impose upon literature the use of a new medium, require writers to practice popular but to them unfamiliar forms, and ask them to draw their material from the lives of people with whom they had had little previous contact. One writer asked, "Why is it that a problem raised more than two years ago is still not put into practice today?"[61] Indeed, in one form or another the issue still persists, and specific literary policies as proposed in the *Yanan Talks* or, more explicitly, during the Cultural Revolution, have only underscored the illusory nature of apparently clear-cut and easy solutions.

Among the issues raised during the popularization debates of the 1930s there was only one where conscious and immediate change was possible: how the writer himself perceived and defined his role. Writers welcomed their integration with the people; the idea of independence or autonomy in their literary activity made no sense in view of the political urgencies impinging on their private lives.

Ding Ling's admonition that writers should submerge their individual identity in the collective had behind it the personal sacrifice that had already been asked of her in Hu Yepin's death.

Another impetus behind the move toward the collective was the disillusion with introspective and subjective writing, and the lonely condition of those who practiced it. The writer whom Ding Ling had depicted four years earlier as the alienated individual at the edge of existence converting a suicidal record into a pitiful means of livelihood, had now been transfigured into the warmhearted, faithful poet singing the "Internationale" with his comrades while facing the firing squad. To be sure, "A Suicide's Diary" and "A Certain Night" are both extreme, melodramatic presentations of the writer's situation, but they do illustrate the fundamental shift between 1928 and 1932, from narcissistic self-pity to self-sacrifice in public commitment, from the writer as suicide to the writer as martyr.

The history of modern Chinese literature is strewn with the dead bodies or broken lives of martyred writers. Harold Isaacs notes in his anthology of 1918–1933 short stories that, "barely five years after May 4, every individual's choices and actions became a matter of life and death for each one."[62] Of the sixteen writers represented in his collection, only one, Guo Moruo, had survived in "lonely eminence" till 1974, the date of Isaacs's preface. Others had been executed by the Kuomintang, killed by the Japanese, purged by the communists, "silenced, stifled."[63] Paradoxically, as George Steiner points out in an essay on Marxism and literature, the persecution of literature is a sign of how *seriously* it is taken by autocratic regimes. To shoot a man for what he writes is a sinister form of tribute, "but a tribute nevertheless."[64] Perhaps this mutual recognition of the power and the seriousness of literature on the part of both writers and dictatorships accounts for the historical phenomenon that the risk of persecution and the writer's commitment frequently increase in direct ratio to each other.

"In countless chapters in our nation's history," wrote Shen Congwen in his *Further Reminiscences of Ding Ling*, "we can see murder become policy. What is strange is that those who in this age and society had the probability of being sacrificed, did not seem to know how to seek ways to avoid their fate."[65] Ding Ling's activities after her husband's execution were not calculated to avoid sacrifice. She petitioned to go to the Soviet area but was asked instead to be chief editor of *Beidou*, the new literary periodical of the League of Left-wing Writers. The editorship subjected her to constant harassments from Kuomintang authorities, her publisher was arrested once, manuscripts and letters were confiscated or intercepted, until finally the periodical was closed down in July 1932. She had joined the party earlier that year and was soon secretary of the party group in the League. She incurred further risks by lecturing at universities, taking part in demonstrations, putting up slogans, and working among factory strikers and at the front during the 1932 Shanghai Incident.[66]

In suggesting that there may have been a kind of willful naiveté or even complicity in the writer who suffered martyrdom, Shen Congwen was expressing half-ironically his pain and anger over the fate of both his friends. Yet for Ding Ling, aware as she was of the dangers involved, to become fully committed to the cause for which Hu Yepin had been killed, seemed the only choice possible.

The Unfinished Literary Work

In spite of the threat of political persecution, Ding Ling's writing continued apace. In 1932, she began a projected 300,000-word novel, a longer form than she had ever attempted before. One motive behind the writing of *Muqin* (Mother) was to present the life of an individual within the context of collective history.

According to a letter she wrote to the editor of *Dalu xinwen* (Continental News), who had originally solicited a manuscript for serialization, the subject came to her during a brief visit to her mother in Hunan. There she heard many stories about the countryside and the small towns that revealed "a social system in the process of historical change" and she determined to write a novel about it.[67] The work would begin with the end of the Xuantong (1909–1911) period, cover the 1911 revolution and the great revolution of 1927, and continue up to the land agitation then spreading in the rural areas. It would take place in a small city and a few small towns in Hunan, the characters centering around a few landlord gentry families. The mother is "one of the characters threading the book together, one who has suffered multiple tribulations under the feudal social system but in the end escapes from them . . . The book would be called *Mother* to commemorate this one who was a mother."[68]

In the book, the daughter Ding Ling appears as Xiaohan, a three-year-old, "her small, round face suffused with innocence and happiness."[69] The death of the young father, which takes place a few months before the novel begins, hastens the decline of this branch of the family, so now there is only one long-term laborer to work the land that has not been rented out:

> Although Changgeng was the only one left, he was still just as happy. As soon as it was almost dawn, the cool morning breeze would steal quietly into his small room, then he would wake up. Whistling he would pull on his short padded jacket . . . open the side door and walk along the stone dike. In the sky, white like a fish belly, clouds were changing into thousands of hues, blue, purple, yellow, red, gold, and the sun would be rising over the other side of the mountains, the roosters in the backyard all merrily crowing.

Changgeng's joy in the morning scene extends into his feelings about his work:

> Then he thought of the time when the field would be covered with small purple flowers. The sun would shine on it, small bees would flit about. And he himself would, in imitation of his father, sit on that high mound, looking around him at that purple sea near and far, his shirt buttons open, lighting up the pipe he had just learned to smoke. He would look quietly about him and think, "Better get going!" Actually he could not rest any more; each day there would be more work, and it would get strenuous. But this hard work produced results. When

he stood on the threshing floor pulling back the ears of grain, the golden ker-
nels pouring into the barrel, and when picul by picul he carried them from the
fields towards the house, how filled with happiness he was![70]

Although he knew that he was farming for the master, "who could
say that this land, and its grain was not his? Only he loved it, like his
own child . . ." These lyrical descriptions of the countryside and of the
peasant who takes pride and joy in his work have their origins in the
happy memories of Ding Ling's childhood, rather than in any ideological
view of the oppressed peasant laborer.

Critics charged that Ding Ling was not writing in accordance with
"objective social reality"; her story of a widow with two small children
struggling to obtain a modern education was criticized for its failure to
reflect the decline of the feudal family structure and the pressures of foreign imperialism.[71] In spite of such ideological shortcomings, the novel
turned out to be one of Ding Ling's most politically exploitable works.
This had little to do with the book's actual content and everything to do
with the fact that it was left unfinished.

Mother is an unfinished work in more than one sense. The leftist
daily paper that originally solicited it for serialization was soon closed
down. Ding Ling had written to the editor that she would merely be submitting a draft that would undergo much revision or even be rewritten
when published in book form. She was summoning "a great deal of courage to begin, planning to spend on it two hours a day, one and a half
hours for thinking, and half an hour for writing."[72] When the daily was
shut down, she stopped writing the novel but took it up again when
Liangyou Press asked to publish it, sending the manuscript out in install-
ments. Because of illness and other things, she was "always writing it one
day and then putting it aside for ten days, so who knows when it will be
finished. From now on I do not intend to write long novels; sloppiness,
premature deaths, all make me sad."[73] The writing caused her great difficulty and her planned revision never took place.

The effects of hurried writing can be seen in the novel. There is little
of the sense of a purposeful structure working towards a clearly conceived end that marks her short stories. The assortment of childhood
memories, elaborated hearsay information about her mother's early life,
plus vague references to historical events, result in an uneven, somewhat
random book that seems to be frozen in the process of evolving into
finished form. In some ways, the groping for form mirrors, although it
does not illuminate, the book's subject — society in the process of revolutionary change. Some staple features of classical fiction find their way
into the portrayal of gentry life of the past.[74] There is even a gesture towards the "banquet pattern" in a wine-drinking game scene, one of those

apparently purposeless nonevents, as Andrew Plaks calls them, which do nothing to advance the plot action.[75] Yet in the hands of a skillful novelist such a "static" chapter could subtly but surely place a character in the social scheme of things. In *Mother*, the scene can be viewed as establishing Manzhen's leadership among a gathering of female relatives and schoolmates, but since it is not developed into a fully discriminated occasion (in Henry James's sense of the term), it remains something of an unassimilated throwback.

The struggle to emerge from the bonds of the past is concretely depicted in the mother's effort to let out her bound feet, a process almost as painful as the initial binding. She soaks them in cold water, and endures the pain of running in gym class in order to hasten the process.[76] This effort is mentioned repeatedly and becomes symbolic of her heroic struggle toward liberation. Most other events in the novel do not achieve comparably clear-cut outcomes or meaning by the time it ends, abruptly and inconclusively, with the arrival of revolutionary troops in the city.

When *Muqin* appeared in book form in June 1933 with only a third of it written, it contained this terse statement from the publisher:

> Since the author began work last fall, sending in parts of the manuscript from time to time, we had received nearly 100,000 words by mid-April. But unfortunately on May 14 the author had disappeared, and no more pages were received.[77]

On that day Ding Ling was kidnapped from her apartment in the Shanghai International Settlement by Kuomintang agents, imprisoned, and amidst speculation and rumors, widely presumed to have been executed.

The poignant fate of the writer immediately transformed for its readers the status and meaning of the novel. The important thing now was not the book itself but the relationship between the personal life of the author and the book. An extravagant expression of this view is the following passage that concludes a discussion of the novel. Using elaborate punning, the word "mother" refers to Ding Ling's actual mother, to the book written about her, and to the book's author in her sacrificial, motherly role:

> *Mother* is unfinished, it is only a fragment; the author of *Mother* has sacrificed everything for light (*guangming*); how forcefully does this show that our times are in the midst of a violent storm! The mother of the first generation "embodied the future aspirations of the people." The "mother" of the second generation has burst through "aspiration" and entered into "reality." In form *Mother* may be a fragment, but in fact, Ding Ling has used her blood to complete this book; can there be any book more valuable, more precious than this? Be content, Ding Ling! Your blood even more forcefully than your pen has instructed the

masses; even those who are weak, because of your sacrifice have awakened and stood up![78]

Metaphorical flights such as these take off from the premise of a direct, two-way flow between the writer's ink and blood, the fusion of the literary work and the personal life.

The very concept of the writer as martyr suggests a denial, on one level, of the literary work's separate, independent mode of existence, a denial which the unfinished state of *Muqin* was seized upon to reinforce. An unfinished book is unenclosed, has no definite boundaries, thus allowing its contents to escape into the real world and become mere extensions of the author's life, or preferably, death. The status of the literary work as an independent, self-contained entity seems to diminish whenever the writer herself has been elevated to the status of a martyr — one who is seen as having dedicated or sacrificed her life to something beyond literature. The suicides of Sylvia Plath or Ann Sexton, viewed as martyrs (in the original sense of the word) bearing witness to the unbearable anguish of the modern artist's condition, have determined and limited the perception of their poetry. The works of writers who lose their lives in consequence of commitment to some higher political vision are similarly reduced to the level of documents that provide evidence or information about history or biography. In either case the books do not stand on their own; their meaning and relevance arise from what happened in their authors' personal lives. The books remain *unfinished*, incomplete, mere fragments in the life-work continuum of their authors. The fact that *Muqin* is such a "fragment", made it unnecessary for critics to consider the book seriously in itself.

Another work by Ding Ling, written of course before her presumed martyrdom, but also neither revised nor put into finished form for publication by the author herself, makes its own very curious contribution to the blurring of all lines of distinction between life and work. This is a story written in 1933, apparently a sequel to "The Diary of Miss Sophie." Compared to the first "Diary," written five years earlier, this second one is slight indeed, comprising the entries of two days only, May 4 and May 5, the second day being the sixth anniversary of Ding Ling's meeting Hu Yepin. One purpose of the story is therefore to come to terms with the past, or rather to put it in its place. The diary begins by reflecting that many things have happened and she herself has changed:

When I read my stuff of a few years ago, I do not feel any melancholy or persistent longings, none of the old feelings rekindle my heart, all is truly past! What is past is not just this little period of the diary; all the dreams, ardor, melancholy, all the enjoyment of love, all are past, fading away so naturally, fading away in such a manner so as not to astonish me, fading away so that I do not feel the least bit held back. How lightly and quickly have I leaped into my present state!⁷⁹

In this passage Ding Ling is speaking as Sophie, or rather as the new Sophie, referring even to that first diary, which had ended by saying that she would go to "where no one knows me to squander the remainder of my life," in order to point out that it has *not* happened. The story then begins recounting Ding Ling's own life with Hu Yepin, making specific mention of his last novel, and, in a passage omitted from many editions of the story, telling of his death. She also writes about the birth of their son, and the visit to her mother in Hunan to leave him in her care. But she will not spend all her days mourning someone who is dead; this is a time for her to start being a person again. The entry of the second and last day of this diary, however, complains that "I'm really no good (*bux-ing*), too many of the old feelings remain."⁸⁰ She has spent the day in vain looking for peonies, which are rare in Shanghai, because six years ago, on the day when they first met, she and Hu Yepin, being "children, who did not know anything," had stolen some peonies then in bloom in Pe-king's Central Park. So the diary ends on the admission that in spite of all her efforts to look ahead, memories of the past retain some hold after all.

Even while commemorating the relationship with Hu Yepin, the writer is stressing that she is now freed from her old self and making a new beginning. This claim is made through the character of a second Sophie, even though, as the author has often repeated, she is not Sophie. Such an illogical merging of herself and her fictional creation introduces many contradictions between the two diaries. But a main statement emerges: it is not "I am no longer Miss Sophie," but "I am no longer the way I was when I wrote about her." With all its overlapping of the past and the present, of the writer and work, the story proclaims that she "could no longer write that kind of literature."⁸¹

There is a question as to whether Ding Ling ever intended to make this second diary public, or at any rate, public in its present form. The manuscript was found among her belongings after her secret arrest and published by her friends as another means of publicizing her disappear-ance.⁸² It was given the title "The Diary of Sophie, Part II," and thus sug-gests a continuity with the best known example of the kind of literature Ding Ling wrote during her first phase. But what the story in fact em-phatically proclaims is a break with the subjective writing of the past, and that she is no longer the writer she once was. At the time of the story's publication in 1933, its author was widely rumored to have be-come, like Hu Yepin, another martyr to the revolutionary cause. Ding Ling was spared however, and three years later she escaped her captors to join the Communist Party at its headquarters in the Border Regions. She had avoided martyrdom at the hands of the Kuomintang; instead she surrendered herself and her writing to the cause of the socialist revolution, only to exemplify in her subsequent career the fate of the writer who makes such a choice. Very early on, in 1931, when she was just beginning her turn toward revolutionary literature, she confronted the self-effacement demanded of the committed writer in her story "One Day."

"One Day"

A passage of time appears as the title of many Ding Ling stories and frequently serves as a metaphor for the moral or spiritual situation within the story. "Ri" (Day) images the endless and futile repetitiveness of a purposeless existence; "Mouye" (A Certain Night) describes the dark tragedy of execution. Very often a particular juncture in time or the passing of time will reflect the progress of the action, as for example, the overcoming of difficulties and the movement toward hope and new beginning in "Nianqian de yitian" (The Day before New Year's) and "Cong yewan dau tianliang" (From Night till Daybreak). Written in 1931, at a time when Ding Ling herself had decided to move left, "Yitian" (One Day) concerns a day in the life of a writer as he begins his participation in the revolution. The title also implies that the frustration and difficulties he encounters during that one day are temporally limited, containable, and transient.

The central character is again the familiar writer caught in a particular dilemma, which he must resolve in order to write. In previous stories writers were confronted with poverty, alienation, love entanglements, self-doubts, the insidious weakness of the female sensibility. Here the challenge to Lu Xiang is a writing assignment demanded by his political responsibilities.

A very short story, "One Day" is not designed to probe deeply into the immensely complex situation of the newly politicized writer — in fact one message of the story is that one must not dwell on such potential sources of anxiety. But it is notable as Ding Ling's only attempt to explore openly the situation at all. It does this without making elaborate literary formulations but simply by following the writer's activities in the course of the day as he goes from one event to the next.

The author's note at the end of the story states that it was written on May 8 and finished in one night. The fictional day of Lu Xiang begins at five in the morning and ends late that evening when he finally comes to terms with what he must do and begins his writing. The brevity of time covered, both in the story and in the writing of it (Ding Ling was probably, as she was so often, racing desperately against another manuscript deadline), does not promise a full treatment of the subject, yet much is suggested about Lu Xiang's situation through his relation to his physical environment.

Many of the details in the setting convey a sense of constriction, intrusion, or dislocation. Throughout the day Lu Xiang alternates between being enclosed in his small room trying to write while being assaulted by loud, distracting noises, and going out to carry out political assignments, attempting contacts with factory workers in areas where he feels utterly out of place and is even maltreated as an intruder.

Lu Xiang is a twenty-one year old student who had

> recently given up the ball courts of the university. It was spring, bright and beautiful and just right for outings, but because of a kind of self-awakening, a kind of faith, he came a week ago to this district in Western Shanghai to begin a different kind of life.[83]

Having left behind him a carefree existence he is now shut in a room off the kitchen which is "dark and gloomy even during the day, and often seems lonely" (p. 113).

> The sun cannot shine in here . . . he glanced out the window, a gray wall blocked his vision. In the dirty alley, there was a child crying. (p. 115).

As the story begins he is staring at the rough pages of an exercise book trying to figure out how to write a report (*tongxin*).[84] The sounds of his crowded poverty-ridden neighborhood bombard him, water blasting from a faucet mingles with the voices of women washing and talking about their sorrows.

> He felt that his head was gradually swelling up. Many images, filthy, desolate, many voices, unceasing, moaning and crying all collected together in one piece, formed a kind of pain and pressed down on his heart in one large lump. (p. 114)

But he cannot leave here. He must stay, "this is not school, not a free place (*ziyou chusuo*)" (p. 115).

A man in a long grey gown comes in, after giving the usual signal by tapping on the window, and asks him to continue to try contacting Xiao Huzi (Small Mustache) and Cai Baozi (Bumpkin Cai), even though Lu Xiang had already waited in vain for them outside the factory from five to six-thirty that morning. This person, an unnamed mentor figure, a party representative perhaps, tells him not to be discouraged, "there are many people doing the same work; you are not alone" (p. 117).

Lu Xiang must go out and look for the two factory workers again, since it was probably out of fear that they did not meet him that morning. In the afternoon he ventures out, "trying hard to carry himself in the manner of the lower classes, his hands in his pockets, wearing an old hat."

He went through a series of vegetable gardens. On both sides of the street, there were piles of human excrement; one had to be very careful walking through them. He reached a spot of low ground; the ground was always wet and emanating bad smells as the spring sun shone on it. Every time Lu Xiang went there he summoned up the greatest forbearance. There were many low houses there, old-style tile buildings that leaned right and left, where the families who worked in the nearby factory huddled and lived. Some frightfully dirty children were crouching there playing with filthy water collected in the small puddles. On the water floated some oily film, showing lots of red and green colors.   (p. 121)

This careful presentation of the physical surroundings is essential to enhance the story's sense of realism — Lu Xiang is now in the *real* world, particularized in all its ugly actuality. As Ding Ling's fiction in this period turns to the outside world, its palpable presence is unmistakably established through the offensive smells and repugnant sights that assail the senses and even arouse aversion. But such aversion is precisely — and this is one theme of the story — what one must overcome in order to participate actively in that external world.

Lu Xiang does not find Bumpkin Cai; instead the old mother comes out, accuses him of leading her son astray, and rushes at him without letting him explain, while a young woman looks on and jeers at his discomfited retreat. His next errand takes him to dormitories built by the factory, where the workers are "in dense rows like pigeon cages, the air is bad, often disseminating infectious diseases." As Lu Xiang approached,

a kind of bad odor that comes from human bodies made it even more unbearable for him, but in order to maintain the appearance of being one of the people, he could not cover his nose. He thought that slowly he would get used to it and not feel it too much.   (p. 124)

He is first mistaken for someone else and grabbed by a big fellow who accuses him of being a thief, but even after he clears himself, the crowd that had been roused and gathered around him continues to taunt and handle him roughly, demanding a *kowtow* or they will beat him to death.

The crowd shouted even louder, came closer. He was so infuriated he wanted to laugh — he looked at that pitiful, ignorant mob.

But it was all useless, he understood now. He must sacrifice (*xisheng*) himself this once in order to satisfy them. He made a deep obeisance towards them and smiled bitterly.

"All right, have your fun!" Then, with a mortified heart, he left, accompanied by their exploding laughter.   (p. 127)

However painful and humiliating this experience of bowing to the jeering proletarian mob and however determined he is to "patiently instruct them in their ignorance," the writer realizes that he is the one who must adapt in order to serve them, *he* who must learn the lessons of humility and submission. This will entail a reexamination of his own function as a writer.

Within the story, Lu Xiang is required to carry out two kinds of writing activity. He goes to meet the worker Zhang Abao at noon outside his factory, walks with him for a while and gets from him the news he wants. Zhang Abao had spoken clearly and provided many details:

> He sorted out and wrote down what Zhang Abao had said. It had to do with brutal treatment, tragic deaths, pitiful sacrifices; it had to do with victories and losses in struggle, it had to do with the exposure of fraud and deception. He wrote it all down and took it to another place, and then on the next day, all who were slaves of the same kind would see it, and tell it also to those who could not read, they would talk about these things, discuss these things, be aroused by the forceful language, they would be awakened, they would unite.
>
> This job was important, indispensable, several hundred people ran about all day for this information, look what rich material this was, these ironclad proofs of oppression and resistance!   (p. 120)

The job may be "important and indispensable," but the role of the individual writer has been minimized. He is reduced to a recorder or transmitter of material, which, because of its richness and authenticity — it comes straight from those involved in actual experience — can almost "speak for itself." Writing it down provides the documents that justify political struggle, and also, since writing has the ability to awaken and unite, the weapons of that struggle. The writer is still an indispensable link in the transmission chain; after all his mastery over words is required to get the information (*xiaoxi*) from one barely literate group to another. Nevertheless this description of what he does assumes that he has no unique, special contribution to make to the total process of communication and awakening. Literature conceived as a gathering and sharing of information for the purposes of collective action leaves but a minimal, subservient role for the writer. On the other hand, the writer confronting for the first time such overwhelming evidence of human suffering and injustice, and the enormous illiteracy of the enslaved, must inevitably question the old assumptions about what he does, and particularly his own individual and privileged creative literary operations.

In his role as chronicler Lu Xiang has little problem in carrying out his writer's responsibilities. His difficulty all morning from the beginning of the story has been with his second assignment, the required report on his work. Only after undergoing the indignities of his day does he discover how to fulfill this assignment:

> Under the yellow electric light the report began. He decided to use a literary form (*wenyi de ticai*) to describe the difficult tasks of the period. And what

must above all be expressed was a kind of steadfast, unextinguishable spirit in the midst of difficulty, even though perhaps he was not yet able to perform so very well.   (p. 127)

After a day of disillusionment, humiliation, and anxiety over what to write in his report, Lu Xiang decides that the transformation through the writing process of these difficult experiences into a source of strength and confidence should constitute his subject. His tremendous faith in the efficacy of language to turn things around is a faith that has been characteristic of China's revolutionary ideology and practice. "All propaganda work in China, of which literature is often considered a part, is directed towards spreading the belief," notes D. W. Fokkema, "that things do exist in reality if words only say so often enough."[85] Indeed the history of the Chinese Communist Party, which has survived repeated disasters on its road to victory, seems to demonstrate that words, or literature, in apparent disregard of reality, make optimism possible in the face of defeat.

There was in truth little basis for optimism for an intellectual writer recruiting and organizing factory workers in Shanghai in the early 1930s. There had been a huge decline in the proportion of proletarian membership in the party, so that by 1930 it was only 8 percent, of whom only 2 percent were factory workers.[86] There was a real question then whether the Communist Party could even survive, much less carry out a successful revolution. The "extermination campaigns" had begun in late 1930, and with increasing efficiency the Kuomintang was also making a determined effort to root the communists out of the cities. During these few years arrests and executions ran into the tens of thousands.[87] In view of such harsh conditions the determined cheerfulness of comrades like Lu Xiang is all the more remarkable, and the expression of it in language — slogans, campaign propaganda, literature — that made "things exist in reality" undoubtedly helped account for the revolution's success against overwhelming odds. On a personal level, Lu Xiang was able to overcome the discouragements for the day by means of language when he finally found a way to write his report.

His "steadfast, inextinguishable spirit" does not emerge suddenly in the penultimate paragraph. Throughout the story he keeps to his course by remembering the advice of his comrades and admonishing himself after each setback. Very early on it becomes clear to the reader that a positive outcome is the only possible one for this story. No matter how raucous, ignorant, cruel or evil-smelling the people are, the intellectual leader will have no choice but to submit to them — for they are the ones in whose name the revolution is being carried out. As encountered in the wretched conditions of the city slum, the actual living representatives of the proletariat may contradict the image with which ideology has endowed them; nevertheless the individual must humbly learn to subordinate himself to them. He must undergo a moral or spiritual education to prepare himself for this subordination. In Ding Ling's earlier stories the individual had to establish a sense of identity in opposition to a hostile society and indeed to a hostile world. Now the relation of the self to the world has been fundamentally altered. The adversary position has been replaced by one in which the individual seeks integration with the large social group at all costs; all self-awareness is directed only toward this one goal.

Various narrative processes advance this ideological proposition in "One Day." The outside world, the others, the people are palpably, indeed assertively, there to challenge the individual, as in the give-and-take of dialogue and the face-to-face encounters between Lu Xiang and the crowd. But this confrontation is also projected onto the physical milieu in which objects become statements or metaphors of the besieged state of the central character. The conflict, which is really located within the individual and rooted in his ambivalent attitude or hesitancy, is thus continually externalized while the internal drama is correspondingly attenuated.

The story is told through the dramatized subjective consciousness of Lu Xiang, but in contrast to the supersensitive, overwrought, or willfully perverse Mengke, Amao, or Miss Sophie, he is completely open and direct. He is and must be very easy to know. As a "vessel of consciousness," in Henry James's phrase, he is not one who would " 'get most' out of all that happens to him." But if Lu Xiang does not "vibrate to many occasions,"[88] it is partly because he is provided with very few of them. Even when we realize that the character is confined by the limits of a short story, and is seen for but one single day, it is striking how narrowly circumscribed his sphere of action and the range of possible "vibrations" actually are. Limitations of space in some of Ding Ling's earlier stories had not prevented the unfolding of intense and complex reflective processes. Much of that was achieved through the dialectical interplay between the dual perspectives of the character as actor and spectator, or between the intersecting points of view of narrator and self-reflecting character.

Such mutual refractions in nonconcurrent points of view allowed the uncovering of levels of personality, and cultivated the possibilities of irony, of surprise, and ambiguities of response, all of which are absent from "One Day." Although the theme of the story is the struggle of a writer to enter the revolutionary experience, the absolute congruence of narrator and character in their single-minded pursuit of a preconceived end removes all suspense from the action. These limitations also preclude a deeper exploration of the story's theme through the interaction of its formal elements, as "The Diary of Miss Sophie" attempted to do.

The reduction of narrative options is a consequence of the revolutionary ideology that Lu Xiang subscribes to. This ideology embraces all human problems and claims to have the solutions for them, at least in principle. It does not leave room for the despair and self-doubt characteristic of Ding Ling's earlier subjectivist heroines. Lu Xiang's difficulties are merely the momentary hesitations of the initiate; after his "one day" is over, once he accepts and is accepted in the collective, his individual problems will be solved.

Its pervading optimism notwithstanding, this story makes a much more realistic and sober assessment of the writer's role in the revolution than the pronouncements, say, of the members of the Creation Society when they dramatically announced their conversion to Marxism in the mid-1920s. Guo Moruo's famous dictum that literature is always in the vanguard of revolution was in fact a dual claim, for the special sensibilities of the poet and for the privileged status of literature.[89] The emotional celebrations of the ipso facto links between literature and revolution were mainly extensions of the artists' glorified self-images. As a 1931 article put it, their fervor included ideas of personal heroism and the feeling that "extraordinary exploits must await extraordinary individuals."[90]

By 1931 such romantic notions of the revolutionary writer had been considerably chastened by the lessons of experience. Lu Xun's address at the inauguration of the League of Left-Wing Writers in 1930 reminded his listeners that revolutions were not the way poets imagined them to be, that "the laboring classes certainly have no obligation to treat poets or literary men in any exceptional or privileged way."[91] Ding Ling's story admits as much, although one could still argue that in her character's self-conscious surrender to the revolutionary cause the writer continues to show a certain hubris and self-importance. Why else should his particular self-effacement or even sacrifice be considered so noteworthy as to become the subject of writing? But while there may be irony in such a query, there is poignancy as well. For it points to the already necessarily defensive posture adopted by the writer of "One Day," the fuller implications of which would not become manifest until Ding Ling's relationship with the party unfolded further.

The events in Lu Xiang's day were no doubt drawn more from actual experience and observation than from romantic wishful thinking. But realistic as these were, they were still limited only to the confines and very special conditions of the foreign settlements in Shanghai. When Shen Congwen returned to Shanghai after several months in Hankow, he was much concerned to find Ding Ling and Hu Yepin deeply engaged in political activities while remaining ignorant of the broader picture. Their faith in the revolution and ideas about the writers' participation in it were built upon the little that they saw and heard within the shelter of the settlements. "As the ancients said," observed Shen, " 'Once they knew one little bit, about the rest, they knew nothing at all' "[92]

Considered as an effort to examine the place of literature within the revolutionary context, "One Day" is only a small initial step taken at a time of relative innocence. It appeared then that for the writer to adapt to the pressures of politics was in a sense a matter requiring but the effort of one day. But the story at least acknowledges the possibility that the writer might falter. Ding Ling could not in 1931 anticipate what was in store for her or for the practice of literature in the future. About that she "knew nothing at all." "One Day" turned out to be the last time she inquired into the role of the writer through a fictional work, with the writer himself presented as the central figure.

3

YANAN AND THE USES OF
LITERATURE

ONE MORE COLLECTION of short stories by Ding Ling was published in Shanghai before she departed for the Communist Party base in the Border Regions to begin a new literary life. After being held for three years, she escaped Kuomintang detention in September 1936, and during a secret stopover in Shanghai arranged for the publication of *Yiwaiji* (Unexpected Collection). The stories only went through one edition and have never received much attention. In the preface Ding Ling expresses her own extreme dissatisfaction with the book, which she is simply "unwilling to read over a second time . . . it is not a good harvest, merely some unexpected dregs."[1] She had often regretted never having a long leisurely time "unpestered by affairs, free of economic pressure" to write:

> But things turned out unexpectedly. I was given an opportunity to leave everything, to live alone in a very quiet place. Time passed and passed; it was a terribly long three years, I had absolute leisure, and a great deal of material right before me, but I did not write.[2]

This time of "absolute leisure" was the period of her captivity. Only the urging of friends who contrived to convey messages to her — "you must write, or people will suspect that you are finished, you must rouse yourself and pick up that pen of yours again" — made her write, with much unease and irritation, the few pieces collected in that volume.[3]

Slim as it is, the *Unexpected Collection* reveals an unusual range of subject matter and formal diversity. "Chen Boxiang" (Chen Boxiang) is a character sketch of an illiterate male laborer told by a first-person narrator whose identity remains unclear. "Bayue shenghuo" (Eight Months), subtitled "An Experiment in Reportage" (*baogao wenxue shixie*), portrays the bitter life of apprentices in a print shop through the first-person narration of one of them. In "Yiyueershisan ri" (January 23rd), a story Ding Ling herself describes as a "photographic lens, shooting here and there without any focus,"[4] moments in the lives of the cozy rich are juxtaposed against those of the wretched poor.

Although Ding Ling comments that she had been "particularly care-ful" about "technique" (*jishu*),[5] only the remaining two stories, narrated in a conventional, straightforward third-person manner, rather than the three experimental pieces mentioned above, evince good control over the material. "Tuanju" (Reunion) spotlights a few days in the life of a large gentry family sliding into poverty. The father's business closed down some years ago as a result of Japanese imperialism; almost sixty now and in poor health, he has retired to live in straitened circumstances in the country. One by one the grown-up sons and daughter come home, each facing dire problems and needing the shelter and support that the family can no longer provide. "Songzi" (Songzi) focuses on a young boy whose peasant family has been driven off the land by floods and drought. Hav-ing now become vagrant beggars, they eke out a miserable existence as brickmakers. While the parents work, Songzi looks after his younger sib-lings. One day the baby brother in his charge was crushed under a truck and the boy was cursed and savagely beaten by his parents. On the moonless evening when the story begins, Songzi sets out to steal a water-melon to appease his continual hunger—the garbage dump often does not yield anything—shooing away the younger sister who tries to follow him. In the field he is caught and miserably assaulted. As he limps up the hill he hears piercing screams coming from the midst of milling dark shadows—his little sister has been attacked and partially eaten by wolves. His heart freezes as he hears his father yelling for him. "Songzi gave another shudder, stealthily turned around, and faded into the dark-ness. Into a darkness without end."[6]

"Reunion," with its mounting despair, and "Songzi," which is, in Ding Ling's own words, "permeated with a gloomy atmosphere,"[7] are her last stories representing the pessimistic view of a world enveloped in pre-revolutionary darkness. Such examples of "critical realism" vanish from her fiction when she begins writing from Yanan.

From Shanghai to Yanan

The full story of Ding Ling's escape from captivity and her journey from Shanghai to Yanan is still a matter of cloudy speculation. But the shift that occurred in her writings as she moved from one city to the other is starkly evident[8]. In joining the Communist Revolution at its base in the Border Regions, she was also relocating her fiction, extending its setting, characters, and events beyond the semi-Westernized coastal metropolis of Shanghai to the hinterland where Chinese civilization had its origins. The move to Yanan signified a mental reorientation, a turning away from Western sources in choice of subject-matter and technique. Com-munist literature and art sought instead to develop national forms, to utilize folk traditions, to tap the roots of cultural consciousness for the purposes of a mass-based revolution. Yanan's discovery and exploitation of the art forms of the people may have been just as shallowly expedient as the hasty importation of half-digested Western forms during the May Fourth era; it certainly carried similar burdens of unresolved contradictions for literature.

Even though the "Shanghai phase" of modern Chinese literature was receding into the past, its legacy could not be so easily discarded. One of the struggles at the Yanan literary front was whether or how to reject or accommodate Western/bourgeois practices and forms. Ding Ling, who was an outstanding presence in Yanan but nevertheless still carried the stamp of the literary reputation she had established in Shanghai, was to become deeply embroiled in this struggle.

During her Yanan period Ding Ling continued to be a writer of fiction. But her more prominent historical role there was to become the concrete case around which pressing literary issues revolved. She was one of the writers who precipitated the confrontation and called down on literature and art the authoritative pronouncements of Mao Zedong in May 1942. With the party's literary policy thus defined and writers required to reform accordingly, Ding Ling's writing underwent a marked change. The narratives she produced before and after Mao's "Talks at the Yanan Forum on Literature and Art" differ significantly, and should be compared for the way they illustrate the effect these "Talks" had on literary practice, particularly on the treatment of character. But what involved her most immediately in contemporary literary controversy were the reports of her experiences in taking art and literature to the front and essays that addressed themselves to "the bright versus the dark side" debate.

The uses of literature was the central issue. Although the activists in Shanghai had already found out that political commitment entailed the waiving of literature's independent status, it had not yet become clear to them that the party's view of the uses of literature sanctioned its direct intervention in the literary process. Yanan was above all the base from which, against seemingly overwhelming odds, the Chinese Communist Party underwent "the most dramatic expansion of a revolutionary movement in all history,"[9] and emerged ready to assume national power. Such an extraordinary achievement exacted a price from literature; literature was commandeered, as was everything else, into contributing its services to the total effort. The exigencies of war and revolution meant that literature could no longer be a commodity freely or randomly turned out, as it had been, for the Shanghai marketplace (albeit within the restrictions of Kuomintang censorship), but had to be redefined as a special product meeting explicit and urgent requirements. From the very beginning, Yanan directed intense efforts towards clarifying the function of literature in the collective striving for an all-subsuming goal.

The need to define the uses of literature within the revolutionary context placed definite strains on its production. Compared with Ding Ling's early prolific output of thirty-seven to thirty-eight short stories and two short novels in seven years (she was in captivity between 1933 and 1936), the Yanan decade of 1936 to 1946 was for her a relatively fallow period. Altogether there were perhaps twelve short stories, two plays, and ten to twelve pieces miscellaneously classified as sketches, reportage, and essays. She was, of course, no longer "just a writer" but engaged in many activities, at various times working for the Women's League, teaching literature and writing, serving as vice-chairman of the Red Army Guard Unit, director of the Northwest Front Service Corps, and editor of the literary supplement of the *Jiefang ribao* (Liberation Daily). Very little time remained for writing, as Ding Ling also contributed her share to increasing material production — she was proud of the quality of her tomatoes and of her fine spinning.[10] Moreover, some of her manuscripts got misplaced or lost.[11] Publishing conditions were difficult, and there was a severe shortage of paper and other materials; the literary pages of the *Jiefang ribao* seem to have been at one time the only outlet available.[12]

Altogether Yanan offered the writer a very different kind of environment from Shanghai. In a 1937 essay Ding Ling describes some of the early activities and conditions of literary production as she found them. She acknowledges that due to other pressing needs, art and literature were indeed "relatively backward areas in the Soviet movement."[13] Although great themes (*ticai*) for literature were to be found everywhere, they inspired few masterpieces. Nevertheless art and literature had become "popular" (*dazhonghua*), fresh, lively, and loved by the masses. Interesting short pieces or poems crowded the army newspapers, often in stencil form, or appeared in the stenciled or handwritten wall newspapers put up in public buildings, factories, and schools. Even if printing was underdeveloped in the Soviet area, "the flowers of art and literature, very small wild flowers though they may be, shine everywhere."[14]

She was also engaged in editing a monumental work of collective authorship, "The Twenty-Five-Thousand-Mile-Long March" (Erwanwuqianli changzheng ji), for which manuscripts, written on all kinds of paper, were being received from all over. A later visitor to Yanan claims to have seen one of the twenty-four handwritten copies then circulating for editorial revision. This draft represented a selection of over a hundred pieces culled from the thousands that had been sent in. In response to a question about her impressions (*ganxiang*) of the project, she replied:

It makes me feel moved and ashamed. I am moved and astounded by these great events, ashamed that I have not done more. From the point of view of writing, the more I read it the more I feel my own life experience is inadequate; great works are not achieved by literary people (*wenren*) playing around with ink and pen on paper.[15]

She noted that the work was nearing completion and "it will certainly spread throughout the world" but despite high hopes it was never finished. (Edgar Snow complained that much of the material he collected from participants in the Long March and lent to Ding Ling was never returned.)[16]

Both the collective emphasis and the ephemeral, nonprofessional form in which much art and literature was "published" in Yanan undoubtedly compelled the writer to question the relevance of his individual creative efforts. But the very activity of writing itself was viewed with uncertainty. Ding Ling's answers to the inevitable question by every outside visitor to Yanan—why so little writing was being produced—reflect some of these problems. Instead of writing for money in Shanghai, where the more you wrote the better, she said, here in Yanan "there was no need to be concerned about one's livelihood. In writing one must consider its effect on the reader, so one's attitude toward writing is naturally more serious (*yansu*)."[17]

Writing had become a more serious and hence uncertain business because of the new stress on the uses of literature. But Ding Ling's position is at times too readily seen as being in direct, clear-cut opposition to that of the party.[18] Similarly, setting up a Shanghai-Yanan polarity is only useful for outlining two distinct intellectual positions, not for ranging individual writers—who might compromise, shift, or vacillate—on an ideological spectrum.

One of the impressions sometimes given in certain descriptions of the events surrounding the "Yanan Talks" is that Mao by fiat declared an end to the "petty bourgeois" writing engaged in by Ding Ling and others, and dogmatically made literature and art subservient to the interests of the party. That would be an oversimplification. Certainly one consequence of the "Talks," as part of the rectification campaign, was the consolidation of Mao's leadership and the assertion of party control and discipline over all activity, including the cultural. But in content the "Talks" did not initiate any radical changes regarding the relation between art and politics and should be seen as a continuation of ideas that had been "in the air" in leftist circles since the early 1930s;[19] indeed, they were a crystallization or theoretical formulation of what had already been literary practice for some time.

Ding Ling's work in the League of Left-Wing Writers, her editorship of *Beidou*, her contributions to the debates on *dazhong wenyi*, and her developing conceptions of the writer's political role anticipate many aspects of the "Yanan Talks." Most of all, it was the record of her experiences as a writer soon after she arrived in Yanan, trying to serve the revolution and the War of Resistance in the most direct way possible, that helped prepare the groundwork for many of Mao's ideas. These practical experiences provide an important link between the "Yanan Talks" and the literary discussions of the early thirties in Shanghai.

With the Northwest Front Service Corps

Ding Ling had no pretensions of being a literary theorist, and did not contribute any fully developed and coherent statement to the emerging Yanan position on literature. Her own understanding of such problems was based instead on what she had learned through practice. As she had written earlier, "only in the actual work of struggle can there be the deepest and most concrete understanding of any theory."[20]

When she arrived at the headquarters of the Communist Party in Baoan in November 1936, she was one of the very first writers to join the ranks of what at that time looked like a ragged bunch that had barely survived the Long March. It was entirely characteristic of her spirit that soon after arriving she should have gone with the Red Army to the Shaangan front and then served as the vice-director of the Red Army Guard Unit.[21] Most of her writing about these experiences is lost or in fragments.[22] Her most sustained, literally "fieldwork" effort to test literature and art in the service of political action was during her experience with the Northwest Front Service Corps, which she organized and directed shortly after the War of Resistance against Japan began in July 1937. Again she did not manage a finished account of this important experience; the book *Yinian* (One Year) is "not a literary work, just a record of their lives, merely the fragments (*lingsui*) of a year."[23] Still these "fragments" are an account of the experimental testing of many of Mao's ideas on literature and art four or five years before his definitive formulation of them. *One Year* may or may not be a factual record of the work carried out by the Northwest Front Service Corps; certainly it makes no claims to being a complete or systematic one. What makes the book a compelling document is not just the information we can glean from it concerning the Corps's activities, but its testimony of the powerful ethos, at once aesthetic and political, that animated them throughout.

When the War of Resistance against Japan broke out, every day in Yanan, as Ding Ling describes it, dozens of students and cadres requested to be sent to the front, "the hearts of young people were all flying among the cannon fire." Mao Zedong's remarks on the playing fields of Kangda (Resistance University) were therefore greeted with much excitement:

> Anyone who is not afraid to die will have a chance to go to the front. Get yourselves ready, the day the order comes, that day you can shoulder your

blanket roll and leave. Yanan does not need you, does not need all these cadres
. . . When you've fixed up China, driven out the Japanese, we'll welcome you
back.[24]

The Service Corps was conceived in this heady atmosphere of patriotic fervor; first formed as a reporters' group (jizhetuan) to write reports
and communications, it was later expanded into a propaganda team
(xuanchuandui). The shift of emphasis is apparent in the Corps's organization charts, which Ding Ling provides in the book. At the beginning
the correspondence section is parallel to the propaganda section, but in
later charts it is subsumed under it.[25]

Among the Service Corps's objectives was to bring "large-scale propaganda through such forms as plays, music, lectures, cartoons,
slogans," to the soldiers and the people, so they will "thoroughly understand the meaning and goals of the national revolutionary struggle."[26]
The Chinese word xuanchuan is a more neutral term than "propaganda";
it means mainly to publicize, to make known, and does not in itself
(whatever its applications) carry the negative connotations of manipulation for a special purpose. This does not mean that Ding Ling and her
group of mostly twenty-year-old university students were not conscious
of their goal of communicating a particular point of view. The central
message stressed at that time was not Communist ideology but the urgent
and direct one of national survival against a war of aggression. It may be
that the Communist Party preempted the issue of nationalism in order to
carry out a social revolution, but certainly at this stage the main efforts
were directed consciously toward the matter of strengthening the will to
fight Japan.

The necessity of spreading such an elementary message becomes apparent when we realize that the itinerary of the Service Corps required it
to pass through small backward villages in Shaanxi and Shanxi whose
names do not appear on even the most detailed map of north China. According to Ding Ling, the village might consist of twenty or so families,
steeped in superstition, the women with bound feet; the head of the Poor
Peasants' Association (set up by the Eighth Route Army that had preceded the Corps) would be a peasant in tattered clothes and an old straw
hat. Performances might take place in town in the God of War Temple,
the City Guardian Temple, or the elementary school, under the light of a
borrowed gas lamp, on a platform hastily put up and decorated with
wild flowers by members of the Corps. The American correspondent
Agnes Smedley describes one such performance on November 9, 1937,
for which the gate to the small town was transformed into a theater by
building a platform about six feet up from the ground across the gateway
and stringing a red curtain across it.[27] The audience in these places were a

very far cry from the public to whom Ding Ling had addressed her fictional art in the Westernized, cosmopolitan cities of Peking and Shanghai. The references she used to make to Beethoven or Salome would have been ludicrously out of place in these isolated cultural backwaters.

In most cases the group played "one-night stands" on the road, arriving at a town or village, going to the market place or street to draw in an audience, prepare the stage, put on a show, and sleep, moving on the next day. A collective report by members of the Northwest Front Service Corps records that during the six months they were on the road in Shanxi, they passed through some sixteen towns and over sixty large and small villages, covering a distance of more than three thousand *li* (one *li* is half a kilometer). During that time they put on one hundred and thirteen performances, not including the street corner talks or story-telling sessions they gave on the way. They then took part in over sixty performances in the city of Xian where they stayed for four-and-a-half months. Their repertory included some works by established playwrights, but in response to the demands of performance they wrote more and more of their own, creating a total of twenty-four original plays.[28] Many of these were written collectively, some were categorized as street theatre (*jietouju*) or people's theatre (*qunzhongju*); most were the products of inexperienced playwrights like Ding Ling herself. The plays tended to very short one-act shows; as she describes them in *Yinian*, "the greater part was made up of rousing slogans, since our audience was either soldiers or workers and peasants, and our objective was to educate them, encourage them . . . but we had hardly studied stage technique and were making slow progress."[29] These performances would be interspersed with political lectures and songs.

Under these conditions both the practice and criteria of art and literature had to be radically revised. Ding Ling always expressed dissatisfaction with her work, but was even more critical of her plays. They were often a product of group pressure, perhaps on an assigned topic, or written because the Corps might happen to need a longer work to perform in Xian. She worried about their quality; praise of them always made her feel "desolate and false."[30] In print her playwriting efforts are hardly interesting, but they seemed to have served their purpose well enough at the time. It could be that the rapport with the audience, the direct appeal to the emotions, or the enthusiasm, if not skill of the performers, were together sufficient to overcome the crudities of the written text.

But regardless of the actual quality of the works presented by the Northwest Front Service Corps — very little survives in printed form — the impression gained from reading Ding Ling's account is that they enjoyed a tremendous success. The circumstances under which the Corps produced its works meant that audience appeal was immediately measurable; actors and playwrights quickly found out what went over and what did not. Peasants walked ten *li* or more to the performances, stayed to watch them even under the most uncomfortable conditions, remained standing for up to five hours, and eagerly demanded more when the program was over. The Corps suffered dangers and hardships on the road and at times ran into rude and unsympathetic district officials, but the people were always wonderfully appreciative; certainly no artists could have asked for a more consistently gratifying audience response. In the God of War Temple of Linfen, a town where the Corps stayed for two days, for example:

> All were hoarse from shouting, the faces flushed with excitement, eyes beaming, those on the platform and those below merged into one (*dacheng yipian*); the brave spirits all together drawn to the light made the crowd into something great; this scene would remain in people's hearts as most beautiful, most memorable, because at that moment we felt emotions that were not the common ones of every day.[31]

The group felt that its experience demonstrated over and over again that people responded most readily to "what originally was theirs (*yuanlai shi qunzhong de dongxi*)"—the popular traditional forms, now updated with a "down with Japan" message, but essentially something familiar. One division of the Service Corps specialized in studying and adapting such forms. These included drum songs (*dagu*), clapper talk (*kuaiban*), two-man acts (*shuanghuang*), comic cross-talk (*xiangsheng*) and many others. Their greatest success was with the modern version of the *yangge*, a song-and-dance form popular in the North. (Performers twisted and turned their bodies in a series of steps, moving forwards and backwards, making various formations, forming pairs; they would also sing, accompanied by drums, gongs, and the *sona*, and might add some clowning.) By adding costumes of workers, peasants, soldiers, students, merchants, and the Japanese with their "running dogs" they could enact a dramatic situation with a patriotic message while maintaining the form's lively movement. When this was performed in Yanan the whole city followed them through the streets, cheering along.[32] The *yangge* could be used to attract a crowd upon arrival at a new place; it could be used also during a performance, with the actors freely moving up and down stage, and in and out of the audience.

One might conclude from her exhilarating account that what Ding Ling offers in *One Year* is not the historical objective reality of the Corps' experience, but rather that experience as perceived and interpreted by her and others who participated in it with such zeal. In either case, the effect of her work on the thinking of those struggling to define a role for art was of course the same. Born in response to the urgent national crisis and adapting itself continually to the needs of its audience, the practical example of the Service Corps suddenly seemed to reduce the tortuous debates begun in the early 1930s over the use of national forms, the necessity of reaching the masses, and the purposes of literature and art, to some obvious and irrefutable facts and solutions.

For the artist now presenting his work directly to the people, the issue of *dazhonghua* so earnestly discussed from the time of the League of Left-Wing Writers took on an actuality it never had before. In spite of the attempts to reach factory workers and organize cultural activities among them, there had been an air of abstract unreality in the strident debates carried on within the pages of magazines published in the enclaves of the foreign settlements in Shanghai. Perhaps the most important reality these debates did reflect was the writer's own sense of anxiety over the relevance and purpose of his work. There was almost a sense of relief when all-out war against Japan broke out because, with stunning clarity, it revealed the task of literature. "From the beginning, all work must be connected with the War of Resistance";[33] "Literature must go to the countryside, literature must enlist" (*wenzhang xiaxiang, wenzhang ruwu*),[34] were the slogans that gave writers their sense of purpose. The war was felt to be forcing literature out of the ivory tower and into contact with a broader reality:

> The fires of the War of Resistance forced writers under the new circumstances to come closer to reality, to break into a brand new life of struggle, to perceive a vision broader and more real than anything they had seen before. Writers are no longer hemmed within their own constricted world, no longer gazing at the blue sky and white clouds through windows but have been liberated from their studies, their back rooms, their salons, their coffee houses, to stride into the field of battle, to the places where the people are; from the cities they are used to living in they have gone into the villages and towns, from the foreign settlements, they have walked toward the interior.[35]

The liberation was not merely physical or geographical, but social and psychological as well — a liberation from the feelings of alienation and frustration in which writers had been trapped. They now found themselves meaningfully engaged with a wider world.

The broadening of a writer's horizon also meant the enhancement of literary possibilities. "Some say that having discussions with two or three friends and reading a few novels in translation constitute the entire culture (*xiuyang*) of our writers";[36] an exaggerated statement that nevertheless evoked the sterility of the modern writer's way of life, his endless cultivation of limited and half-understood Western sources of creativity.

Ding Ling was one writer who very early translated the rhetoric into action. The issues of adapting national forms, of reaching out to the masses, of using literature and art to serve broad political and social ends, issues that had been discussed in inevitably abstract terms since the early 1930s, were through her experiences with the Northwest Front Service Corps tested in practice. Before the Corps left on its mission, Mao gave them a lecture on "The Problem of *dazhonghua*." Their subsequent experience showed that popularization could work, at least in a limited context. The concrete success of this venture and similar efforts by other artists provided a practical base for the approach to literature and art that Mao was to outline five years later in his "Yanan Talks." That these same "Talks" were by then directed *against* Ding Ling, among others, is an example of the irony of history, or even more, a testimony to the recalcitrance of literature.

The Bright Side of Reality

One of Ding Ling's ambitions when she became director of the Northwest Front Service Corps had been to do more writing; instead she became "a person who did the chores." The only time in nine months that she was able to sit down and write with any sense of leisure was during the two days when enemy planes were flying overhead bombing Yuzi[37] — presumably because public performances were ruled out. But however difficult the conditions, Ding Ling never relinquished her self-image as a writer and constantly worried about the paucity of her output. The work she did manage to produce between 1937 and 1941 drew mainly upon immediate wartime experiences in the Border Regions. The content is therefore inevitably harsh or tragic, yet she contrives to end each piece on a generally optimistic and hopeful note, acknowledging that it is the duty of literature to contribute positive support to the collective effort. But these endeavors were not enough to spare her from being a target of criticism during the 1942 rectification movement,[38] when her writings were used as damning evidence against her. In spite of the general convergence of principles between Ding Ling's *One Year* and Mao Zedong's "Yanan Talks," there was an undeniable conflict over the writer's basic right to portray and interpret reality. This conflict was at the core of the bright versus the dark side debate.

The "Talks at the Yanan Forum on Literature and Art" must be viewed within the context of the rectification movement, which was launched to discipline and streamline the party in response to a crisis. A series of natural disasters and the prolonged Kuomintang blockade exacerbated the hardships of existence in what was already an impoverished, poorly developed area. Intensified Japanese offensives were causing severe losses of lives and supplies. That the Chinese Communist Party was able to surmount these incredibly difficult conditions and forge itself into the unique and effective instrument that later won the revolution was due in large measure to the success of the rectification movement. Its purpose, and that of the many subsequent campaigns of which it turned out to be a mild prototype, was not to enforce a passive acquiescence in party policies but to transform each individual into a committed worker actively supporting them on his own initiative. Mao's conception of revolution as above all a process of mass consciousness-raising had of necessity assigned to literature and art a crucial role, but one that, ineluctably, had to be clearly defined and strictly controlled.

The conditions of war underlie the predominantly military images used in the "Yanan Talks." Literature and art as weapons in processes of struggle was by then a threadbare cliché, but Mao gave the metaphor new clout by repeatedly speaking of the cultural and military fronts as parallel in the revolutionary war, and of the cultural army as "absolutely indispensable for uniting our own ranks and defeating the enemy."[39] It is the never-to-be-forgotten presence of the enemy and obligatory ranking of people into "those who are for us" or "are against us" that restricted the room for literary maneuver, since all material and characters became subject to a preliminary political classification. But though the "Yanan Talks" were produced under the pressure of a grave crisis, they have remained the fundamental scripture of the party's literary policies; more than thirty years after the successful establishment of the revolution the "siege mentality" still prevails in the field of literature and art.

Under siege conditions, any criticism will be seen as undermining in effect. The "Yanan Talks," delivered in May, were specifically addressed to a group of writers who had indeed undertaken to criticize the party in a series of articles that appeared from March to April in 1942. Without mentioning names, Mao engaged in a point by point rebuttal of issues raised by Ding Ling, Luo Feng, Wang Shiwei, Xiao Jun, and Ai Ching, in the literary pages of the *Jiefang ribao*, of which Ding Ling was then editor. More particularly, Mao's comments on the bright versus the dark side problem and the use of the *zawen* form (critical or satirical essays) referred directly to the question of whether, and to what extent, criticism itself should be permitted. In retrospect this was the overriding issue.[40]

In a brief article Ding Ling had published in 1939 on satire (*fengci*), she wrote: "People want to speak, to say what they see as the truth, but at certain times when you are not allowed to speak the truth, then many things must be disguised."[41] Lu Xun, she said, was skilled in his use of this sort of weapon, but now "during our sacred national revolutionary struggle," satire is not needed. However, in October 1941, she urgently invoked his critical spirit in an essay entitled "Women xuyao zawen" (We Need *zawen*):

> We are still in the period of Lu Xun . . . there is corruption, darkness, the murder of progressive elements . . . even in progressive areas, where there is incip-

ient democracy, there is even more need to exhort, to be vigilant. The deeply rooted feudal evils of China, which have lasted for several thousand years, are not easy to eradicate. What we call progressive areas do not fall down from heaven, they are linked with the old society. Still we say it is not appropriate to write *zawen* here, that here we should reflect only the democratic life, the great constructions.

She goes on to praise Lu Xun, then concludes: "Today I think we would do well to emulate his steadfastness in always facing towards truth, to dare to speak for the truth, not afraid of anything; our age still needs *zawen*."[42]

Ding Ling herself dared "to speak for the truth" about the condition of women in Yanan a few months later, in her essay "Sanbajie you gan" (Thoughts on March 8) published on March 9, 1942. It is an impassioned report on the situation of women even in the liberated areas. They are forever the objects of attention or criticism, damned if they marry or if they don't, have children or don't, stay at home or don't. Divorce is usually initiated by the man; if the woman wants it, "then there must be something even more immoral and it is entirely the woman who should be cursed." Then women grow old, never having escaped the fate of being "backward" (*luohou*). In traditional society a woman might have been considered "pitiful," "ill-fated"; now that she is supposedly equal and can choose her marital status, if she suffers it is "her own doing," "serves her right." Ding Ling stresses that women in Yanan are much more fortunate than women elsewhere in China, but the bitter contradictions of their existence remain.

> I am a woman myself, I understand women's shortcomings better than most, but I understand even more their suffering. They cannot be above their times, they are not ideal, they are not forged of steel. They are unable to resist society's temptations and silent oppressions, they all have a history of blood and tears, they have all had lofty emotions (whether they have risen or fallen, are fortunate or unfortunate, still struggling alone or have joined the crowd). To say this about the women comrades who have come to Yanan is not unjust. Therefore it is with a great deal of leniency that I consider those who have sunk to become female criminals. I hope that men, especially men in high positions, and women themselves will see the shortcomings of women more as based in society.[43]

She soon discovered that it was indeed not "appropriate to write *zawen* here" and was led to confess her errors at a public meeting on June 11. Her self-criticism, of which we only have published fragments, was included in a statement denouncing Wang Shiwei, the only public example of the rectification movement. She begins by responding to those who had written to express their agreement with her:

I want to say to all those who hold similar views: this article is a bad article. You must not, because it has spoken up for you, obstinately insist that it is a good article and express sympathy for me personally. Let me now tell you (perhaps you are already only a very small minority) that the main thing wrong with the article is its standpoint and ideological method . . . Though I had poured my blood and tears into that article, infusing it with many years of pain and investing it with fervent hope, yet it shows that I merely spoke for a part of the people and not from the standpoint of the entire party. I talked only about some unimportant shortcomings, taking a lopsided view of the problem. I merely pointed out some of the darkness and forgot to affirm the bright future.[44]

The strong personal and emotional tone of this piece (as well as of the offending article) is so rare in a writer of fiction who normally expresses herself behind the mask of an assumed narrator, that one wishes for the entire text. But little has been published of the exchanges between Ding Ling and her critics during the rectification campaign. Fortunately, unlike Wang Shiwei, she was not a target of harsh public criticism at this time. In fact, little was known of her difficulties in Yanan until they were brought up during the antirightist campaign some fifteen years later. By then the record was no doubt distorted by the vehemence of the attacks on her. The quoted fragment implies that Ding Ling admits the validity of the charges about her article's divisive and negative character, but she does not recant the basic truth of its contents. Furthermore, the somewhat defiant address to her supporters, even while pointing out that their sympathies towards her may have been misguided, suggests again that what she wrote about the conditions of women was at least partially true, that some "darkness" did indeed exist. As far as can be deduced from the fragmentary evidence, the "charge" that she was confessing to was not her erroneous views concerning women in Yanan — there was little inclination on the part of the leadership then to look into the actual situation even just to refute her argument — but the fact that she had been critical at all.

According to Ding Ling's conception at that time, *zawen* was unquestionably a tool for criticism. In the hundred-and-first issue of the *Jiefang ribao*'s literary page she had referred to her previous call in October 1941 for everyone to write "short pieces that would be criticisms of society and literature and art."[45] But that issue of March 12, 1942, also marked the approaching end of a forum for critical writing. Ding Ling was leaving the editorship of the literary page and the *Jiefang ribao* was being reorganized into a paper that could be counted on to give more militant support to the party. Meanwhile the rectification movement was gaining momentum, was soon in full swing, and the question of *zawen* was peremptorily closed by Mao Zedong in the "Yanan Talks":

To take *zawen* and Lu Xun's method (*bifa*) as satire is correct only in terms of the enemies of the people[46] . . . but . . . where democracy and freedom are granted in full to revolutionary writers and artists and withheld only from the counter-revolutionaries, the style of the *zawen* should not simply be like Lu Xun's . . . To criticize the people's shortcomings is necessary . . . but in doing so we must truly take the stand of the people and speak out of whole-hearted eagerness to protect and educate them.

How rigorously the principle of taking "the stand of the people" was to be defined was yet an open question, or so Ding Ling thought when she wrote "Guanyu lichang wenti wojian" (My Views Concerning the Question of Standpoint), presented to the Yanan Forum before Mao delivered his concluding address:

Some say that in the Border Regions there is only brightness and no darkness, so that one should only write about brightness; some say that the Border Regions are bright, but the sun has black spots; while the sun should be praised, the black spots should not be tabooed (*huiyen*) . . . I believe that while on the surface this seems a matter of choosing material (*qucai*), actually it is a matter of standpoint and method. So-called defects or darkness (*heian*) are merely debates over phraseology. If we have a firm and clear standpoint, and follow the method of Marxism-Leninism, it will not be a problem even to write about darkness. Since there are ways [to deal with] its origins and removal (*you qi laiyin quguo*), not only will brightness (*guangming*) not be impaired, but will because of it shine even more. If we limit ourselves to arguing over this problem as a matter of choosing material, then we will be trapped in the particulars of whether something is real or not real (*zhenshi*), seen or not seen, and will not be able to arrive at proper conclusions.[47]

In other words, once the writer is politically committed to the proper standpoint, he need not be further bound by the questions of whether darkness is real or not real, should or should not be written about. Clearly, Ding Ling did not realize then how explicit and prescriptive party policy was to be. Indeed the question of whether darkness existed in reality was losing its relevance, since it was becoming apparent that reality was not necessarily the proper subject of literature. Zhou Yang, who between 1942 and 1966 increasingly took on the role of chief interpreter of Mao's ideas on literature, wrote soon after the Yanan Forum:

What I mean by writing about the bright side, means to advocate writing about the positive, the growing, the developing side of reality, the side with a future . . . Brightness is not an abstract concept, it concretely and actually exists. To demand that a writer write about the bright side is to demand that he write about something already contained in reality or new and about to be born [from it].[48]

He draws a distinction between "old realism" and "revolutionary realism" (*geming de xianshi zhuyi*). The old realism criticized and exposed the defects and evils of the existing social system, but revolutionary realism

> does not have such a negative character at all; while negating the old it affirms the future. The tendency of history's development is always advantageous to it, it naturally always has the courage to look to the future . . . In this sense, the basic spirit of a revolutionary work of art, regardless of its theme or subject matter, should always be to reveal brightness (qishi guangming).[49]

The vision of reality as determined by the party is primarily oriented toward the future. The task of literature is therefore quite clear. To write as prescribed about the bright side is not to reflect a contemporary reality but to create an image of the reality that is coming into being. Maoist revolution is a continual process of projecting into the future, so literature and art should parallel the revolutionary process and manifest the same qualities of heroism and optimistic confidence needed to realize that future.

The supremacy of the party in the realm of literature and art was established with the "Yanan Talks." Beyond committing himself to the correct political standpoint, the writer was henceforth expected to comply with guidelines specifying that the bright side, the vision of reality that unequivocally reinforced revolutionary goals, constitute his proper subject. But even with the writer's acceptance of the party's leadership, some residual intractability in the literary process continued to activate tension between the two that would later erupt time and again into open conflict. On one level there was real improvement in the writer's lot: although life in the Border Regions was difficult, he was well rewarded and better off than most. The psychological gain was perhaps even more important; with a clearly defined political role, the writer was no longer a marginal person or a social outcast, uncertain of his function and alienated from his public.

Ding Ling did not struggle long to come to terms with this designated place of the writer in the overall revolutionary scheme. Along with self-criticism she joined in the criticism of her colleagues who had followed her lead in the *Jiefang ribao* in voicing their dissatisfaction with the way things were. She had not viewed herself as occupying a position of dissent vis-à-vis the party; her demurrals and questions must be seen within the wider context of her support and indeed anticipation, in her own thinking and practice, of many aspects of party policy. Nevertheless the confrontation she helped bring about in Yanan marked the beginning of the campaigns that were to be waged against writers for the next thirty-odd years.

The above account of Ding Ling's part in the Yanan experience may give the impression that all the events and issues at the time formed around her and were, so to speak, determined and defined by her. She was, of course, only one writer among others, but her established reputation and her Shanghai background did endow her with a larger representative value. She continued setting the pace as, soon after the dust of the Yanan controversies had settled, she quickly translated the lessons learned into literary practice. When she resumed writing in 1944, after two years of thought reform and study in party schools and in the countryside, she turned to the bright side. The effect her reformation had on her narratives can be seen most dramatically in her treatment of character.

Characters and Models

When the writer's perception of reality is extrinsically defined for him, he may manifest great uncertainty in determining what precise narrative genre he is writing in. A generic label commits him to placing his work in a particular relation to that defined reality. This may be why generic terms proliferate in Ding Ling's various prefaces and afterwords to her works of the Yanan period. Whereas in the earlier writings the single term *xiaoshuo* (fiction), which includes novels and short stories, seemed serviceable enough, now she refers to individual pieces variously as *yinxiangji*, "impressions"; *tongxin*, "communications"; *zuopin*, "literary works"; *shenghuo shilu*, "actual record of life"; *baodao*, "reportage"; *duanwen*, "short prose pieces"; *lishi*, "history"; as well as *xiaoshuo* based on real incidents. These manifold labels were used by others as well and the distinctions between them are not at all clear, but together they appear to suggest that in the wide spectrum between fiction and reality, genre should be an indication of the work's approximate position in that spectrum and a measure of its relative distance from the real. The inconsistent use of these labels and their diversity, more than anything else, reveal the quandary in which the author found herself when contemplating the relationship between a particular work and reality.

If the right relationship between literature and reality becomes a central concern, character can take on a great, perhaps disproportionate importance. "For many readers," according to Jonathan Culler, "character serves as the major totalizing force in fiction — everything in the novel exists in order to illustrate character and its development."[50] Yet along with its "totalizing force," the ability to hold the novel together for the reader, character is also, paradoxically, the most abstractable of all the elements that go into the making of a work of fiction. Character can be most readily picked out and isolated, most easily lends itself to being judged as to whether it is life-like or whether it embodies the proper values the work is supposed to present. For these reasons, character is the touchstone of Chinese Marxist criticism.

Marxist revolutionary ideology, while politically oriented toward a utopian future, is unyieldingly conservative in its aesthetic tastes, insisting still on the nineteenth-century (actually "bourgeois") conventions of realistic fiction with their emphasis on the creation of character. Together with its adoption of Marxism, China has taken over these conventions of realism; indeed considers them the only method appropriate to all literature. The state of affairs at times deplored in the modern West as the "retreat from character"[51] in both experimental fiction and the new criticism has not yet reached China. Characters in Chinese novels are very much discussed and politically evaluated as if they were real people for their readers and had an existence outside the books in which they appear.

The notion of character not only represents something the reader can readily identify with, but can also be used to "identify" the author. Mencius' exhortation, "Can one read a man's books and not know him?" (du qi shu er bu zhi qi ren, ke hu?), an important principle in traditional criticism, has now at times been carried to extremes. In the past, much critical discussion had centered on the individual writer's personality and moral qualities, usually as revealed in the work, in order to add another dimension to the understanding and appreciation of the work itself. Communist criticism has used this tendency of deducing the author from the work not so much to "characterize" the poem or the essay, but to praise or discredit the author himself. For the political purpose of excoriating any given writer, the notion of character has proved to be infinitely malleable. It is always possible to damn a writer's character through clues provided by the characters in his work.

Character is the "major totalizing force" not only in fictional narratives, but also in the real world these narratives are supposed to represent. Through character, more than anything else, the institutions, values, and self-images of China's revolutionary society have found the most powerful means of expression and reinforcement. The ideal revolutionary is embodied in real persons (though often after their death, as, for example, Lei Feng). But words, literature, and art are essential to compose and publicize the inspirational portraits of these individuals for emulation. As in the past, "knowing verbal descriptions of exemplary things is almost the same as knowing the actualities."[52] One effect of the "Yanan Talks" is the increasing tendency in subsequent literature to replace characters with models, or lifelike, complex personalities with types (dianxing) who exemplify ideals.[53]

Changes in the selection and treatment of character in response to political orientation have always been quite marked in Ding Ling's writings. In Yanan she continued what she had already begun doing in 1931: to expand the range of the age group and occupations of her characters and to observe closely the physical and social environment in which they moved. One new feature of the Yanan stories is that the main character is usually already a member of a collective—the army, the party, school—or will join one in the course of the story. The story concentrates on assessing that character's role in the collective; its action is the demonstration of his qualifications for that role. In spite of the similarity in plot outline, the action, in the works written before the "Yanan Talks" can still be fraught with uncertainty, and the characters, while sympathetically treated, are not yet idealized, stereotyped, nor elevated into models, as they will be in her reportage pieces (*baodao*) written after 1944.

Many of the characters are children or have what may be considered childlike qualities. Such people may be older people, peasants, or soldiers. One of her first Yanan stories, written in April 1937 about events just before the formation of the Second United Front, "Yike wei chu tang de qiangdan" (A Bullet not yet Fired from Its Barrel), begins with an encounter between a thirteen-year-old boy and an impoverished old peasant woman. He turns out to be a Little Devil (*xiaoguei*) from the Red Army who was inadvertently left behind by his unit during an air raid. The old woman takes him in and the whole village befriends him. When the Kuomintang army comes through he is captured and about to be shot, but he asks to be killed by a sword: "Keep the bullet, save it for fighting the Japanese."[54] This little speech on behalf of the United Front policy moves his would-be executioners to tears and they spare his life.

Several other pre–1944 stories or sketches feature children who turn out to be precociously patriotic, running away from home to join the Red Army and fight the Japanese. Ding Ling also describes some of the youngest members of the Northwest Front Service Corps, which included a unit composed of twelve- and thirteen-year-olds. These writings no doubt represent Ding Ling's genuine interest and experiences with children during these years—in 1938 her own son and daughter joined her in Yanan—but this literary emphasis also makes an ideological point. The mass line being worked out in Yanan was based on the assumption that all people have unsuspected, untapped sources of energy; the strength of the revolution would come from their mobilization. Therefore children, old peasant women, all were capable of rising to heroic and extraordinary heights.

"Xin de xinnian" (New Faith), written in 1939, concerns an illiterate grandmother who, after experiencing and witnessing shocking atrocities committed against her family and others by Japanese soldiers when they attack her village, apparently loses her sanity. She becomes compulsively talkative, telling over and over again in horrible detail what she has seen. She is asked to speak at a patriotic rally, where her account, hesitant at first, deeply moves and inspires the audience. Her morbid volubility is thus turned into a source of strength and consolation for herself and for the group.[55]

The story affirms that we need words, we need the act of telling, both to bear witness and to help us confront, or even transcend, the horrors of war and existence. While the rambling narratives of the old peasant woman are only minimally fit to be called literature, they are an example of the sort of use literature, under extraordinary conditions, can have. They show that the capacity for literature exists even in the lowliest of places. Furthermore, portraying the masses extended the range of literature to include subjects that had never been taken seriously before. The humblest, "lowest common denominators" of the community were being discovered in both their revolutionary and aesthetic potential.

The choice of peasants as characters was also determined by the fact that, in the absence of the urban proletariat in the countryside, they had taken over its exemplary role to become the vanguard of revolution. By far the majority of characters in Ding Ling's Yanan works are peasants.

The 1941 story "Ye" (Night) is about a cadre, He Huaming, from "almost the poorest small village in the area." Walking home one night after a late meeting, along the road that shares so many of his memories, past the graves of his two young children, he worries that his party work has made him neglect for some twenty days now his few patches of land. He is anxious about his cow about to give birth. His wife, thin and sallow, and twelve years his senior, is waiting for him, "every line in her face the ambush for a storm."[56] In the middle of the night he anxiously goes out to check on his cow, and finds that the calf will probably not be born until tomorrow. He repels the advances of his young neighbor's wife who had come out there to wait for him. Back in bed, he decides not to divorce his thin sallow wife, "it will be a bad influence," and tries hard to fall asleep,

> but all he could see were meeting rooms, people, and hear things like "the propaganda work is not adequate, the village is backward, the work among women has amounted to nothing." As he thought of these he began to fret, how can we improve the village, there is no one here to work. Who was he himself? He didn't understand anything, he had never been to school, he could not read, he did not even have a son, and now he was county leader (*xiang zhidaoyuan*) and tomorrow he must report on the meaning of the meeting.[57]

He sinks into a doze while the sky gradually brightens. By bringing together the pending birth of the calf, the movement from night to dawn, the shifting attitude toward the wife, the story beautifully captures and holds in suspension that mood, that moment of consciousness, when one can acknowledge all the doubts and hardships of the present yet feel poised, ready, at the edge of a new beginning.

In a story dating from the same year similar self-doubts and hardships are experienced by a young intellectual rather than an illiterate peasant, but this story was subjected to severe censure. "Zai yiyuan zhong" (In the Hospital) is about a single young woman from Shanghai, so critics could score obvious points by stating that the story represented a reversion by its author to her early unregenerate "petty bourgeois" days. The twenty-year-old Lu Ping is trained in Shanghai as a midwife, and after a period of wandering arrives in Yanan. She becomes a communist, studies at Resistance University, and answering the "needs of the party," is assigned to a newly opened hospital forty *li* away. Taken aback by her inhospitable reception, by the primitive conditions, above all by the incompetence and irresponsibility of some members of the staff, she nevertheless dedicates herself to her duties, determined to improve the quality of care for her patients. Her outspokenness arouses criticism and, after a harrowing episode in the operating room where tragedy caused by deficient equipment is narrowly averted, she falls ill. She leaves for further study knowing the new life ahead will have "new thorns," but "to be truly useful one must undergo much tempering without dissolving. It is through hardship that one grows."[58] The ending and message of the story is forward-looking, but one that has duly recognized the internal and external difficulties of struggle.

Both "Night" and "In the Hospital" — the titles themselves are metaphors of their themes — dwell on the dark side of revolutionary experience yet unequivocally affirm a bright future. They are narrated in the third person primarily through the dramatized consciousness of the central characters, but the character of Lu Ping is done much more intensively from the inside. Could the internal state of a peasant character be described in comparably intimate detail? The true portrayal of the peasant, the vanguard of China's revolution, poses this dilemma: any proficient writer, due to his cultural background and specialized education, is alienated from the real peasant mind; on the other hand, any peasant who has acquired the linguistic skills and socially determined conventions of literate narrative, will unavoidably "distort" his own material. The party's constant exhortation to writers to go among the masses and learn to speak their language in order to give authentic expression to their thoughts and feelings, is in acknowledgment that the right medium of expression for such a purpose does not yet exist. This lack is one reason why writers often resort to idealized stereotypes when they attempt to represent the peasant.

In "Night" the central figure is not idealized, which is one reason for the story's emotional impact, but his thoughts are expressed in language very far from that of an illiterate peasant. This need not matter to those who do not believe that a character's true-to-life authenticity is the only criterion for judging a story's success. The details of He Huaming's internal experience do not in any event dominate the action. But Lu Ping's case is different; in a sense, she determines the reality of the "hospital" in the story.

Beginning with the opening paragraphs, the cold weather, the frozen rivers, the darkening twilight, the shivering crows, do not simply set the scene but are also charged with a personal meaning. In the cave that is to be Lu Ping's living quarters the frightening cold air assaults her, the weak evening sun hovers on the black mud walls shedding a sad and lonely light, so that "one seems to be situated in a dim, but semi-transparent world, as if isolated from the present world."[59] Her blanket is thin, but determined not to be disappointed or feel depressed, and not to depend on others, she says, "I'm not too afraid of the cold." This "isolated" world comes into existence, as it were, with her arrival, and reflects both her state of mind and the challenge of her environment. The readers are not shown the objective world where the character is placed, but rather her perception and subjective response to a world.

Even when the narrative distance is shifted slightly and Lu Ping is described from the outside, the focus is still on her alone or on her effect on others, but only as it ultimately affects herself:

> She went to meetings . . . she had sufficient enthusiasm, and little savoir-faire (shihgu); she described, argued, poured forth the unreasonable things she saw every day; she did not know how to observe other people's expressions, and said things that many people were afraid or unwilling to say . . . she had become a small odd person in the hospital; there was no question that she was looked at by the majority of people with curious eyes.[60]

Since all events, persons, landscapes, atmospheric conditions are "imprisoned" within the subjective experience of a twenty-year-old, sensitive, anxious, high-strung, insomniac woman, our only view of the world is the singular one of Lu Ping. There is no access to the external, objective reality of the hospital, whatever that might be, or to any alternative or corrective viewpoints.

The device of narrating a story from a subjective point of view is a well-established one; it had been carried to an extreme in "The Diary of Miss Sophie," but it was clearly not compatible with the revolutionary ideology being forged in Yanan. This ideology itself embodies a firm and specific view of reality, historically determined yet collectively propelled. Such a view of reality is locked out of "In the Hospital," however, because of its particular narrative approach. Thus, according to one critic writing in the Jiefang ribao during the rectification campaign: "The writer has substituted the particular or the individual (gebie) for the general (*yiban*), phenomenon (*xianxiang*) for substance (*benzhi*). What we demand is a more realistic description of reality."[61]

The problem with Ding Ling's description of reality was the substitution of "the individual for the general," an ideological shortcoming which, although the critic does not make this deduction, was implicit in her choice of narrative point of view. One might speculate whether it is conceivably possible through an extended dramatization of an individualized subjective consciousness to do justice to a vision of the world or history "created by the people"—not the people as a group of heterogeneous individuals, but the *people* collectively as a unitary idea. "In the Hospital" demonstrates the ideological implications not only of character itself, but of the techniques used for the presentation of character.

When Ding Ling returned to writing in 1944 after two years of reform, a dramatic change occurred in her portrayal of character, both in her selection of subjects and in her use of narrative devices. She wrote a number of reportage pieces (*baodao*) about "real people," in which characters through her treatment largely became models. It was, as she said, a "new beginning . . . after reading Chairman Mao's 'Talks at the Yanan Forum on Literature and Art.'"[62] A sketch of Tian Baolin, the director of a peasant cooperative, brought her a dinner invitation from Mao, who congratulated her on her "new literary path."[63] Her achievement was praised in a history of Chinese literature published in 1957:

> New heroic figures continue to emerge through struggle; they are the positive creators and builders of the new life; naturally they also become the central characters in literary works. To portray them realistically, to place before the broad public vividly alive models for emulation is precisely the primary responsibility of a fighting realistic writer's literary undertaking. In this regard the character sketches of Ding Ling assume a great significance.[64]

The accounts are full of detailed information, production statistics, place names, battle incidents; but against the solid specificity of the context, the characters themselves are deliberately flattened. It is as if they were on a shallow, lighted stage, performing assigned roles and presenting only what can be seen by the public out front. The complexity of motives,[65] the inner recesses of personality and its darker impulses are simply omitted as irrelevant. The individual's existence has meaning only through his public activity; as a heroic figure, a model for emulation, he has incorporated the ideals and institutions of his community into his own personal behavior. The rest of him, the qualities that might make him a unique, fallible human being, the attributes that constitute his private self, would detract from his public image; therefore information about him is severely selective. "Comrade Yuan Guangfa, we support you, we will learn from you!"[66] is the culminating sentence of one of Ding Ling's sketches, the end that discloses the meaning and purpose of the work.

The writing focuses on the model hero who stands alone, aloof; there are hardly any secondary characters who might involve him in private relationships. He exists only as much as and in the way that his role as hero requires him to. But as he increases factory production or expands the cooperative, the people collectively are always present, expressing support and approval, speaking at times as though in unison, "all the workers said he was progressing quickly."[67] "All the people from the Changqu Gou area had said good things about him, said that he was a peaceful and honest person, an upright person."[68] One of the most important characteristics of the model hero is that he is perfectly in tune with the people; they recognize him, understand who he is, realize that what he does is done for them because he truly represents them.

The "implied author"[69] himself identifies with this voice of consensus; his presentation and evaluation of each act of the hero is such as would have been perceived and approved by the community. The "chorus" of the people is heard now and then in the work really to confirm the points the narrator is making. By limiting himself to being merely one among many applauding spectators of the figure on center stage, the implied author is disclaiming any of the privileges of narrative omniscience; he claims no access to information not immediately apparent to the public eye. Neither the model character, then, nor the self-effacing author is a unique individual in his own right; the author verbalizes the aspirations and sentiments of the community, while the model character exemplifies them. Both are mirrors of an image of the people. For this meshing of character, narrator, and public to work, the writer must refrain from indulging in irony, criticism, stylistic complexities, or oblique angles of vision; these literary tricks would merely interfere with the mirroring process and call undue attention to the independence of the act of writing.

A very different type of character, community, and narrator relationship exists in the important story "Wo zai Xiacun de shihou" (When I Was in Xia Village),[70] written in 1940 before Ding Ling had embarked on her "new literary path." The girl Zhenzhen from Xia village falls into the hands of the Japanese, whereupon the party gets her to work among them as a spy. When she becomes severely ill with venereal disease, she is released from her intelligence mission and returns home for medical treatment. The story does not focus on her horrendous experiences but on her reception by the villagers upon her return. Toward a woman who has been brutally exploited by both sides in the war — the physical use by one is means to information by the other—the reactions of the community are passionate and contradictory. Younger people, including her former lover, appreciate the heroism of her sacrifice. The more traditional attitude condemns her because she has violated the chastity code with a vengeance. But Zhenzhen cannot accept being made into an object either of scorn or of pity. As she confides to the "I" narrator who arrives in the village on the eve of Zhenzhen's return, she must struggle to make a future for herself, leave the village, and avail herself of the care and education the party will provide.

This story, like "In the Hospital" and the essay "Thoughts on March 8," shows a deep concern for the plight of women. Zhenzhen is, to be sure, drawn as a resilient character who not only survives physical abuse but also manages to preserve a strong enough sense of self to refuse to exist in the way women usually do, as an object defined and perceived by others. She has developed this strength through the experience of working for a larger cause: the party in its fight against the Japanese. Yet a woman comrade in reflecting on Zhenzhen's fate laments the "wretchedness of being a woman", for the story also points to the reality of the female condition against which Zhenzhen must assert herself. During the 1957 antirightist campaign these three works by Ding Ling were singled out from all of her Yanan writings as targets for the most ferocious condemnation. One might well ask whether this choice suggests an antifeminist bias on the part of the critics.[71]

The case can be made that since the essay is critical of Yanan, and the two stories, in the words of one critic, "blatantly express an opposition between the individual and the masses,"[72] Ding Ling's overriding offense was her undermining of collective revolutionary goals. The particular issue of feminism would be incidental to the larger divisive effect of her writings. On the other hand, once the attack got underway, it followed the familiar pattern of criticizing a woman not so much for what she writes but for what she is, for her personal character, or more particularly her sexual conduct. "When I Was in Xia Village," criticized as a glorification of a prostitute in the enemy's camp, was quickly linked with Ding Ling's own allegedly immoral behavior. Her attackers charged that she had sold out the Communist Party by selling herself and living with a man who had been a spy for the Kuomintang when she was under arrest in 1933-1936. Thus she was herself guilty of violating the chastity code (shijie, to be disloyal or unchaste, applicable in both senses of the word in her case).[73] Again extrapolating personal morality from fiction, her accusers concluded that Lu Ping was an incarnation of the much earlier Miss Sophie—sexually obsessed and selfishly manipulative of men—who was in turn an incarnation of Ding Ling. Thus the usual identification of the character of an author with the characters in her fiction turned on the issue of sexual behavior, where women are most vulnerable and, because of the double standard, judged more harshly.

The sufferings of Zhenzhen in "When I Was in Xia Village" are fully "available" only to women: arranged marriage, rape by enemy soldiers, exploitation of her body by both armies, and after her return to the village, ostracism for violating the chastity code. One problem raised by the story was how to see correctly these examples of brutal oppression of women in the context of a revolutionary society. If total social revolution is the precondition of women's liberation, then how much attention should be paid to the specific oppression of women during the early stages of the revolutionary process? Ding Ling's emphasis on the female condition was denounced because "facts have long proved that it is the reactionary class that suppresses women's liberation, not males [nanxing] in general."[74] But it was difficult to shift the onus from sex to class in Zhenzhen's story, since those responsible for her suffering, apart from the enemy, included members of the people's army and peasants in her liberated village.

Another source for possible ideological deviance in "When I Was in Xia Village," which was not noticed by the critics, exists in the story's narrative procedure. The harmony between narrator, character, and community, so important in the sketches of model heroes, is absent here. In fact it is precisely the separateness of three kinds of perceptions and attitudes that *makes* the story. The first-person narrator arrives as an innocent outsider, becoming aware of the commotion caused by Zhenzhen's anticipated return long before the notorious girl makes her actual appearance in the story. This outsider's stance enables the "I" to perceive that, far from embodying the aspirations of the community, Zhenzhen jars on its collective nerves. At the same time, the gradual unfolding of Zhenzhen's personal response to what she has been through, and her struggle to survive in spite of it, contrasts with and exposes the shallowness of the villagers' moral judgment, which is rooted in antifeminist modes of thinking. Ding Ling has said that her story was based on an incident told to her by a woman comrade in the Women's Association of the area, and that she herself had not met the real protagonist.[75] All the more noteworthy then is her effective use of the "I-narrator", a passive outsider who innocently comes upon the scene and slowly discovers the painful disjointedness between a victimized yet heroic character and her chauvinistic society.

By contrast the model hero in Ding Ling's post-reform sketches presupposes a near-model community; he may be the leader, the exemplar, but he is possible only because of his community's support and appreciation; he is the realization of its inherent potential for greatness; whether labor hero, cooperative manager, or artist of the people, he shines because of the overall brightness of reality.

"The People's Artist Li Bu"

As a work of reportage (*baodao*), "Minjian yiren Li Bu" (The People's Artist Li Bu),[76] like the other works that make up the collection entitled *Scenes of Northern Shaanxi*, claims to be firmly based on fact. Ding Ling wrote it when attending the Border Regions Literature and Art Workers Conference during which Li Bu, a conference representative, had reported on his own life. Certain other pieces in the collection were inspired by the meeting of cooperatives in the Shaanganning Border Regions and the meeting for labor heroes. "Sanri zaji" (Miscellaneous Notes of Three Days) was based on a visit to a Mata village to witness a spinning contest. In all these works historical truth is stressed as all-important. Ding Ling reports a typical comment made by General Commander Zhu (De) when she was writing "Shibage" (The Eighteen) at his suggestion:

> At Taolin [the headquarters of the General Commander] I read telegrams for two whole days. I understood General Commander Zhu when he said, "There's untold quantities of material here; these events are all absolutely true, go ahead and read them."[77]

In all these reportage pieces veracity is a fundamental assumption and a presumed source of their value. The need to record true heroic events drives the author to praise "The Eighteen": "so many heroes sacrificed, so many brave warriors still struggling bitterly; I did not consider whether my writing would be successful or not, I began to write about these people who had so moved me."[78] Similarly, the inspirational labor heroes and cooperative managers could not serve their exemplary functions if they were not modeled on real people.

The relationship between text and reality, the question of verisimilitude, can usually be considered on at least three levels. On the first level the text is assumed to reflect reality or truth directly. Such a "naive" claim is no longer taken seriously in modern Western criticism, particularly in its structuralist variety. Instead many critics would proceed to the second level and see literary discourse as corresponding not to reality (in any case a questionable concept) but to what people believe to be reality; in the words of Tzvetan Todorov, discourse is seen as consistent not with its referent, but with "another (anonymous, impersonal) discourse,"[79] another "generalized text," which may be called "common opinion." On the third level, verisimilitude refers to the system of rhetorical devices used to convince the reader that the text conforms to truth, it is "a mask assumed by the laws of the text which we are meant to take for a relation to reality."[80]

Because reportage by definition claims always to be a direct, true reflection of actual reality, it insists only on verisimilitude in its first sense and consequently plays down or denies its other two possible levels of meaning. After the "Yanan Talks," the revolutionary attitude was that the ideological interpretation of reality coincides with reality itself, and is by no means "another discourse" or "generalized text." Therefore, "true representation" will inevitably be consistent with ideology, since the ideological truth is inherent in all actual events and will always be revealed almost without conscious effort and as an incidental byproduct of verisimilitude. Following the same principle, the writer should avoid all conscious exploitation of literary devices or techniques in the text, in the interest of directly reflecting reality. In fact the narrative text will cultivate a transparent look, assume an air of rhetorical innocence or naivete, as we can see in "The People's Artist Li Bu," in order to allow the material to speak directly to the reader.

"In 1925, in the area of Pingliang and Longde in Gansu province, there came Li Bu," opens Ding Ling's account, with the vagabond actor strolling on to the scene,

> Wearing an old unlined jacket, and an old wheat straw hat, a small packet wedged under his armpit, he would walk up to someone's front door or to a sales counter, plunk himself down, cross his right leg over his left knee, as if he were still on the stage, then take out his clappers, and, his small eyes blinking, he would start to sing. (p.36)

Down and out at this time in his life, the artist is little more than a vagrant beggar, singing good-luck chants to beg for a few strings of cash. At night he curls up to sleep in the empty halls of a temple.

Li Bu had been a good carpenter and cement worker in his youth, but his fondness for singing opera, particularly the regional variety known as *meihu*, led him to join a theater group. In the old society, the actor was particularly vulnerable to oppression by warlords and officials. Li Bu had been kidnapped by military officers and forced to take part in their decadent life of prostitution and gambling, but he ran away and turned into a homeless vagabond singing for his living. In time he became an opium addict, wandering from village to village in an area where opium was a bigger crop than grain. He organized a troupe, married a widow, and, although still very poor, began to settle down. In 1940 he attended a performance of the People's Drama Troupe (Minzhong jutuan) and his comments on its performance of a Shaanxi opera (*qinqiang*) show that he has an immediate and intuitive understanding of the proper approach to traditional art forms:

> The show is a good show. It's a new show in an old form. They're telling people to fight Japan, to be good. The singing and the technique are not too hot; it doesn't matter much. It would be better for them to sing *meihu*, the diction would be clear, easier to hear. (p. 40)

He thus finds his true vocation, joins the drama group and travels with them, teaching them the techniques of performance. At the same time he begins to understand the "relationship between the Communist Party and fighting Japan, and the relationship between the war and the people." Although no one applies pressure on him, his realization that everyone is good, and he alone is backward, makes him grimly determined to break his addiction. "So, astonishingly, at the beginning of his fifty-first year, in spite of his bad legs and back, with his teeth falling out," the old opium habit that had lasted for dozens of years is broken in one stroke. (p. 43)

Li Bu raises the technical level of the People's Drama Troupe. Young music students from the Lu Xun Art Academy come and learn from him. Others are stimulated to use the old form to create new plays. The Border Regions Literature and Art Workers Conference asks him to attend as a delegate. During the discussion, when someone speaks about the difficulty of reforming old actors, he stands up and offers his own "short history to explain the situation." He explains that

> the old actor indeed had many bad habits but they could be corrected. In the old society these people had been oppressed; once they understood the idea of revolution, got their heads cleared up, it was easy to reform them. Take himself for example, an opium addict of dozens of years, wasn't he, after taking part in the new life, able to kick it just like that? In the past he had liked to fool around, had put aside his carpentry skills, preferring to beg. They all knew this about him in the People's Drama Troupe, no one was after him to do things, but he himself became aware that what was the group's was his own, the group's business was his own business, so he started to go at things with all his might. (pp. 45-46)

His remarks continue in the form of a direct quotation:

> When it comes to technique, the old actors are conservative. The only thing I'm afraid of is not being able to teach it to someone. When I've taught it to others, they can use it to teach the people. To see my old goods become new stuff in their mouths only makes me happy. I'm an old man, I want to reform myself, and reform others too. (p. 46)

Li Bu's statement is supported by the whole meeting, and he is loved by all.

The bare, straightforward narrative of the old artist's life culminates in this moment of public praise. Like all model heroes, Li Bu achieves a close, harmonious relationship with his community. But because he is an artist, rather than a labor hero managing a factory or a cooperative, such a relationship cannot be taken for granted from the start; it is complicated by the problematic role of art within the Yanan context, and must to some extent be earned by the model hero through a regeneration process. Li Bu is referred to as an *yiren* by profession, a term that would apply to a performer in regional drama, an acrobat, or a storyteller. He is therefore the kind of artist who is closer to the people to begin with. The biographical sketch frequently implies that Li Bu was a "natural" for his exemplary role. His impoverished background, his oppressed status in the old society, his suffering, and of course his own intuitive under-standing of the relation between the new and old art — all eminently qual-ify him for the part even before his reeducation process is actually begun by his comrades in the party. In such a clear-cut situation there is no ap-parent need for the narrator to indulge in explanatory detail or analysis; he merely has to record, or assume the attitude of recording, what is self-evident in a plain, matter-of-fact way.

Normally a work of fiction will include several distinct types of lan-guage, ranging from dialogue that "imitates the speech characteristics of the kind of people who are supposed to be speaking," to the description that "may display a far greater freedom and bear the hall-mark of a per-sonal, idiosyncratic 'style.' "[81] One of the characteristics of Ding Ling's narratives of that period is the deliberate leveling of language, in an at-tempt to obscure as much as possible the distinctions between the speech of the character and the voice of the narrator. A few snatches of direct re-ported dialogue with idioms and a colorful metaphor or two give Li Bu's speech a more individual flavor, as in his remarks to Ke Zhongping, the leader of the Drama Troupe:

> Look, with all the culture (wenhua) you have, and a bellyful of literature (wen-zhang), yet you're working so hard to teach the people. An old actor like me (za), shouldn't I bring out my bean-size ability and teach some of these young-sters? (p. 42)

But for the most part the language of the entire work aims toward a homogeneity that is marked by a simple vocabulary, short sentences, and a straightforward syntax with few modifying elements.

The new style developed by Ding Ling in her reportage is a measure of the distance she had traveled since the days of her 1920s fiction. The distinctly "literary" style of those early stories can be seen in their man-nered vocabulary and in their long, complex, and "Europeanized" clauses. Here is Mengke, the innocent girl in Ding Ling's first story, being educated by her sophisticated cousins into the ways of the world:

> But this was not so very enjoyable either, especially when she was alone with the two young ladies. They would unrestrainedly ridicule the people they had been so affectionate to during the day; they compelled her to learn many secret formulas for conducting herself in the world and for dealing with men. Mengke often had to listen patiently to their laughter as they recalled making fools of others, listen to the meanings of the strange philosophy of life they ex-pressed. There were times, of course, when she laughed at their mischievous-

ness which seemed so close to innocence, but when she saw their demonic intentions and manipulations, she would be so astonished as to cry out; her fists would then open and clench in the dark.[82]

Mengke's shifting and contradictory responses to this way of life and behavior, itself hedged with ambiguity and cynicism, is mirrored in the convoluted modifying clauses and phrases and the elaborate comparisons that nevertheless fail to clarify. She is so unsettled by what she learns of corrupt society that she ends by "selling" herself to the film industry and is led down the road to perdition. But when Li Bu is introduced to the new revolutionary world of Yanan by his comrades, the conclusions he draws from his observations are quite simple and direct:

> After he got to Yanan, he looked around a bit, he also saw a lot of old friends, everyone was doing well, everyone was at peace. He also saw some of those who were in charge of things, they all treated him very well, as an equal, not at all like the officials of the old society. They always very patiently explained things to him, he was happy to listen to them, he truly was deeply moved, so that whenever there was something he could do, he would make nothing of the trouble it took. (p. 44)

The bare narrative style ranges the necessary facts, which are clearly apprehended by Li Bu and result in his unquestioningly adopting the correct course of action.

The Shanghai of Mengke and the Yanan of Li Bu are worlds apart, both morally and politically, and this distance is reflected in two divergent literary styles. The styles manifest also a different relationship between the "implied author" (obviously not identical in the two narratives) and her work. While in Mengke's story the reader's attention is arrested by the self-conscious complexity of the style, by the heightening and deformation of "normal" language, in the portrait of Li Bu the self-effacing language points directly to the objective facts concerning him. The writer's technique is totally subservient to the simplicity of the character's vision.

To write about the masses meant also to write for the masses, and furthermore to become a part of the masses. Mao Zedong noted the new phase of Ding Ling's work and congratulated her on the "beginning of my writing about workers, peasants and soldiers."[83] He had clear ideas on what writing should be like. Three years earlier, in his introduction to Gao Kelin's "Lu Zhongcai changzhengji" (The Long March of Lu Zhongcai), which had appeared in the *Jiefang ribao* on September 14, 1941, Mao had praised it as "a report which uses simple, clear language to reflect actual conditions," an example of "what we need and what everyone should learn," in order to do away with "subjectivism" and "formalism."[84] The discussion of "popularization" versus "raising standards" (*puji* and *tigao*) in the "Yanan Talks" a year later again emphasizes simplicity and a direct use of material, instead of a style that has been "worked up," processed, elaborated, or refined (the original phrase is *jiagong*, much used at the time but omitted from the *Collected Works* version). "Popular works are simpler [*jiagong jiao shao*—less polished, less finished] and therefore more readily accepted by the broad masses of the people today."[85] The plain simple language Ding Ling used in writing about a simple artist of the people was part of a conscious effort to be "popular" by minimizing the "worked up" literary nature of her text.

Deflating the pretensions of literature was a common Yanan theme, to which Ding Ling had made her own contribution soon after arrival. For example, Tian Jian had to overcome his identity as a poet before he was fully accepted in the Northwest Front Service Corps. She confesses that she had been prejudiced against him: "It's because there have been a few people who somehow become a bit famous; these so-called poets and novelists then put on dazzling laurel crowns and never forget to exude constantly an artistic air . . . and strut about in public."[86]

The 1940 story "Ruwu" (Enlistment) has a similar theme. A writer-journalist[87] visits the guerilla areas and the young orderly Yang Mingcai is assigned to serve him. The boy, recovering from a battle wound, grumbles about his assignment; all he wants is to rejoin his unit. But he feels a sense of awe toward such visiting writers, whose incomprehensible jargon makes them appear to him as a different species of people. His commander has told him that they wield a "five-inch-long gun as powerful as a thousand rifles."[88] On their way to "see action," the village where they stop to spend the night is attacked by the Japanese but the two manage to escape into the hills. Displaying resourcefulness and courage, Yang Mingcai finds food and shelter and after five days leads them both to safety. During the ordeal the writer behaves like a frightened child, cravenly dependent on his young companion, but once safe, he cannot wait to write about his exciting adventures and "heroic exploits."

Thus the claims of literature and the status of the writer are reduced to nothing in comparison with the practical survival skills of the uncultured boy-orderly, who even turns out to be the morally superior character. Yanan sought to elevate mass art while diminishing the status of the individual professional literary artist. From this perspective Li Bu, an artist of the people, a performer rather than a creator, can therefore be a model hero. The paradox was that popular art forms, of which he was such a successful and well-loved practitioner, were not themselves plain or artless (*jiagong jiao shao*) or in any way free of formalism. Indeed, one problem confronting the advocates of a popular art was that many of the traditional art forms *already* popular among the masses did not quite fit the advocates' preconceptions of what art should be like. The *meihu quzixi*, Li Bu's specialty, was a highly formalized and stylized regional operatic form. Like other local forms of theater, it included, in the words of Ma Jianling, a composer of modified *meihu* and other Shaanxi-type operas,

> many undesirable things. But the forms (*xingshi*) of regional theater also contain many things that can express the life, character, temperament and thoughts of the people. If it did not have these things, are our Chinese masses all simpletons (*shagua*) that they would all foolishly love this old theater? To reject the bad, adapt the good, then refine and give it substance, in order to express a new progressive content, is both completely possible and absolutely necessary.[89]

Since the early days of the Yanan period the theater, the most important art form in terms of the number of works produced and the size of the audience reached, was the arena where the most vigorous experiments were tried to infuse what was popular but inherently formalistic with a "new progressive content." *Baimaonü* (White-Haired Girl), one of the more durable works produced at the time, was based on the traditional *yangge*. Ding Ling had described the versatility of that popular song and dance form, and how it was used to dramatize up-to-date patriotic themes, in her account of the activities of the Northwest Front Service Corps. In an essay on the reform of the Peking opera, she discussed further the problem of adapting traditional forms, noting particularly the difficulties in using such a heavily symbolic art form to treat contemporary and realistic material.[90]

Caught in the general trend to adapt traditional forms, Ding Ling too experimented with writing a novel in the manner of the *Sanguo yenyi* (Romance of the Three Kingdoms). But her attempt to write about revolution in northern Shaanxi by imitating the greatest traditional example of the *yenyi* genre, which specialized in presenting popularized, expanded versions of history, did not get beyond the first two chapters.[91] As one who began writing under the iconoclastic impulse of the May Fourth period, Ding Ling's attempts to adapt traditional forms in her creative writing remained limited. Her next major achievement, *The Sun Shines on the Sanggan River*, included little that was traditional in conception and form.

4

THE SUN SHINES ON
THE SANGGAN RIVER:
LITERATURE AS HISTORY

TAIYANG ZHAO ZAI SANGGANHE SHANG (The Sun Shines on the Sanggan River) is the only novel Ding Ling ever completed. The writing of *Mother* was interrupted by her arrest in 1933 and only one-third of the projected manuscript was published, and that in an unrevised form. Other attempts to produce long fiction were aborted. In Yanan Russian novels were popular reading among the writers gathered there — Mao Zedong had mentioned Alexander Fadeyev's *The Debacle* in his "Yanan Talks" — and Ding Ling was busy borrowing and reading *And Quiet Flows the Don, War and Peace, Anna Karenina,* and others.[1] But because of the shortage of paper and the absence of a sophisticated readership, few long novels were produced. When the war against Japan ended in 1945, there was a rush to make up the deficiency and Ding Ling too was encouraged to try her hand. For one who for more than twenty years had been primarily a writer of short stories, *Sanggan River* was a remarkable excursion of the fictional imagination into a vastly extended area.

The center of attention in the shorter works was often one character or a very small group of characters, whereas *Sanggan River* contains almost forty characters with established identities and, even more important, all with specified roles within the community to which they belong. In fact, the interrelatedness of their individual destinies is deeply tied to the central theme of the book. Although the time span covered within the novel is a little over a month, and thus much shorter than, say, a model hero sketch giving an account of a lifetime, the additional length (232,000 words) allows an intent focus on change over time, for the subject of the book is nothing less than the passage of China from its traditional past into the new revolutionary future.

In one important respect, however, *The Sun Shines on the Sanggan River* retains an affinity to the short story. For example, the terms by which Fredric Jameson distinguishes the short story, myth, or the tale from the novel would place Ding Ling's work in the first category. The shorter forms, in Jameson's view, are "characterized by a specific and determinate type of content" and "their laws can be the object of investigation," whereas each novel is different, "a leap in the void, an invention of content simultaneous with the invention of form." Because Ding Ling's novel, in spite of its length, is governed by a "specific and determinate type of content"—the experience of land reform—many of its formal features will to some extent be predetermined. It is in this sense that her book can be seen as a kind of extended short story or tale and as such have laws eminently suitable for investigation. Though her novel manifests a profound historical consciousness, it could thus be considered a synchronic work, exhibiting as it does an "atemporal and object-like unity."[2]

Another possible approach to the generic classification of such a fictional work is mentioned parenthetically as Jameson speaks of "those sub-varieties of the novel which do have laws—I am thinking, for instance, of the detective story or the historical novel . . . evolutionary oddities and dead-end streets rather than illustrations of any general tendency."[3] One could argue that the historical novel may be a special case following rather more elusive laws, but it is certainly possible and useful to see the land-reform novel, a "dead-end street" in its own way, as a sub-variety of the novel, and comparable as a formulated generic system to the detective story or even, to introduce another "novelistic" parallel, the picaresque tale.

The works within each of these genres will be found to share features or characteristics that have a reciprocal relation: such elements as character, plot motivation, and narrative mode will interact with and reinforce one another in prescribed ways. Furthermore, these interacting features together postulate a specific external order, a clearly formularized world view that informs the human experience contained within the work. Just as the axis in the detective story may be considered the "triumph of reason over the irrational"[4] and the basic premise in a picaresque novel "the half-outsider's lasting but ambiguous estrangement from society, reality or established values,"[5] the central theme or ideology in a land-reform novel may be formulated as the power of raised mass consciousness to change the world. My intention in considering the land-reform novel as falling into a distinct genre is not that generic classification is always necessary; what I want to emphasize is that the various elements in *Sanggan River* will add up if we see it as a specific kind of novel, and that, of its kind, it is a highly integrated one.

The Knowable Community

The story takes place during the early phase of radical land reform (1946–47) in a small village along the Sanggan River in southern Chahar province. Since its liberation by Communist forces the villagers had done some settling of accounts and taken over the land of a few landlords, while some others have fled. But, as everyone knows, the real struggle still lies ahead. Soon after the novel opens a land-reform team of three arrives to assist the village cadres to complete the work. Some twenty days later, their task accomplished, the team leaves and the novel ends.

Although the catalysts for the action are outsiders—in addition to the land-reform team there is the mentor figure, Zhang Pin, the District Propaganda Head who makes a brief but decisive appearance toward the end—the novel is bound by the village of Nuanshui. All human transactions, all the experiences that matter, must take place within this confined space.

In the carrying out of land reform, each village is considered an isolated entity in redistributing its own resources, no matter how limited they might be. Of course neighboring villages were also engaged in land reform and rumors and gossip drift in from time to time to heighten the suspense of what is going on in Nuanshui, but the confiscation and distribution of land and the accompanying classification of people take place within that village as if it existed alone. The principle can be seen being rigidly applied in nearby Liyu, "a really poor village" where only one family owning over thirty *mou* (one *mou* is roughly one-sixth of an acre) can be classified as rich peasant; the others are all poor. Thus land reform there is a matter of "forty-nine families struggling against one."[6] For the purposes of land reform and therefore for the purposes of the action in the novel, each village is a self-contained universe.

An occasional relative from a neighboring village will turn up, daughters do marry out of the village and return to visit, villainous landlords may even manage to make their escape, but essentially the community of about two hundred families in Nuanshui must stay there and await the working out of their fate. Within the village there is mutual visiting and gossip exchanging, a constant to-and-fro motion in a confined space creating a claustrophobic atmosphere. This feeling is intensified as anxiety and uncertainty mount throughout the novel over the impending land-reform struggle, which is repeatedly described—it is an oppressively hot summer—as a storm that is about to break.

Somewhat analogous to a literary structure in which the various elements are closely interrelated, Nuanshui is an enclosed community in which every person is linked with everyone else. "All of us have grown up in one village, we're either relatives or neighbors," (p. 110), is a constant refrain. These ties are further complicated by landlord-tenant, or lender-borrower relationships. The novel meticulously establishes the bonds created by blood, property, custom, and power, because the complex human network that is formed by them defines each person's place in the world. The most unsettling prospect of land reform is that it will overturn the age-old social structure and cause a radical relocation of everyone.

Basic to the novel's outlook is the sense, always important in China, that each individual achieves his identity through being a member of his community. Such a view is in apparent agreement with that currently held by some American social psychologists who see the self, performing in and shaped by society, as nothing more than a structure of the roles it plays:

> The learned repertoire of roles is the personality. There is nothing else. There is no "core" personality underneath the behavior and feelings; there is no "central" monolithic self which lies beneath the various external manifestations.[7]

This approach to personality contravenes the cherished "bourgeois" notions of the autonomous and unique individual character, long the staple of the Western realistic novel. The author's conception of character and the attributes he supplies will be determined by the kind of novel he is writing. Whether the "core" personality exists or not, it is not involved in the land-reform process; for this type of novel, the only relevant aspects of a character are the "external manifestations" that are easily visible to the community.

Apart from the scheming villain, Qian Wengui, whose deviousness is precisely what sets him apart, all the other characters are fully knowable. Even Dong Guihua, an outsider who marries into the community, has already been thoroughly sized up by her neighbors. She is therefore qualified to assume responsibility in the revolution and in the novel's plot development:

> The head of the Women's Association had come here from the north as a refugee over four years ago. A village relative brought them together and she started living with Vineyard Li. It was to his advantage to marry her since it would cost him nothing, and she saw that he was a straightforward man, so both sides agreeing they married without much ceremony. She was a woman of almost forty, very sharp, not a bad match for this thirty-year-old tramp. The two got on well, and gradually set up something like a household. People all said Vineyard Li was lucky to get such a wife. She had suffered a lot, understood the cares and hardships of life, knew how to manage, was good tempered. All the people who lived in the mud houses in that western section spoke well of her. Last year, when Nuanshui Village was liberated and they wanted to set up a women's association, they picked her. She said she didn't know anything, and wasn't a native of the village, but it didn't matter, and she was elected. When anything came up in the village the cadres would ask her to call people to the meeting. Later on when the literacy class was organized she was very responsible there too. (pp. 24–25)

Nothing is obscure, perplexing, or complex about Dong Guihua. This short passage is a succinct summing up of her history, her role in the community, and her potential for contributing to the unfolding drama of the novel — the suggestion is that she will be more progressive than her husband. All that one needs to know about her can be and is already clearly known. The crises of identity and self-knowledge suffered by Ding Ling's earlier characters and their frustrated longings to be understood by those about them are simply unthinkable in this fictional context.

The focus on the self's "external manifestations," on its repertoire of social roles, implies an actively perceiving and evaluating community that continually forms conclusions about its individual members. This community then is also an important "character" in the novel, indeed the most powerful human presence in the book. "Bad elements" are obviously excluded from the generalized, impersonal collective, but it is not otherwise discriminated or identified. The community often begins by expressing a variety of attitudes towards a particular event or person through a collection of anonymous voices, then gradually arrives at a consensus. When it is discovered that the landlord, Li Zijun, had suddenly run away,

> Li Baotang returned to the village and told his nephew, the nephew told a neighbor, and slowly the news spread. Some tenants became anxious and quietly told the cadres. Again in the street there appeared the idle squatters; before the door of the co-op gathered groups who were not there to buy. Some said, "If the landlord has given us the slip, what's there to reform?" Others said, "Everyday we have meetings, dry thunder without rain. How can there be a revolt without using weapons?" There were those who scoffed at Zhang Zhengguo: "Were your militiamen going after the women?" But there were those who said quietly, "Li Zijun is a weakling, he can't stand being scared, someone scared him by saying that in this reform he would be the first; he heard that and couldn't stay put any longer." Someone else said, "We heard that too, that the struggle would start with him."
>
> No matter what, everyone's hatred of him was intensified. "Who said this guy was straight? Umph! From the moment he heard about reform he hid in the orchard every day selling his fruit. Before he didn't mind giving heaps and heaps of money to the secret police, the traitors, the rich people, but as soon as he hears about reforming his land, he makes off! Well, now you've gone off, don't you come back! The monk can decamp but not the temple, let's see if you can hold on to that bit of land, are we scared to touch it now that you've fled?" (pp. 156–157)

This gathering of opinions is to arrive at a unanimous, unambiguous verdict, the correctness of which is ensured by the collective sagacity of the people. Everyone knows that "the eyes of the people are bright as snow" (p. 242). The knowable community is also the knowing community.

Central to the ideology of land reform is this confidence in the people's capability, given time and the proper leadership, to understand and do the right thing. People like Dong Guihua and the anonymous villagers squatting in the street or gathered before the cooperative will constitute the available human material for carrying out the immense revolutionary experiment. They are the ones who will transform the world. This simplified yet exalted view of human nature in which the revolution places its faith governs the conceptualization of character in Ding Ling's novel; at the same time it requires that characters be portrayed undergoing change. Land reform was not just a matter of redistributing land and material possessions but, as the novel repeatedly emphasizes, a process also of *fanshen*, a "turning over," a literal "revolution" in one's being and self-perception.

This subjective dimension is emphasized in William Hinton's *Fanshen*. As the subtitle indicates, Hinton's monumental book is indeed "a documentary of revolution in a Chinese village," but it is also a demonstration of the revolutionary ideology in action. *Fanshen*, a word created by the Chinese revolution, meant to China's hundreds of millions of landless and land-poor peasants,

> To stand up, to throw off the landlord yoke, to gain land, stock, implements, and houses. But it meant much more than this. It meant to throw off superstition and study science, to abolish "word blindness" and to learn to read, to cease considering women as chattels and establish equality between the sexes, to do away with appointed village magistrates and replace them with elected councils. It meant to enter a new world. That is why this book is called *Fanshen*.[8]

Science, literacy, sexual equality, and political elections are not the issues that *The Sun Shines on the Sanggan River* concerns itself with, or rather these will be byproducts of the more fundamental transformation of the people's consciousness. The world will be restructured when the people's perception of themselves in it is restructured. It is therefore necessary, within the time encompassed by the novel, to show characters in development, to show, in the words of a contemporary critic, how "the peasants in the course of struggle overcome the shortcomings in their own thinking, develop, and mature."[9]

Developmental characterization does not necessarily imply a profound interest in the details of the inner life or exploration of character for its own sake. Characters in a land-reform novel "develop and mature" in ways comparable to those described by Scholes and Kellogg in their discussion of *Parzival* or the knights in *The Faerie Queene*. In those works the "developmental formulation itself is primarily a plot formulation"; personal traits are attenuated, irrelevancies are filtered out, so that the progress and "change against a particular background may be readily apparent."[10]

Cheng Ren, the chairman of the peasants' association, is one of the important developmental characters in the novel. He believes that his love for Heini has prevented him from facing up to the fact that her uncle is the most evil person in the village. Although he has turned away from her, he has not really fought hard against this enemy whom everybody hates. One thing he does not fully realize as he examines his own conduct is that Heini, like many other women of the land-owning class, is herself a victim of oppression. She had lost her father when she was five years old, and was then claimed by her uncle when her mother remarried two years later. Treated like a maid in the household, she grows up to be a good-looking girl; her uncle harbors hopes of getting a good sum for her when she marries. Clearly she does not share her uncle's class prejudices, or she would never have become friendly with Cheng Ren, an impoverished hired laborer. Later, when the village is liberated by the Eighth Route Army and Cheng Ren is made chairman of the peasants' association, he deliberately avoids her since his position now makes it impossible to marry the niece of a landlord. At the party meeting, when the crucial decision is made to select Qian Wengui, the uncle, as the chief target of struggle, Cheng Ren recognizes that he had been less than resolute in facing up to that necessity.

> He felt as if he had committed a crime, and done something wrong to others, and could not hold up his head. This was something he had never felt before . . . He had always been a straight person, who never deceived people, but now he felt that he had not been honest; he had deluded himself. He discovered that what he had always said about not marrying Heini was only a falsehood; it was only because he was afraid of criticism that he forced himself to avoid her. His staying away from her was only to deceive others, and not because he bore towards her uncle, the most evil man in the village, the man whom everyone hated, any enmity . . . He had forgiven him everything for the sake of his niece . . . At what point had he considered the poor people? He had only been considering himself, afraid that he would give offense to the niece of a landlord, the niece of a rotten egg . . . In his heart he had been secretly protecting her, that is protecting them, the interests of the landowning class. (pp. 247–248)

It does not become clear to him until the end of the book that the struggle against uncle Qian Wengui, far from hurting his niece, actually liberates her along with everyone else. Although the political roles of the women characters in the novel are in most cases clearly delineated, the somewhat romanticized and ambiguous figure of Heini does raise questions about certain women who belonged to the landlord's household and their place in the class struggle. This dilemma is the principal cause of Cheng Ren's agonizing self-accusations, as his feelings for Heini interfere with the wholeheartedness of his commitment to the party.

Nevertheless any resemblance perceived here to the "love and revolution" theme of Ding Ling's 1930 fiction would be illusory. In the land reform novel there can be no real, extended conflict between the two. Love is toned down, it is one of the "irrelevancies filtered out"; it is acknowledged but not *experienced* by the characters within the novel. There is no intimate scene of the lovers together, since to portray it, even if only to repudiate it, could make love a dangerous counterweight to revolution. Cheng Ren had indeed stayed away from Heini. The severity of his self-criticism does not stem from any external offense, therefore, but from his falling short of the relentlessly high standards of revolutionary morality; he had failed to be undeviatingly pure in his class hatred. For its participants, land reform, almost as unsettling to the individual as a religious experience, can indeed provoke a spiritual or moral crisis. Characters frequently ask themselves, Am I doing the right thing? Am I doing it for the right reasons?

Towards the end Cheng Ren succeeds in redeeming himself during the confrontation scene between the peasants and the uncle of his beloved. When the landlord-tyrant Qian Wengui is brought before them, the peasants stand silent and hesitant, in awe before this representative of "several thousand years of tyrannical power" (p. 271). But Cheng Ren leaps on to the platform, curses the landlord and pushes him, forcing him to kneel down. This action dramatically changes the mood of the crowd, as their feared and hated oppressor is instantly transformed before their eyes into their captive and prisoner.

The decisive battle (*juedou*) against the landlord is the climax of the book, not just because of its violence and drama, but because at that moment there occurs, through the degradation of the landlord, the clear and sudden revelation that the old society has now indeed been overturned to stand on its head. The scene also represents the final, supreme test for all the developmental characters; like Cheng Ren they must prove that they are able to rise to the occasion and actively, in fact, physically, demonstrate their commitment to the revolution. They join together in the brutal attack. Qian Wengui is reviled, spat upon, forced to kneel down, humiliated with a dunce cap, savagely trampled upon and beaten, but for the time being his life is spared.[11] In the confrontation scene the polarities of good and evil are definitively established, and each character, through his participation in struggle, arrives at a clear state of definition in his political consciousness. All the tensions and self-questioning explode into the open and dissipate in this unleashing of the community's fury. This decisive battle is the moment the world of the novel has been waiting for; it is the violent storm that at last clears the air.

Nature and the Imagery of Struggle

Natural setting plays an important part in the overall strategy of the narration. In the first chapter, "The Rubber-Tired Cart," physical objects and features of the landscape selected for description evoke an appropriate fictive world for the enactment and the reflection of the novel's major themes.

The arrival of the rich peasant Gu Yong, his daughter, and grandson in a cart with rubber-tired wheels introduces the reader to Nuanshui village. This journey takes place in an environment fraught with challenges that must be overcome. The weather is oppressively hot, the heat from the setting sun is like fire, the cart track resembles a muddy river. White Nose, the mule, must strain and strain to pull the cart. When they cross the two swollen rivers, the cart's wheels almost totally submerged, the mule's great back looking as if it were floating on the water, they are repeatedly bogged down. In the first few paragraphs words like *lihai* (severe), *youjing* (energetic), *haurongyi* (with great difficulty), and *nan* (hard) occur again and again to indicate effort and struggle.

Yet nature is also the source of the peasant's hopes and rewards. The travelers pass a place where the rice is growing thick and tall,

> the height of a man's shoulder. *Gaoliang* [Chinese sorghum] screened everything, their leaves as broad as those of corn. The soil was moist and black. An odor rose steaming from the groves of vegetation. They passed these fields and reached the vegetable fields, encircled by irrigation ditches, neatly divided into squares of dark and light green. Every time Old Gu passed by here he felt an inexpressible envy, how could he himself get such a piece of good land? His longing for land was insatiable.   (p. 2)

It is of course the peasant's hunger for land that provides the motive force behind the whole land reform movement. But even this elemental hunger must yield to justice. At the end of the book, Gu Yong is almost ready to relinquish voluntarily some of his own land—a sign of how far he has traveled and the mark of the beginning of his political redemption.

As the travelers proceed toward the village they pass the fruit orchards that will likewise function importantly in the book. Now "still mostly green, only a few here and there with a touch of tempting red" (p. 4), the steadily ripening fruit registers the passing of time and is a reminder of the growing urgency to act decisively. The peasants' first revolutionary step will be their taking over the orchards to forestall the sale of fruit by the landlords. The fruit, when divided among themselves, will be their "fruits of victory" (*shengli guoshi*), a signal that the land reform movement is really under way. In the orchard also grows Gu Yong's pear tree, crushed under a fallen willow from Qian Wengui's land and slowly dying. But Qian Wengui will not permit the willow tree to be removed. The image of the two trees is a small but concrete example of that evil tyrant's oppressive, but not fully understood, local power.

Finally the cart reaches the village proper, passing some people squatting before the doorway of the elementary school, a large empty platform, more people sitting by the wall, and others gathered outside the window of the cooperative. This is the center of the village where the meetings and big public events will take place.

Through the choice and treatment of features of the physical setting, Ding Ling is providing in this first chapter what Eudora Welty has called, in a discussion of "place in fiction," the "achieved world of appearance, through which the novelist has his whole say, and puts his whole case."[12] But as we have seen, the Chinese revolutionary experience assumes a much more interdependent relation between man and the natural environment. Details of setting not only form the location—here is where everything will happen—they make up the objects, and also the imagery of struggle.

Beginning in the heat of the seventh lunar month, with its fearful forecast of violent storms, the novel ends on the calm moonlit evening of the midautumn festival. The struggle against the landlords is concluded just in time for the harvest. On the tenth day of the eighth month the confiscated household things are given out, on the fourteenth day the distribution of land is discussed, on the fifteenth day the momentous little red strips of paper marking each family's new land acreage and the money from the fruit are given out. Then on the next day the people will prepare to measure the land and begin the gathering of the harvest: "The tension of more than twenty days was almost over. They were waiting for the festival tomorrow, the midautumn festival, and also the celebration of their standing up (*fanshen*)" (p. 306). It would be an easy date to remember, to tell their children and grandchildren, so they would never forget—the day they got their land and began anew.

That evening the land-reform team takes leave to go on to their next assignment. They wade across the Sanggan River as the full moon rises behind them. Willows by the road gently sweep against the sky. All about them they hear the beating of gongs and drums to celebrate the festival mixed in with the joyful sound of people. "It was the same everywhere. Everywhere in this past month there had been a change of heaven and earth! With the people in charge of the world, what hardships could not be overcome!" (p. 315).

One of the expressed goals of the Chinese revolution is to alter fundamentally man's relation to nature. From a position of helpless dependency on nature, the peasants through collective efforts will increasingly be able to gain mastery over it. The broiling sun, the swollen river, the soggy mud path, the ripening fruit, the rising harvest moon, symbols of challenge or of success, all reflect aspects of this process of change in the man-nature relationship. Thus, every object in the natural world has its place and meaning in the intensive and purposive structure of the novel's universe.

The most elaborate use of physical setting to project theme is in chapter thirty-seven, "The Orchard Comes Alive." The cadres decide to take over the orchards that belong to the landlords and divide the fruit among the villagers.

> Just as the great earth was awakening in the faint light of dawn, clear sounds of laughter floated up from the still, cool orchards. The joy of the people rose above the sparrows' chirping, and the small scaly insects that love to flit about in the morning breeze darted uneasily in all directions. Thickly growing leaves trembled slightly on the extended branches, but could not hide the bunches of heavy fruit. In the groves there still remained some sparkling dewdrops, like stars twinkling in a foggy night. On the red fruit there was a soft down, or a layer of thin frost, making them look soft and moist. Colored clouds drifted; through the gaps in the thick green leaves shone dots of gold. In the groves were reflected lines of transparent, faint purple and light yellow rays. (p. 186)

Such a lyrical description of the orchard in the morning light is a lapse from plain writing and the novel's frequent imitation of peasant speech but nevertheless provides the "objective correlative" of the peasants' state of mind. For them, the fruit, now that it has become their own, has assumed a totally new and alluring appearance. This is especially true of old Li Baotang:

> He had watched other people pick the fruit or had picked it for them for twenty years. He never liked to talk, but worked quietly, incessantly, as if completely unmoved inside; as if he did not realize that this fruit was sweet and fragrant, as if what he held had been clumps of clay or bricks and there was no joy in it. But today? His sense of smell seemed to have woken together with the great earth; he had discovered for the first time this green, luxuriant, rich environment, like a beggar suddenly coming across many gold coins. All the fruit was shining, all winking at him. (pp. 186–187)

With the people taking charge of the world, it is transformed into a different kind of place. As the narrative draws toward its joyous conclusion (somewhat tempered by the grave civil war situation and the need for the village to send volunteers), the novel becomes a celebration of the dream of revolution come true, an exhilarating vision of hopeful fantasy turning into reality.

One character in particular embodies the incredulous joy over the near miracle that is changing his life: the old man Hou Zhongquan. Once Hou Zhongquan had been a clever and lively youth, quite prosperous and educated, a story-teller and a great singer of opera. But a series of disasters—drought, law suits, and illness—put him deeply in debt; he lost his land and became a tenant farmer, miserably exploited by his landlord uncle. Hou therefore adopted a fatalistic view of life, "he had surrendered himself to fate, forgave all past injuries done to him, and attributed all his sufferings to his own fate" (p. 100). When he received one

and one-half *mou* of land after the earlier score-settling session in the
spring, he insisted on returning the land to the landlord saying that he
must have owed it to him in a former life. "From all that he had read and
heard, he knew that never once in several thousand years had the poor
ever been master" (p. 100).

The morning after the people's victory over Qian Wengui, the landlord of old Hou Zhongquan, fearful of suffering a similar fate, comes
to prostrate himself before Hou and his wife, and begs them to accept
the title deeds for fourteen *mou* of land. The event is hard to assimi-
late:

> After he left, the two old people looked at each other, afraid that they were in
> a dream. They turned the title deeds over and over, then rushed to the door to
> look, then they ended up laughing; they laughed until they became sad. Hou
> Zhongquan sat on the steps of the courtyard, wiping away his tears and think-
> ing back on the hard life he had always had. He had led camels in the desert,
> blown about by the wind and snow; he had trudged the plains, the endless
> sand dunes, while hope like the horizon at dusk faded farther and farther
> away. He remembered his illness, when he had nearly died; he thought then it
> would have been better to die, but he lived. Living was so much harder than
> dying! Gradually he came to believe in fate and retribution, placing truth in
> the invisible future life, using the illusion to console himself. But now the
> future was a fact, reward had come so quickly! This was something he had
> never thought of, had never dared to think of. He should be happy and he was
> happy, but his happiness was no longer something that he could bear, his tears
> were flowing because of his happiness. He had come to life again, his senses
> were reawakened, he was not a dead old man anymore.

As he walks out with the deeds, his wife thinks that in his old stubborn
way he is going to return them to the landlord again. "No," he said, "I'm
taking them to the peasants' association. I want to tell them, I want to tell
a lot of people, the world has really turned over!" (p. 288).

After everyone has heard him out, they joke about his old supersti-
tions, "Buddha never paid us any attention even though we burned in-
cense before him every year, but with one command from Chairman
Mao land is offered to us. Chairman Mao is our Buddha; from now on if
we make offerings, we should make them to him." The peasants may
seem to be teasing old Hou for merely substituting one deity for another,
but the point of their remarks is that his consciousness has been raised;
the change from Buddha to Chairman Mao means that he has turned
away from the old fatalism to a new perception of the world. While land
reform is a process in which the individual, the community, and the natural elements all play essential roles, it can succeed only because old Hou
and everyone else have reached a new understanding of the forces of
history.

Plot, History, Reality, and Literature

The coming events that are to change the world and their true significance are disclosed only as the story unfolds. But the uneasy sense that
something unusual is about to happen arises early in that first chapter, so
important for setting the scene of action, when Gu Yong and his
daughter and grandson arrive in their rubber-tired cart. Obviously an
outside object, and much too fine for those parts, the cart arouses
curiosity among the bystanders who do not realize that it is a warning
signal that land reform is approaching their village. Gu Yong is driving
the cart because he has been asked by his son-in-law in nearby Baliqiao
to take it temporarily to avoid its being confiscated during the impending
land reform there. The inexplicable cart — Gu Yong cannot admit the true
reason for its being there — causes much speculation in Nuanshui village
and immediately introduces the note of apprehension that will pervade
the novel until the resolution of all issues at the end.

Gu Yong, a "well-to-do middle peasant" later wrongly classified by
the land reform committee as a "rich peasant", is politically the most ambiguous figure in the book. The difference between the two classifications
lies in the degree to which income depends on the exploitation of
others.[13] But only after forty-eight years of hard work, of "dropping their
blood and sweat on the barren land, investing in it their hopes, year after
year" did Gu Yong and his brother gradually prosper and expand their
land holdings. "First paper was used to wrap his title deeds, then he
changed to a piece of cloth, then he put them in a wooden box" (p. 5).
The family is able to buy a house with two courtyards from landlord Li
Zijun. Because of his intermediate status, Gu Yong has a network of relatives and in-laws that extends into the highest and the lowest classes in
the village. He is therefore an efficient point of entry into the fictional
community. Moreover, in his continual anxiety over his political classification upon which would hinge his fate, his livelihood, and actual survival — if there is a struggle session, "the old man would not be able to take
it; even if he didn't lose his life, he'd be as good as dead" (p. 90) — Gu
Yong also exemplifies the tensions, fears, and attendant ambiguities in
the complex land reform process.[14] As Dong Guihua, the head of the
Women's Association, whose own extreme poverty would seem to give
her impeccable class credentials, wonders, "If even Old Gu's family is
struggled against, then who can live secure (an sheng)?" (p. 93).

One of the most important activities in the early part of the book is
that of people visiting back and forth, exchanging news and seeking information. A frequent question they ask one another is, "what's the
news?" The visits are a device for linking chapters and introducing new
characters, but they are also a means for reinforcing the sense of anxiety.

Uncertainty also surrounds the enigmatic figure of the despotic landlord Qian Wengui. He will turn out to be the chief object of the land-reform struggle but is not firmly identified as such until chapter forty-five. Only when the cadres determine their true target can the "decisive battle" begin: "In going after the villains, you must get the head; in eating persimmons, there's no point in picking the soft ones!" (p. 52). But which is the head? Most of their meetings are spent debating this question.

There were many accounts that needed to be settled (*qingsuan*), "but among these there was no typical figure (*dianxingderen*) guilty of the most heinous crimes, so that by means of him the fires of anger could be kindled in the masses" (p. 103). Qian Wengui was not the kind of landlord who possessed conspicuous wealth, nor was he a murderer or rapist who would arouse the people to a struggle unto death. Compounding the confusion, Qian Wengui has cleverly sent one son off to join the Eighth Route Army and married a daughter to the village security officer. So he

> sat at home not doing a stroke of work, smoking his tobacco and fanning himself . . . Who would dare touch a hair of his? Villagers smiled when they greeted him, "Uncle Qian, have you eaten?" But the best thing was not to meet him, to keep out of his way, in case he found you distasteful, and you could be injured without seeing how. It was easy for him to trap (*keng hai*) people, he might say a few words somewhere, and you would suffer without knowing where it all started, whose doing it really was.   (p. 8)

People fear Qian Wengui but his evil power is shrouded in mystery; he's a *sai Zhuge*, as smart as Zhuge Liang, the superhuman strategist in the old novel *The Romance of the Three Kingdoms*. In *Sanggan River* Qian's villainous practices are neither obvious nor directly presented; he is mainly seen scheming with the schoolteacher, Ren Guozhong, to undermine confidence in the Communist Party, subvert the land reform movement with rumors of the Kuomintang's victorious return to the area, and to insinuate conniving between cadres and other landlords. A clear decision to focus the struggle on Qian is not made until the arrival of Zhang Pin, the District Propaganda Head, who warns the cadres: "If you don't touch Qian Wengui the people will be afraid to stand up and speak out" (p. 237).

When the time comes, the full exposure of the tyrannical landlord is undertaken by Liu Man, who tells the big meeting how he has been reduced to bankruptcy; his father was hounded to death, his brother had turned insane, and all his family was destroyed through the nefarious schemes of Qian Wengui. Liu Man is to some extent a surprise witness, for there are those who think he too has gone mad after his terrible sufferings. His impassioned account inspires others to follow suit; one by one they rise to denounce Qian Wengui until the crowd is stirred up into a state of frenzied anger over the itemized disclosure of the evil he has perpetrated.

From the opening paragraphs the enigmatic objects, characters, and situations become structuring devices in the novel. They fall under what Roland Barthes has termed the "hermeneutic code"[15] in the organization of narrative: that which in the text functions to formulate questions, delay answers, and raise problems. These enigmas and questions provide the sources of narrative suspense and form the mainspring of the plot as the whole novel moves toward their solution.

Different novels will pose different kinds of questions, depending on what matters. The choice of questions is determined by the very specific view of history the novel subscribes to. As Jurij Lotman has observed: "A plot is organically related to a world picture which provides the scale for determining what constitutes an event and what constitutes a variant of that event communicating nothing new to us."[16] In another context, the question of classifying a peasant as rich or middle, or of identifying the archvillain in the village, both critical events in *Sanggan River*, would be meaningless issues. The drawn-out enigma of Qian Wengui, developed, modified, complicated, and eventually solved, is important to the plot structure here because of the world picture of which land reform was a part. Only if the archvillain is identified can the evil of the old feudal society be seen in concrete form, and only when he is degraded or destroyed will the collapse of the old order become immediately visible and irrevocable. Participation in this process is what enables the downtrodden to gain a new perspective on their world. The emergence of the true villain brings out into the open the hidden, pervasive powers of oppression and offers the masses a dramatic lesson in historical understanding.

Although the dividing up of village land into small plots for individual peasants proved later to be only a temporary phase in the Chinese Revolution that would soon give way to more radical forms of restructuring in the countryside, such as cooperatives and then communes, land reform was nevertheless a key historical experience of the Communist Party. Certainly it was an effective means for mobilizing peasant support against the Kuomintang and played a critical role in the party's ultimate victory in the Civil War. But the main purpose of land reform was the total destruction of the traditional rural system of economic and political power and it took place even where landlords were not a problem.[17] More important, the land-reform process contained the formula for revolution in a nutshell: the activation of mass struggle. Once the political consciousness of the peasant masses was raised, they could act in powerful ways to overturn the structure of their community. In the traditional view everything, including one's poverty and lowly station, had been decided in a former life (*qiansheng zhuding*). A person who was doomed to misery could only bow to fate in resignation. But the land-reform experience changes all that — it makes the peasants realize that "the world has changed" (*shidao bian le*); "it's a new world now" (*rujin shi xinshijie*); "the poor have become masters" (*qiongren dangjia le*).

The actual history of the period of radical land reform would, if it were to be written properly, consist of the aggregate of thousands of separate case histories of individual villages in 1946 and 1947. These histories would manifest unequal degrees of success and show the range of human cost resulting from the disruptions and injustices inevitable in such cataclysmic upheavals.[18] But like the Long March, an example of the heroic spirit turning a disastrous retreat into victory, the land-reform movement similarly takes on the instructive, inspirational aura of a special legendary episode in the historical memory. Land reform represented the moment of the peasant's awakening, the vital turning point when he suddenly saw that his centuries-old poverty and oppression could indeed be lifted and his world became for the first time a place where hope and a new beginning were possible. Ding Ling's account does not ignore the ambiguities and the potential for failure and excesses, but her novel is essentially a hymn of praise to that special moment as it occurs in the lives of humble individuals in small places.

It is these individuals, the ones whose homes were in the village alleys, that Ding Ling particularly recalled when she discussed several years later her motivation in writing *Sanggan River*. She had gone to participate in land reform in Huailai and Zhuolu (in southern Chahar) in July 1946, shortly after the May Fourth Directive that marked the official shift from rent reduction to the inauguration of land reform. The evening after the land distribution meeting, which was also the midautumn festival, as the "moonlight poured like water into each small courtyard and a gentle breeze lightly wafted the fragrance of autumn flowers," she went from door to door visiting people who were celebrating the "midautumn festival, the first halfway decent one (*xiangge yangzi de*) in their entire lives." They were so full of life; she suddenly felt toward them a deep emotion, as if she had known them not just for the twenty-odd days of their mutual struggle, but a long time ago. These people thronged into her mind, she was unable to sleep or eat, they

> brought me excitement, tension, unease, apparent discomfort, but I felt happy. I lived in their universe, weaving imaginary colored clouds. I wished to work; I said to myself, "Get started, don't wait!"
>
> When I returned to Kalgan, the party asked me whether I was still going to the Northeast. I said, "Get me a desk, I need to write." My novel seemed already finished; it only needed to be written down.[19]

In the novel the conclusion of the land-reform campaign likewise coincides with the midautumn festival, but the novel as a whole is not a direct account of that one particular experience. Ding Ling began to write the book in November 1946, stopping at intervals to work on land reform elsewhere. She also attended a land-reform conference and read documents and materials on the subject, which led her to discover errors in her earlier work:

> I saw people and events that I had not been able to see in my work; I thus utilized my knowledge and criticism of real life, interweaving them with those concrete people and events to write the story and action of my novel.[20]

That the novel is the "interweaving" of actual personal experience and ideas absorbed from various party documents and conferences is apparent from the work itself, even without the confirmation of Ding Ling's own recollections. The only character she mentions as having been based on a real person is Zhang Pin,[21] who was the leader of the Land Protection Team of Sanggan, and he emerges in the novel as an image of the ideal cadre. As District Propaganda Head, his brief appearance towards the end makes him function almost like a *deus ex machina*: his unerring reading of the people's wishes points the way to the final identification of Qian Wengui as the central target of struggle. Zhang Pin is one example of the fusion of the ideal and the historical or actual in Ding Ling's fictional treatment of the land-reform process.

The historical experience of the land-reform movement was quite explicitly informed by the ideals and self-images of the Maoist revolution. The constant reiteration of Lenin's theme of the indissoluble unity and interdependence of theory and practice, makes it unnecessary and even impossible at any given moment to distinguish clearly between the two. Although the claim that the novel is based on personal participation in the process is obligatory — every writer in the land-reform genre prefaces his work by telling the time and location of his own actual experience — *Sanggan River* is not a direct account of historical reality, even supposing there were such a thing. Rather it is a fictional work in which the selection and arrangement of events, their sequence as cause and effect, the end to which all progresses, the whole structuring of the plot, are determined by the ideological meaning of land reform. Land reform is more than the downfall of the landlord tyrant and the redistribution of land to the exploited peasant, often by violent means; it also entails the overturn of age-old social structures, a radical process that is premised on the revolutionary ideology of mass awakening and mass struggle. This world view in its singleminded totality underlies the narrative choices and procedures in the book. The basic story the novel will tell, the central action of the plot, the question it will try to answer, is how the masses attained the requisite new perception of themselves and of their own role in history.

But if literature and art are to participate legitimately in the revolutionary process they must be, in the Marxist view, accepted as historical reality. A fictionalized treatment of an ideological version of past events —a novel, twice removed, as it were, from an unrecoverable historical experience—must nevertheless be judged according to its fidelity to history. *The Sun Shines on the Sanggan River* was thought to have achieved this kind of fidelity even by critics who attacked Ding Ling during the antirightist campaign: "It [the novel] makes those who have not taken part in land reform feel as if land reform is in process; it makes those who have taken part in land reform feel there are things they have seen before."[22]

The criterion of historical truth seems important because, as many discussions about the value of art and literature show, audiences often respond to works literally as reality. This was especially true for the works written and performed by propaganda troupes, which drew on material from the everyday lives of the audience for their dramatic presentations. The literalness with which the peasant masses, whose past experience of drama, if any, was likely to have been limited to stylized Peking or other regional forms of opera, responded to such contemporary plays, provided the artists involved with eyeopening, exhilarating demonstrations of the power of literature.

Ding Ling has given several accounts of this sort of audience reaction.[23] In *Sanggan River*, Gu Yong's eldest daughter describes to her family a play (*xi*) she has seen in a neighboring town. It was about a tenant farmer's daughter whose father has been hounded to death. She sells herself into bondage to repay his debts, is beaten by the old mistress, raped by the young master, has an illegitimate child, and is later sold. Many in the audience wept at the performance, especially a neighbor whose own life was not too different from that depicted in the play: she herself had been sold in just the same way (p. 13). Such an emotional response comes from the empathetic recognition that there on the stage is something finally and truly "about us," about our actual experiences. By drawing on material that is immediate and relevant and by diligently working for close interaction between work and audience, the artist could have the satisfaction of knowing that he was playing a "real" role in people's historical lives. Although Ding Ling's novel was not written for the average semiliterate peasant, she was seeking to share through its writing a contemporary historical experience with her readers; she wrote about land reform then because land reform was what was happening to everyone.

It is tempting to see the Marxist novel's claim to be contemporary history as a return, albeit with a difference, to the Chinese narrative tradition in which historiography served as the central model of narration. In the past, history and fiction shared certain formal features, such as structured dialogues and an episodic framework, but even more relevant to our consideration is the traditional idea that the final justification for the narrative enterprise in either its historical or fictional variety "may be said to lie in the *transmission* of known facts." "The sense that what is recorded," in Andrew Plaks's words, "is ultimately true — either true to fact or true to life — remains a fundamental underpinning"[24] in both the historical and fictional branches of the Chinese narrative tradition.

The line between history and fiction has always been difficult to draw, and in the broadest sense all narrative genres represent versions of history, of what is, provisionally at least, taken to be true. The question one may ask then concerning the Chinese idea of the novel is, at what point is the fictitious character of fiction explicitly acknowledged? Since the Chinese term for fiction as a category of literature does not in itself imply that it is imagined or feigned, there has been no need to conduct endless discussions about illogical concepts like "realistic fiction" — so much critical ink in the West has been spilled over an etymological accident as it were — on the other hand, there is less pressure to conceptualize the real differences that in the end do exist between history and fiction. Much of the narrow dogmatism of Chinese Marxist literary criticism stems from this reluctance to separate fiction from history, to recognize fiction's ultimate independence from history.

In addition to the acknowledged duty of transmitting what is true to fact or to life, traditional historiography and Communist fiction share the notion that truth is what is consensual or officially sanctioned. Chinese traditional history, leaving aside its claim of factuality and objectivity, may also be regarded as a record of the scholar-bureaucrat ideal, or the principles of Confucian statesmanship, in action. From one perspective, Chinese literature after the "Yanan Talks" is simply replacing the scholar-bureaucrat ideal with the worker-peasant-soldier ideal, and has been written to demonstrate the operations of Maoist revolutionary ideology. Just as traditional history was often regarded as a mirror (*jian*) from which the principles of statecraft could be learned, "readers within and without the country could through the events of Ding Ling's novel understand the Chinese land-reform movement,"[25] and for a time it was recommended for study by those about to engage in land reform.

Both traditional history and socialist fiction rely on set situations and typical, even stereotypical, characters to embody quite explicitly formulable ideologies. D. C. Twitchett has written on the standard categories and the "repertory of formulae" used in the biographical entries (*liezhuan*) of the dynastic histories.[26] A similar repertory could no doubt be drawn up for the characters in the novels on land reform, by substituting such categories as "Oppressive Landlords," "Progressive Peasants," "Backward Intellectuals," for "Loyal Ministers," "Oppressive Officials," and "Literary Recluses." The traditional popular novel on the other hand, always proclaiming its moralistic aims yet often criticized for "teaching lust and banditry" (*hui yin hui dao*), appeared less bound to conform to an official ideology. Its relative freedom, its in some ways half-acknowledged subversive nature, encouraged a greater plurality of fictional characters and diversity of situation.

The comparison between traditional historiography and the land-reform novel can only go so far. Even if presenting literary characters as exemplifications of ideological precepts is one of those unconscious legacies or inherited assumptions from the Confucian past, the more immediate derivation for this kind of fiction is, of course, the theory of socialist realism. This theory, officially defined at the First Soviet Writers' Congress in 1934 as a "truthful, historically concrete representation of reality in its revolutionary development," has been applied by the Chinese Marxists with greater determination than by their Russian mentors. Socialist realism accounts for at least one fundamental difference between traditional history and socialist fiction. No matter how closely traditional history was bound by Confucian principles, it had an open future; beyond the narrative, events could take an unpredictable course and reveal untold possibilities, whereas "reality in its revolutionary development" always moves towards a clear-cut end and a predetermined future.

Of course all novels have endings and must be enclosed in a way that traditional history never could be. The last pages of *Sanggan River* describe volunteers from the village marching off to build fortifications at the front, so the battle is far from over. By the time Ding Ling was writing her novel, she knew that Zhuolu was again "under the occupation of Kuomintang bandit troops, and the people back in a hard and even more brutal struggle."[27] Still the novel concludes with a fixed vision of the new world that is coming into being and a confident sense of victory. Every novel must have an *end*, a conclusion, but also a goal which it has been striving for, so that at its termination, the "resolution of its form is somehow consonant with the disclosure of meaning."[28] There is nevertheless a special conclusiveness about the endings of novels that are written in accordance to a revolutionary ideology. The disclosed meaning resides in the eschatological or utopian vision of history that must in the long run be the conclusion of every human event.

The land-reform novel's linear and purposeful progression toward a preconceived end contrasts strikingly with the "heterogenous and episodic" plot characteristic of traditional Chinese fiction. According to Lin Sheun-fu, traditional plot structure was related to the Chinese "synchronistic" view of the cosmos as a self-centered, self-generating, harmonious, and organic whole. Such a cosmic view, as well as the narrative structure based on it, has its own coherence, but the deemphasis of causality or sequence produces fiction in which events apparently exist in simple conjunction, "characters appear, meet one another, vanish, and reemerge almost at random, as if entirely governed by mere chance and coincidence."[29] The world view in *Sanggan River* allows no room for such spontaneity and heterogenous looseness. Every element in its highly integrated plot structure has a defined and fixed place and is there to serve a clearly demonstrable purpose.

There is a basic homology between how characters function in a teleologically organized fictional structure and how man's role is perceived in an eschatological view of history. According to the Marxian concept man is both a determined being, that is, a product of social circumstances, and yet a maker of his own history.[30] The characters in a land-reform novel must exist and operate precisely at the dialectical crux created by these apparently contradictory propositions. They must not be allowed the "illusion of freedom" essential in Western novels, which so often focus on autonomous characters making critical moral choices. Characters undergoing land reform must be seen in the process of making momentous decisions, of energetically affecting the outcome of an action that is actually following a predetermined course. The end, when it comes, will undoubtedly provide the solutions to all their problems. (In fact, there are hardly any human problems outside the realm of class struggle.) Yet human beings must struggle with uncertainty and endure tension even if we know that there is only one way the historical process — and the plot of the novel — can come out.

In addition to being purposive structures with unifying ends, all novels, especially those of the realistic variety, contrive to convey the impression of being a copy of life. Thus the "basic convention governing the novel is that readers will through their contact with the text, be able to recognize a world."[31] But the land-reform novel also aims beyond that to provide its readers with a model of the world. Through the integration of character and community, setting and imagery, action and plot, *The Sun Shines on the Sanggan River* seeks to construct a working model of historical forces in operation; it gives us a microcosm of the quintessential revolutionary experience in which the present world is transformed by the activation of mass struggle into the world to come.

Counterbalancing this grandiose conceptualization of the novel is the self-deprecating image, familiar since Yanan days, of the novelist. In the heart of her book Ding Ling inserts an episode that would appear to deny the legitimacy of a writer's qualifications for doing his own work. It implies that the writer's mastery of the conventions and techniques of his art interfere with his ability to speak directly to and for the people in whose name he is writing.

Nuanshui village has a blackboard newspaper (*heibanbao*). The articles written for it by schoolmaster Liu (he is the progressive intellectual) are criticized by red-nosed old Wu, the janitor, because they are like the "esoteric texts of the Heavenly Mother (*Jiuniangniang de tianshu*); they do not make sense to anyone" (p. 150). Hearing this, schoolmaster Liu tears up his manuscripts. In a burst of enlightenment he understands that his task from now on must be to record the doggerel verses that come spilling out of red-nosed old Wu, who knows and can describe everything that is going on in the village. Liu realizes that "our blackboard newspaper is written for the people . . . it should be like ourselves talking, according to what everyone is thinking; we must talk about our own bitter feelings, recall the injustices done to us" (p. 152). The experienced writer considers himself to be less qualified to perform such a role than the man in the village street speaking spontaneously, in his own voice.

Ironically this disparagement of the writer is contained within a work that could have been produced only by the concentrated application of an individual, highly self-conscious artist. The paradox reflects the hazards and incongruities that can beset the writer's fate. When *The Sun Shines on the Sanggan River* won the Stalin prize in 1951, it was described as "a great decisive victory of our socialist realistic literature"[32] and hailed for the great honor it had brought to Chinese literary history. A few years later during the antirightist campaign this same achievement was used to discredit its author. Ding Ling was condemned for harboring exalted notions about literature, for a superiority complex and arrogance based on the success of this one book. By 1958 she was in exile, her career put to an end, the book banned. In the Chinese literary histories written during the next twenty years, one looks in vain for some sign that the book and its writer ever existed.

CONCLUSION: THE COMMITMENT
TO LITERATURE

THE MAIN ISSUE during the antirightist campaign was that Ding Ling had allegedly opposed the claims and achievements of literature against party leadership. Regardless of what she might have said elsewhere on the subject of the writer's role, one particular lecture was frequently singled out and attacked for what it supposedly revealed about her pernicious glorification of literature. This talk, "Dao qunzhongzhong qu luohu" (Go Make Your Dwelling among the Masses), was addressed to the Second Congress of Representatives of China's Literature Workers in September 1953. She began by saying that literary creation is very complex and hard labor; to write a good piece requires much preparation and overall effort. Some critics have over emphasized the need for analysis and study, thinking that it is all a matter of understanding Marxist-Leninist policy and thought. But the main problem in creative writing is getting deeper into life (*shenru shenghuo*). Some writers only go into the life of the masses, to the countryside, or to the factory for a short period when they need to write; they use as material what they can see on the surface. But Cao Xueqin, Shi Naian, Tolstoy, Gorky were not like this:

> What they wrote was about the people and events that had been most meaningful to them in their lives, their whole lives. These people and events were used to express a lifetime's summation of feeling and life. From life they established and discovered certain truths, which they wanted to publicize. In order to do it well, they used the form of literature. They did not write for the sake of being writers, nor did they search for a subject because they wanted to write, nor search for material because they had a subject. This is just the opposite of what we do. The path we take is the opposite to that of these great writers.[1]

Writers, she continued, are living in a wonderful time; never in history have they had such good fortune, have they been regarded so highly.

> Responsible cadres everywhere understand the importance of literary work, they are willing to help you, do everything they can to help you understand life, understand policy, provide the best conditions. The masses of people are all hoping that you will be able to portray them, to write a good book for

144

them; they are waiting for you most eagerly with the greatest
expectations. . . . In such a heroic time, we should also have an ideal, and a
heroic spirit. We should have a goal to struggle for: to write a good book, not
a slovenly book, but a book that has a high degree of consciousness and art,
not just for one's own enjoyment, or the praise of a few friends, but to be cherished by hundreds and thousands of readers, pondered over and forever im-
printed in their hearts, a book they are happy to quote from, not just popular
for a time, but lasting into the future.[2]

After expressing these high aspirations for the good literary work,
she very briefly touched on constraints attributable to party guidance,
even though earlier she had gratefully acknowledged the support of "responsible cadres":

I do not oppose the writing groups and such organizations that we have now.
But I believe it is wrong if a writer is never without guidance [lingdao]. A
writer is not like a child who can never leave his nurse; he must grow indepen-
dently. No matter how literary creation is guided, a work is created by an individual.[3]

Then the lecture ends on a personal, semiconfidential note:

I look at myself as a writer striving to achieve my ideal. I have many shortcomings, particularly I feel that I must still make great efforts, but I want to be with
you, to strive to change my environment, to find my way. Let me now secretly
tell you: I still have some ambition, I still would like to write a good book, I
ask you to urge me on.[4]

In 1953 the party's policy toward intellectuals and writers seemed to
have relaxed somewhat.[5] Nevertheless, this talk is remarkable for its assertion, even in passing, of the writer's need for independence, and for
the frank confiding of her own hopes. Ding Ling's references to the great
masters of Russia and traditional China as standards for comparison
were not so much an indication of her own presumptuous aspirations[6] as
an affirmation of the transcendent possibilities of literature as a tradition,
and its responsibility to communicate a personal vision of life and truth
in an enduring form. But such a claim clearly transgressed the principle
that literature should be subordinate to immediate revolutionary needs,
that is, to party leadership, and was used as part of the evidence in 1957
for consigning her to silence.

With her rehabilitation twenty-two years later Ding Ling was able to
resume her literary career, but her writings since then, which are beyond
the scope of this study, have been mainly in the form of essays, reminiscences, and reviews.[7] Apart from the rewritten *Du Wanxiang*, a sketch of
a model labor heroine she met in the Great Northern Wilderness, and the
still unfinished "During the Coldest Days", a sequel to *The Sun Shines on
the Sanggan River*, she has not added to the corpus of her fictional writ-

ings. Whether Ding Ling has indeed or will ever be able to carry out her goal and write that good book that would last into the future is not a question we need to pose or answer at this time. Nor can we glibly assume that the potential for the production of great masterworks has been in her case stifled by a particular political environment. The task of literary study is not, in any case, to speculate on what might have been, but to describe and analyze what has already been done. What we do observe in Ding Ling's work is a compelling commitment to literature realized in whatever ways were possible. The result is a record of narrative works uniquely precise in registering ideological change.

Applying a broad, neutralized concept of ideology as an entering wedge to approach the texts, enables us to perceive more readily how the various elements of the narrative structure function together as her fiction continued to develop. It so happens that this integration is particularly evident in two works that stand at opposite poles, both chronologically and ideologically, of her literary output. In "The Diary of Miss Sophie," as the central character struggles to record her reactions to a disillusioning love affair, the world is constructed around the isolated self in the act of writing; in *The Sun Shines on the Sanggan River*, it is shaped by the concept of revolution underlying the collective experience of land reform. Totally opposing world views are in each case actualized through story, form, and narrative technique. Her other works, some more successfully than others, provide further instructive examples of the diverse ways in which ideology and narrative can be interrelated.

The final assessment of Ding Ling's stature as a writer in terms of "the verdict of the ages," or the appreciation, in her own words, "of hundreds and thousands of readers", may have to depend on such commonly used external criteria as universal relevance or enduring interest, which are less amenable to the kind of structural analysis I have used in examining her works. Perhaps such long-range criteria are ultimately incompatible with the immediate political demands that Ding Ling's narratives attempted sincerely to meet. It is possible that literature produced to further specific collective goals of the moment will serve only for the short run, and must forego hopes for a place in that timeless, transcendent tradition of immortal names evoked in Ding Ling's talk.

The idea of achieving immortality through writing (*liyan*) — parallel aspirations have frequently found expression in Western culture — had been central to the Chinese literary tradition. This confidence in literature's ability to transcend time and defeat death was no doubt reinforced by the stable character and seeming permanence of the unchanging written language. But the lofty conception of literature, as well as the peculiar Chinese script itself, were closely bound to the self-image of the Confucian scholar-literati. The establishment of a literary tradition, and in fact, the definition of what constitutes literature, are always, for each historical culture, matters determined by the prevailing ideology. One question still under debate in revolutionary China is how to receive and evaluate the literature of the imperial past. Significantly no writer from the tradition of the established classical forms was mentioned by Ding Ling in her 1953 talk.

Although Ding Ling talked hopefully then about a book "lasting into the future," about the persistence of literature through time, the idea of literary tradition had been fatally undermined long before by the extreme iconoclasm of the May Fourth period, when she was just starting out as a fledgling writer. Rebellions against the past, in which she herself had vigorously participated, are necessary and regular phenomena in literary history. Upon such rebellions the foundations of new literary traditions are normally laid. But after breaking loose, the young writers of May Fourth were allowed hardly any time to follow through on their free experimentations to create a new tradition before they were all caught up by the sweep of public events. The war for national survival, the turmoil of total revolution, made an "independent" literature seem a dispensable luxury if not a sheer impossibility. We are left with the problem of just how to characterize a literature that is so intimately bound to the momentous changes in modern Chinese history.

There still remains a firm belief in the importance and powerful uses to which an *engaged* literature can be put. The heartbreaking history of modern Chinese literature, its pages bespattered with the blood of martyrs, testifies to this belief, on the part of both those who have written literature and those in power who have persecuted them for it. While many have continued to stake their lives on this faith in literature, others have decided to relinquish writing, not so much because of the personal risks involved, but out of a sense of uncertainty — given the shifting ideological context — over what literature ultimately is, or is for. For these writers the alternative to accepting definitions regarding the nature and function of literature imposed by political ideologues has been abdication from the creative effort.

This has not been Ding Ling's choice. For the sake of writing she has confronted the risks of personal martyrdom, and indeed suffered persecution from both right and left. As a revolutionary writer she has persistently sought to produce genuine literature in circumstances that continually raise questions about the notion of literature itself. But the body of her fiction, through its various phases of development, with its constant explorations into the meaning of writing, and revised notions of the writer's role, does not provide any clear-cut answers. It serves rather to intensify our awareness of the contradictions, ambiguities, and precariousness of literature as it tries to survive in a radically changing world.

The career of Ding Ling ultimately demonstrates that even as our uncertainties concerning literature multiply, the commitment to literature remains. What she was able to achieve with the sequence of her narratives as they continually adapted to ideological change, reinforces our faith in the validity of the literary enterprise.

NOTES

WORKS CITED

CHRONOLOGICAL LIST OF
DING LING'S FICTION

INDEX

NOTES

Introduction

1. Harold R. Isaacs, ed., *Straw Sandals: Chinese Short Stories, 1918-1933* (Cambridge, Mass.: The M.I.T. Press, 1974), p. lviii.

2. Helen Foster Snow, *Women in Modern China* (The Hague: Mouton, 1967), pp. 190-221. See also Helen Foster Snow, *The Chinese Communists: Sketches and Autobiographies of the Old Guard* (Westport, Conn.: Greenwood, 1972), II, 262-266.

3. Shen Congwen, *Ji Ding Ling* and *Ji Ding Ling xuji* (Reminiscences of Ding Ling; Further Reminiscences of Ding Ling) (Shanghai, 1940); Yao Pengzi, "Women de pengyou Ding Ling" (Our Friend Ding Ling), in *Ding Ling xuanji* (Selected Works of Ding Ling), ed. Xu Chensi and Ye Wangyou (Shanghai, 1936), pp. 7-35.

4. In addition to Helen Snow's two books, see Gunther Stein, *The Challenge of Red China* (New York: McGraw Hill, 1945), pp. 251-259; Robert Elegant, *China's Red Masters: Political Biographies of the Chinese Communist Leaders* (New York: Twayne, 1951), pp. 145-162; Robert Payne, *China Awake* (New York: Dodd, Mead, 1947), pp. 381-386; E. H. Leaf, "Ting Ling, Herald of a New China," *T'ien Hsia Monthly* 5 (October 1937): 225-236; and L. Insun, "Ding Ling zai Shaanbei" (Ding Ling in Northern Shaanxi), in *Nüzhanshi Ding Ling* (The Woman Warrior Ding Ling) (Shanghai, 1938), pp. 25-73.

5. Chang Jun-mei discusses the reasons why she gives 1904 as the year of Ding Ling's birth, although other dates have been given in various sources, in *Ting Ling: Her Life and Her Work*, Taiwan: Institute of International Relations, National Chengchi University, (Taipei, 1978), p. 1. The same year is given also in a 1980 chronology said to have been checked by Ding Ling herself; see Zhong Chen and Ling Yuan, eds., *Ding Ling zuopin xinian* (Chronology of Ding Ling's Works) *Jilin shida xuebao* (Journal of Jilin Normal University) supplementary issue, 1980, p. 1. The frequently cited date of 1907 is accepted by Lin Zhihao, ed., *Zhongguo xiandai wenxueshi* (History of Modern Chinese Literature) (Peking, 1980) II, 592. For a list of the dozen or so pen names Ding Ling used in her writings see Ye Xiaoshen, "Ding Ling de biming" (The Pen Names of Ding Ling) *Gansu shida xuebao* (Journal of Gansu Normal University) 1 (1981): 56-58.

6. Ding Ling, "Wo de chuangzuo shenghuo" (My Life in Creative Writing), in *Chuangzuo de jingyan* (Experiences in Creative Writing) (Shanghai, 1935), pp. 21-22. See also Helen Snow, *Women in Modern China*, pp. 200-201.

7. Ding Ling, "Wo zenyang fei xiang le ziyou de tiandi" (How I Flew towards a Free Heaven and Earth), in *Kuadao xinde shidai lai* (Stride into the New Era) (Peking, 1953), pp. 157-158.

8. Ibid., p. 160.

9. Ibid., p. 161; Helen Snow, *The Chinese Communists*, p. 264.

10. Ibid., p. 265.

11. Helen Snow, *Women in Modern China*, p. 191; *The Chinese Communists*, pp. 264–265.

12. Helen Snow, *Women in Modern China*, p. 204.

13. According to Shen Congwen, the friendship with Wang Jianhong was one that Ding Ling greatly treasured, and the characterizations of the tubercular woman in fragile health but with a strong personality who appears in the stories are sketches of this friend; see *Ji Ding Ling*, p. 27. Ding Ling has written about Wang Jianhong and the marriage with Qu Qiubai in "Wo suo renshi de Qu Qiubai tongzhi—huiyi yu suixiang" (The Comrade Qu Qiubai I Knew: Memories and Rambling Thoughts), *Xinhua yuebao wenzhaiban* (Xinhua Monthly, Literary Digests) 5 (1980): 155–163.

14. Ding Ling, "Yige zhenshiren de yisheng—ji Hu Yepin (The Life of an Upright Man: Reminiscences of Hu Yepin), in *Hu Yepin xiaoshuo xuanji* (Selected Stories of Hu Yepin) (Peking, 1955), p. 7.

15. Shen Congwen, *Ji Ding Ling*, p. 85.

16. Ding Ling, "Yige zhenshiren de yisheng—ji Hu Yepin," p. 8.

17. Ibid., p. 17. The *Honghei yuekan* (Red and Black Monthly) ran from January to August 1929, ceasing publication after its eighth issue; the *Renjian yuekan* (Human World Monthly) began in January 1929 and folded after its third issue.

18. Manjia (pseudonym of Ding Ling), "Xu" (Preface), *Yepin shixuan* (Selected Poems by Yepin) (Shanghai, 1929), p. 5.

19. Shen Congwen, *Ji Ding Ling*, pp. 160, 162.

20. Ding Ling, "Yige zhenshiren de yisheng—ji Hu Yepin", p. 9.

21. Ibid., p. 12.

22. Harold Isaacs, *Straw Sandals*, pp. xxvii–xxviii, xl–xlii. See also Tsi-an Hsia, "Enigma of the Five Martyrs," in his *The Gate of Darkness: Studies on the Leftist Literary Movement in China* (Seattle: University of Washington Press, 1968), pp. 163–233. Luo Zhanglong, who was then secretary of the party's working committee in Shanghai, asserted some fifty years after the event that the Wang Ming faction was responsible for betraying the meeting to the Kuomintang police; his account thus confirms the speculations of Isaacs and Hsia. See "Shanghai dongfang fandian huiyi qianhou" (Events Surrounding the Meeting in the Shanghai Eastern Hotel), oral account by Luo Zhanglong recorded by Qiu Quanzheng, *Xinwenxue shiliao* 1 (1981): 141–145.

23. Shen Congwen, *Ji Ding Ling xuji*, p. 64.

24. Ibid., p. 109.

25. Ibid., p. 110.

26. Ding Ling's own incomplete account can be found in her interviews with several foreign journalists. See Helen Snow, *Women in Modern China*, pp. 217–221; Gunther Stein, *The Challenge of Red China*, pp. 255–256; and L. Insun, "Ding Ling zai Shaanbei," pp. 39–45. Agnes Smedley records an eyewitness account she heard in the spring of 1933 from a man named Li, an engineer who claimed he saw Feng Da, under threat of torture, betray Ding Ling's address to Kuomintang agents. Feng had been Smedley's former secretary and translator. Li was also present when Ding Ling was kidnapped. See Agnes Smedley, *Battle Hymn of China* (New York: Knopf, 1943), pp. 118–119. More than two months after the kidnapping one of Shanghai's English-language newspapers quoted an

extensive account by a Li Chie-chen, said to have been an eyewitness to the incident. See *The Shanghai Evening Post & Mercury*, June 15, 1933, pp. 1 and 7. During the antirightist campaign Ding Ling was accused of having surrendered and confessed to the Kuomintang in 1933 and of concealing this history from the party after arriving in Yanan. See Zhou Yang, *Wenyi zhanxianshang de yichang dabianlun* (A Great Debate on the Literary Front) (Peking, 1960), p. 14.

27. This is the opinion of Xu Enzeng, director of the Central Investigation and Statistics Bureau of the Kuomintang government from 1927 to 1944. His account of Ding Ling's detention is contained in his memoirs "Andou" (Invisible Conflicts). Chang Jun-mei includes excerpts translated from the unpublished Chinese draft, made available through the Institute of International Relations, Taipei, in her *Ting Ling, Her Life and Her Work*, pp. 62–64.

28. L. Insun, "Ding Ling zai Shaanbei," pp. 36–37.

29. Ding Ling's account of her experiences abroad appeared in her *Ouxing sanji* (Random Notes on Travels in Europe) (Peking, 1952).

30. Two collections of these writings have been published: *Kuadao xinde shidai lai*, which includes essays written between 1942 and 1950, and *Dao qunzhongzhong qu luohu* (Go Make Your Dwelling among the Masses) (Peking, 1954), which includes essays from between 1950 and 1953.

31. Ding Ling, "Zuowei yizhong qingxiang lai kan—gei Xiao Yemu tongzhi de yifengxin" (To Be Viewed As a Kind of Tendency: A Letter to Comrade Xiao Yemu), in *Dao qunzhongzhong qu luohu*, p. 11.

32. Ding Ling, "Wei tigao women kanwu de sixiangxing, zhandouxing er douzheng" (To Struggle for the Elevation of Consciousness and Fighting Spirit of Our Journals), in *Dao qunzhongzhong qu luohu*, pp. 12–24.

33. A detailed account of this history can be found in Merle Goldman, *Literary Dissent in Communist China* (Cambridge, Mass.: Harvard University Press, 1967). For other accounts of the antirightist drive and Ding Ling's difficulties with the party, see D. W. Fokkema, *Literary Doctrine in China and Soviet Influence, 1956–1960* (The Hague: Mouton, 1965), pp. 160–163; C. T. Hsia, *A History of Modern Chinese Fiction*, 2nd ed. (New Haven: Yale University Press, 1971), pp. 341–349; and Chang Jun-mei, *Ting Ling, Her Life and Her Work*, pp. 120–145.

34. Information about Ding Ling's experiences between 1958 and 1978 is based on conversations I had with her between March and August 1981, a talk she gave to foreign students at the Peking Language School on July 25, 1979, and on the following journalistic accounts:

Fang Mao, "Ding Ling he ta de nüer" (Ding Ling and Her Daughter), *Dagongbao* (Ta-kung-pao), November 4, 1978, p. 3, November 5, 1978, p. 3; Bai Ye, "Dangguo jizhe de Ding Ling" (Ding Ling Has Been a Reporter), *Xinwen zhanxian* (News Front) 2 (1979): 57–61; Shen Mo, "Ding Ling ersan shi" (Two or Three Things about Ding Ling), *Dagongbao*, May 19, 1979, p. 3; "Nüzuojia Ding Ling zhengzai zhuanxie xinzuo" (The Woman Writer Ding Ling Is Now Writing New Works), *Guangming ribao* (Guangming Daily), June 14, 1979, p. 2; Bai Jieming, "Ding Ling tan yangji de gushi" (Ding Ling Tells Stories about Raising Chickens), *Huaqiao ribao* (China Daily News) August 8, 1979, p. 6; Bai Jieming (Under his English name Geremie Barmè), "Ding Ling manhua ershinian zaoji" (Ding Ling Talks Informally about Twenty Years of Her Experiences), *Qishi niandai* (The Seventies) 115 (August 1979): 90–92; Dong Xiao, "Zoufang Ding Ling" (Interview with Ding Ling), *Kaijuan* (Book Reviews Monthly) 2.5 (December 1979): 22–26; Feng Xiaxiong, "Ding Ling's Reappearance on the Literary Stage",

Chinese Literature 1 (1980): 3–16. Some events of her confinement in the "cow shed" are described by Ding Ling in one of her few direct accounts of this period: " 'Niupeng' xiaopin (san zhang)" (Three "Cow Shed" Sketches) *Shiyue* (October) 3 (1979): 196–202.

35. Ding Ling, in a note to "Du Wanxiang," *Renmin wenxue* (People's Literature) 7 (1979): 58.

36. The sequel began to appear in *Qingming* (Brightness) 1 (1979): 4–92.

37. "Nüzuojia Ding Ling zhengzai zhuanxie xinzuo," p. 2.

38. Zhou Yang, *Wenyi zhanxianshang de yichang dabianlun*, p. 19.

39. Ibid., pp. 19–20; Wang Ziye, "Fengming xiezuo" (Writing to Order), *Renmin wenxue* 10 (1957): 8–9.

40. "Jianchi shehuizhuyi de wenyi luxian" (Hold Fast to the Socialist Line in Literature), editorial in *Wenyi yuebao* (Literature Monthly) 10 (1957): 3–5.

41. "Fensui Ding Ling, Chen Qixia, Feng Xuefeng fandang jituan: baowei dang dui wenxue shiye de lingdao" (Smash the Antiparty Clique of Ding Ling, Chen Qixia, Feng Xuefeng: Protect the Leadership of the Party in Literary Matters), *Renmin wenxue* 9 (1957): 1–3.

42. Clifford Geertz, "Ideology As a Cultural System," in his *The Interpretation of Cultures* (New York: Basic Books, 1973), p. 193. Geertz is arguing for the development of a "genuinely nonevaluative conception of ideology," p. 196; "that part of culture which is actively concerned with the establishment and defense of patterns of belief and value," p. 231. While he is primarily concerned with the social sciences, ideology can be similarly useful as a conceptual tool for the analysis of literary texts, once it is neutralized and no longer "ideologized." In this broader, nonpolitical sense, ideology is roughly equivalent to what Roland Barthes and other structuralists have called the "cultural code": the generalized assumptions, the body of common knowledge, the implicit proverbs and system of values that can be said to form a kind of substratum of literature. Ideology may thus be viewed as one of the strands of *vraisemblance* that is interwoven into the text to give it pattern and meaning. Of Barthes's five codes this is the one most in need of clearer definition. See Roland Barthes, *S / Z, an Essay*, tr. Richard Miller (New York: Hill and Wang, 1974), especially pp. 20, 97, 98, 100. The cultural code or cultural *vraisemblance* is discussed with reference to Barthes in Robert Scholes, *Structuralism in Literature: An Introduction* (New Haven: Yale University Press, 1974), pp. 154–157; and in Jonathan Culler, *Structuralist Poetics, Structuralism, Linguistics, and the Study of Literature* (Ithaca: Cornell University Press, 1977), particularly pp. 142–145.

These discussions are mostly concerned with the cultural or ideological code from the perspective of reading, of how the reader assimilates, interprets, or naturalizes the text by, among other things, giving it a place in a world defined by the available culture. From the point of view of the writing process, however, one could make the case that the cultural or ideological code precedes the others in that it is what makes the world of experience initially intelligible and coherent as the writer begins to write. This would be even truer in the case of ideology that is overtly political or prescriptive, when the writer starts out by accepting certain explicitly formulated views of the world, although his text may still contain other implicit assumptions. But for the critic or student of literature, ideology is mainly an effective conceptual tool for sharpening our awareness of what is there within the text and interrelating its various elements.

43. Jonathan Culler quoting Gérard Genette, *Structuralist Poetics*, p. 144.

1. Subjectivism and Literature

1. The number of stories Ding Ling actually wrote cannot be established with absolute certainty. Both Yao Pengzi and Shen Congwen speak of stories by Hu Yepin that appeared under Ding Ling's name. See Yao Pengzi, "Bianwan zhihou" (After Editing), in *Ding Ling xuanji* (Selected Works of Ding Ling), ed. (Yao) Pengzi (Shanghai, 1939), p. 317; Shen Congwen, *Ji Ding Ling*, p. 67. Shen suggests the reason for this confusion: "When magazines requested writings, they often asked Ding Ling, but not the naval student. When both of them sent their works to certain places, those of the naval student would alone be returned. When both of them sold the publishing rights of manuscripts to certain book-stores, those signed by the naval student would not be accepted, but those with Ding Ling's name would be published without any difficulty." Shen himself confused the attribution of at least one story: see discussion below of "Qian laile ke de yueye" (A Secret Visitor on a Moonlit Night). The following pieces which are included in various collections of Ding Ling's works appeared first as stories by Hu Yepin in *Xiaoshuo yuebao* (Fiction Monthly): "Shaonian Mengde de shimian" (The Insomnia of the Youth Mengde), 20.2 (1929): 409–412; "Xisheng" (Sacrifice), 21.12 (1930): 1713–1722; "Zai yige wanshang" (During One Evening), 20.3 (1929): 557–559. There may also be stories of joint authorship to complicate even further the problem of drawing the boundary around Ding Ling's oeuvre and establishing definitive texts. Stories that do not center on a young woman include "New Year's," about an eight-year-old girl, and "Summer Vacation," about a group of young women teachers.

2. Leo Ou-fan Lee, *The Romantic Generation of Modern Chinese Writers* (Cambridge, Mass.: Harvard University Press, 1973).

3. *The Dream of the Red Chamber* may be the great exception. This lack in China is in striking contrast with Western novels, so many of which have as their subject the growth of a young man or woman. "The *Bildungsroman* is not merely a special category: the theme of the novel is essentially that of formation, of education"; Maurice Z. Shroder, "The Novel as A Genre," in *The Theory of the Novel*, ed. Philip Stevick (New York: The Free Press, 1967), p. 16. The "confessional increment" is due to the youthful hero's subjective self-consciousness.

4. May Fourth literature is not merely that which was produced for a few years before and after the student demonstration of May 4, 1919, but includes the literature written between the fall of the Manchu dynasty and Mao Zedong's "Talks at the Yanan Forum on Literature and Art" in May 1942, more particularly the literature of the 1920s and 1930s. See Merle Goldman, ed., *Modern Chinese Literature in the May Fourth Era* (Cambridge, Mass.: Harvard University Press, 1977), p. vii.

5. Helen Snow refers to a study by Olga Lang of the most popular writers among Chinese students and to a listing by Lu Xun of the best short-story writers and novelists; in both Ding Ling is the only woman listed. These are merely slightly more "objective" proofs of what was generally assumed concerning her status as a writer. See Snow, *Women in Modern China*, p. 191.

6. He Yubo, "Ding Ling nüshi lunping" (Critical Discussions on Miss Ding Ling), in her *Zhongguo xiandai nüzuojia* (Contemporary Women Writers of China), 2nd ed. (Shanghai, 1936; 1st ed., 1931), pp. 102–103.

7. Mary Clabaugh Wright, *China in Revolution: The First Phase, 1900–1913* (New Haven: Yale University Press, 1968), pp. 32–34.

8. For a discussion of some images of women prevalent in traditional literature see Yi-tsi Feuerwerker, "Women as Writers in the 1920s and 1930s," in *Women*

in Chinese Society, ed. Margery Wolf and Roxanne Witke (Stanford: Stanford University Press, 1975), pp. 147–151. Even the women who did write tended to be poets with a limited subject matter who adopted the modes of thinking and feeling defined as feminine by the dominant male tradition.

9. Ding Ling, "Yijiusanlingnian chun shanghai (zhiyi)" (Shanghai, Spring 1930, I), in *Ding Ling wenji* (Collected Works of Ding Ling) (Shanghai, 1936), pp. 190–191.

10. Olga Lang, *Pa Chin and His Writings: Chinese Youth between the Two Revolutions* (Cambridge, Mass.: Harvard University Press, 1967), p. 3.

11. Leo Ou-fan Lee, *The Romantic Generation of Modern Chinese Writers,* p. 110.

12. Ezra F. Vogel, "The Unlikely Heroes: The Social Role of the May Fourth Writers," in *Modern Chinese Literature in the May Fourth Era,* ed. Merle Goldman, p. 153.

13. Ding Ling, "Wo de zibai" (A Personal Statement), in *Ding Ling xuanji* (Selected Works of Ding Ling), ed. Xu and Ye, pp. 146–147; "Shenghuo, sixiang yu renwu" (Life, Thought, and Characters), *Renmin wenxue* 3 (1955): 126.

14. Yao Wenyuan, "Shafei nüshimen de ziyou wangguo – Ding Ling bufen zaoqi zuopin pipan, bing lun Ding Ling chuangzuo sixiang he chuangzuo qingxiang fazhan de yige xianso" (The Free Kingdom of the Miss Sophies: A Criticism of Some of Ding Ling's Early Works, and a Discussion of a Clue to the Thought and Direction of Development in Ding Ling's Creative Writing), in his *Wenyi sixiang lunzheng ji* (Polemics in Literary Thought), p. 212.

15. A 1958 article attacking her 1941 Yanan story "Zai yiyuanzhong" (In the Hospital) is typical of this kind of criticism. See Zhang Guangnian, "Shafei nüshi zai Yanan – tan Ding Ling de xiaoshuo 'Zai yiyuanzhong'" (Miss Sophie in Yanan: A Discussion of Ding Ling's Story "In the Hospital"), *Wenyi bao* (Literary Gazette) 2 (1958): 9–11. Although Sophie (the main character in Ding Ling's famous 1928 story) had "put on a cotton military uniform, was under a new name . . . and had become a member of the Communist Party, her character had not changed."

16. Jianru, "Ding Ling yinxiang" (Impressions of Ding Ling), in *Ding Ling pingzhuan* (Critical Biography of Ding Ling), ed. Zhang Baiyun (Shanghai, 1934), p. 183.

17. Shen Congwen, *Ji Ding Ling,* p. 143.

18. Ding Ling, "Qian laile ke de yueye" (A Secret Visitor on a Moonlit Night), in *Ding Ling wenji* (Collected Works of Ding Ling) (Shanghai, 1936), p. 488.

19. Ibid., p. 499.

20. A name that carries an autobiographical reference. It is the name of the little girl in Ding Ling's novel about her mother, and homophonic versions of it appear as pen names in her writings. Ding Ling has told me she was actually two years older at the time of the events in the story.

21. (Yao) Pengzi, "Bianwan zhihou," p. 317.

22. He Yubo, "Ding Ling nüshi lunping," p. 107.

23. Ding Ling, "Guonian" (New Year's), in *Ding Ling wenji,* pp. 518 and 519.

24. Ibid., pp. 519–520.

25. Ibid., pp. 506–507.

26. Shen Congwen, *Ji Ding Ling,* pp. 87, 92.

27. Ibid., p. 294.

28. Ding Ling, "Mengke," in *Zai heianzhong* (In the Darkness) (Shanghai, 1933), p. 71.

29. Ibid., p. 58.

30. Ding Ling, "Amao guniang" (Miss Amao), in *Zai heianzhong*, p. 215.

31. Ibid., p. 220.

32. Ibid., pp. 222–223.

33. (Zhang) Baiyun, "Ding Ling zhuan" (Biography of Ding Ling), in *Ding Ling pingzhuan*, p. 3; Shen Congwen, *Ji Ding Ling*, pp. 78, 87.

34. There are other interesting parallels in the two works: the figures of the father and mother-in-law, the "dumb" husband, glimpses of a "higher" way of life, a "near-hysteria" scene in the hills towards the end, the death agonies, as well as the narrator's practice of being both in and out of the dramatized consciousness of the protagonist. Gary J. Bjorge sees some interesting parallels between *Madame Bovary* and another Ding Ling story, "The Diary of Miss Sophie"; see his "Sophia's Diary: An Introduction," *Tamkang Review* 5.1 (1974): 97–110.

35. Ding Ling, "Qingyunlizhong de yijian xiaofangli," (A Small Room in Qingyun Lane), in *Ding Ling wenji*, p. 159. In some anthologies, such as *Ding Ling xuanji* (editor's preface dated 1956, Hong Kong), the title is given as "Qingyunli."

36. Ding Ling, "Shafei nüshi de riji" (The Diary of Miss Sophie), *Xiaoshuo yuebao* 19.2 (1928): 214–215, 219–220.

37. Ibid., p. 223.

38. Robert Scholes and Robert Kellogg, *The Nature of Narrative* (New York: Oxford University Press, 1966), p. 191.

39. Cao Xueqin, *Hongloumeng* (Dream of the Red Chamber) (Peking, 1953), p. 1.

40. Jaroslav Průšek, *Three Sketches of Chinese Literature* (Prague: Oriental Institute in Academia, 1969), pp. 92–97.

41. Leo Ou-fan Lee, *The Romantic Generation of Modern Chinese Writers*, p. 285. In a 1946 interview Ding Ling said "My early works were a kind of continual *Sorrows of Werther*"; see Robert Payne, *China Awake*, p. 383.

42. Jaroslav Průšek, *Three Sketches of Chinese Literature*, p. 45.

43. Yizhen, "Ding Ling nüshi" (Miss Ding Ling), in *Ding Ling pingzhuan*, p. 107.

44. Jaroslav Průšek, "Subjectivism and Individualism in Modern Chinese Literature," *Archiv Orientální* 25 (1957): 262.

45. Ding Ling, "Shujia zhong" (Summer Vacation), in *Zai heianzhong*, p. 145.

46. Ibid., pp. 151, 150, 149.

47. Ding Ling, "Xiaohuolun shang" (On a Small Steamboat), in *Zisha riji* (A Suicide's Diary) (Shanghai, 1937), p. 97.

48. For a discussion of these writers and their perceptions of the female condition, see Yi-tsi Feuerwerker, "Women as Writers in the 1920s and 1930s" in *Women in Chinese Society*, pp. 143–168.

49. Ding Ling, "Wo de chuangzuo jingyan" (My Experience in Creative Writing), in *Ding Ling xuanji*, ed. Xu and Ye, p. 142.

50. Ding Ling, "Yige nüren he yige nanren" (A Woman and a Man), in *Ding Ling wenji*, pp. 535, 532, 552.

51. Ding Ling, "Ta zou hou" (After He Left), in *Ding Ling wenji*, p. 182.

52. Boris Uspensky, *A Poetics of Composition: The Structure of the Artistic Text and Typology of a Compositional Form*, tr. Valentina Zavarin and Susan Wittig (Berkeley: University of California Press, 1973), p. 42. The divergent possibilities open to the narrated monologue, the ways in which it can be distinguished from the narrator's report of the character's thinking, and the "rela-

tively common ambiguous situation where it is difficult to know whose voice speaks," are discussed in Seymour Chatman, *Story and Discourse: Narrative Structure in Fiction and Film* (Ithaca: Cornell University Press, 1980), pp. 203–209.

53. Ding Ling, "Ta zou hou," p. 178.

54. Yao Wenyuan, "Shafei nüshimen . . .," p. 218.

55. Shen Congwen, *Ji Ding Ling*, pp. 101–102.

56. Shen Congwen, *Ji Ding Ling xuji*, p. 145.

57. Shen Congwen, *Ji Ding Ling*, pp. 83, 67.

58. Bing Xin wrote some children's stories and essays but little else after her early writings; Lu Yin died in childbirth at the age of thirty-six; Ling Shuhua became a diplomat's wife and a painter; Su Xuelin and Feng Yuanjun abandoned creative writing to become literary historians and teachers.

59. Ding Ling, "Yecao" (Yecao) in *Ding Ling wenji*, p. 312.

60. Ibid., p. 318.

61. Ding Ling, "Zisha riji" (A Suicide's Diary), in *Ding Ling wenji*, p. 138.

62. Ibid., pp. 144–145.

63. Ibid., p. 144.

64. Ibid., p. 152.

65. Shen Congwen, *Ji Hu Yepin* (Reminiscences of Hu Yepin), 3rd ed. (Shanghai, 1935), pp. 42, 45.

66. Ibid., p. 25.

67. Ding Ling, "Amao guniang," p. 243.

68. Raymond Williams, *Culture and Society, 1780–1950* (New York: Harper & Row, 1966), pp. 32, 34.

69. Perry Link, "Traditional-Style Popular Urban Fiction in the Teens and Twenties," in *Modern Chinese Literature in the May Fourth Era*, pp. 327–349.

70. Ding Ling, "Wo de chuangzuo shenghuo," (My Life in Creative Writing) in *Chuangzuo de jingyan* (Experiences in Creative Writing) (Shanghai, 1935, p. 23.

71. Ding Ling, "Yige zhenshiren de yisheng—ji Hu Yepin," p. 8.

72. "Shafei nüshi de riji" (The Diary of Miss Sophie), *Xiaoshuo yuebao* 19.2 (1928): 202–223. Subsequent references to this story appear in the text. I have benefited from consulting the translations of A. L. Chin, "The Diary of Miss Sophia," in *Straw Sandals*, ed. Harold R. Isaacs, pp. 129–169; and of Joseph Lau, "Sophia's Diary", *Tamkang Review* 5.1 (1974): 57–96.

73. Qian Qianwu, "Ding Ling," in *Ding Ling pingzhuan*, p. 39.

74. Yizhen, "Ding Ling nüshi," in *Ding Ling pingzhuan*, p. 112.

75. Mao Dun, "Nüzuojia Ding Ling," (The Woman Writer Ding Ling) in *Ding Ling xuanji*, ed. Xu and Ye, p. 37.

76. Huang Ying, *Xiandai zhongguo nüzuojia* (Women Writers of Contemporary China), 2nd ed. (Shanghai, 1934), p. 186.

77. Susan Sontag, *Illness as Metaphor* (New York: Farrar, Straus, and Giroux, 1978), p. 29: "Many of the literary and erotic attitudes known as 'romantic agony' derive from tuberculosis and its transformation through metaphor."

78. An important episode in "Mengke" takes place when the central character goes with her cousin to see the film *Chahuanü* (Camille). She "shared in the sorrow, as if she herself had suffered a similar fate." Mengke also falls in love with the actress, a preparation for her own later career in film. In his *Ji Ding Ling*, Shen Congwen refers several times to the important influence of Dumas's book (in English translation) on Ding Ling's writing and her own decision to try out for a

film career; see pp. 46 and 85. When Ding Ling was in the seventh grade, she wept so bitterly on rereading *Dream of the Red Chamber* that the next morning her eyes were swollen shut. Her mother then took the book away. Helen Snow, *Women in Modern China*, p. 201.

79. Mao Dun, "Nüzuojia Ding Ling," p. 37.

80. Liu Shousong, *Zhongguo xinwenxue shi chugao* (Draft History of Modern Chinese Literature) (Peking, 1957), I, 357.

81. Wayne C. Booth, *The Rhetoric of Fiction* (Chicago: University of Chicago Press, 1961), p. 150.

82. David Goldknopf, *The Life of the Novel* (Chicago: University of Chicago Press, 1972), p. 59.

83. Meir Sternberg, *Expositional Modes and Temporal Ordering in Fiction* (Baltimore: The Johns Hopkins University Press, 1978), p. 278.

84. Seymour Chatman, "The Structure of Narrative Transmission," in *Style and Structure in Literature: Essays in the New Stylistics*, ed. Roger Fowler (Ithaca: Cornell University Press, 1974), p. 240.

85. Georg Lukács, "The Ideology of Modernism," in *Marxism and Human Liberation: Essays on History, Culture, and Revolution*, ed. E. San Juan, Jr. (New York: Dell Publishing Co., 1973), pp. 277–307.

2. Toward a Revolutionary Literature

1. Ding Ling, "Wo de zibai," p. 146.

2. Ding Ling, "Wo de chuangzuo shenghuo," pp. 24–25. Jiang Guangci (formerly Jiang Guangchi) was expelled from the Communist Party in October 1930, only a few months before his death in 1931. However, he was posthumously reinstated as a writer in 1953. Both Tsi-an Hsia and Leo Ou-fan Lee discuss him as a writer of "love and revolution" fiction. See Tsi-an Hsia, "The Phenomenon of Chiang Kuang-tz'u," in his *The Gate of Darkness*, pp. 55–100; and Lee's chapter on Chiang Kuang-tz'u in his *The Romantic Generation*, pp. 201–221. Ding Ling's story "Shiren Ya-luo-fu" (The Poet Alov), written in 1932 and satirizing a white Russian prostitute named Li-sha, is an apparent attack on Jiang Guangci's novel *Lisha de aiyuan* (The Sorrows of Lisa), published in 1929, whose central character, Lisa, is a sympathetic and tragic figure. Ding Ling thus completes her disentanglement from the "love and revolution trap."

3. Leo Ou-fan Lee, *The Romantic Generation*, p. 274.

4. Tsi-an Hsia, *The Gate of Darkness*, p. 176.

5. Ding Ling, *Wei Hu* (Hong Kong, 1953), p.17.

6. Ibid., pp. 14, 67, 89.

7. Ibid., p. 147.

8. Ibid., pp. 16, 151.

9. Ibid., pp. 138, 146. In a 1980 article commemorating Qu Qiubai, the literary critic and leader of the League of Left-Wing Writers, Ding Ling writes of the regret he had expressed in 1930 for having neglected the literature he loved because of his political activities. "I had always known his great love for literature. I had taken him as model in writing a love and revolution novelette. But I was not satisfied with it. I had not adequately treated the revolutionary side of the protagonist; it was not something I was able to achieve at that time." "Wo dui 'duoyu de hua' de lijie" (My Understanding of "Superfluous Words"), *Guangming ribao*, March 21, 1980, p. 3.

10. Ding Ling, "Yijiusanlingnian chun shanghai (zhiyi)" (Shanghai, Spring 1930, I), in *Ding Ling wenji*, pp. 210–211.

11. Ibid., p. 236.

12. Ibid., p. 202.

13. Ibid., pp. 190–191. This passage is quoted and translated by Leo Ou-fan Lee, *The Romantic Generation*, pp. 271–272, and Tsi-an Hsia, *The Gate of Darkness*, p. 188.

14. Ding Ling, "Yijiusanlingnian chun shanghai (zhiyi)," p. 233.

15. Ding Ling, "Yijiusanlingnian chun shanghai (zhier)" (Shanghai, Spring 1930, II), in *Ding Ling wenji*, pp. 309, 306.

16. Ding Ling, "Nianqian de yitian" (The Day before New Year's), in *Shui* (Flood) (Hong Kong, 1954), where the title is given as "Nianqian de yinian" (The Year before New Year's), p. 142. It is tempting to see a self-portrait here; certainly the detailed account of the joint life of struggling writers and their self-doubts seem invested with a personal meaning.

17. Ibid., p. 143.

18. Ibid., p. 157.

19. The 1929 story "Ri" (Day) begins with a long description of Shanghai waking at dawn, its sights and sounds evoking the sordidness, poverty, and injustice of the semicolonial city. In spite of the detailed account of the physical environment, unusual for Ding Ling before 1931, the focus of the story is still the isolated, futile existence of its heroine Yisai. The sounds of the garbage cart or of excrement buckets being emptied early in the morning are mainly a source of vexation. See *Ding Ling wenji*, pp. 576–586.

20. Ding Ling, "Tianjiachong"(Tian Family Village), in *Shui*, p. 56.

21. Ibid., pp. 82–83.

22. Ding Ling, "Wo de chuangzuo shenghuo," p. 25.

23. Literally, the "Fairyland of Peach Blossoms." Ding Ling, "Tianjiachong," pp. 75–76.

24. Ding Ling, "Wo de chuangzuo shenghuo," p. 25.

25. Ian Watt, *The Rise of the Novel, Studies in Defoe, Richardson, and Fielding* (London: Chatto and Windus, 1957), p. 26.

26. Ding Ling, "Fawang" (The Net of the Law), in *Yehui* (Night Meeting) (Shanghai, 1933), p. 47.

27. Jonathan Culler, *Structuralist Poetics*, pp. 159 and 193.

28. Harry Levin, "On the Dissemination of Realism," in his *Grounds for Comparison* (Cambridge, Mass.: Harvard University Press, 1972), p. 259.

29. Ding Ling, "Ben" (Flight), in *Yehui*, pp. 201, 199.

30. Ibid., pp. 201–202.

31. Ibid., p. 215.

32. Meir Sternberg, *Expositional Modes and Temporal Ordering in Fiction*, pp. 210–211, and p. 225.

33. Ding Ling, "Shui" (Flood), in *Shui*, pp. 5, 20, 31.

34. Bonnie S. McDougall, *The Introduction of Western Literary Theories into Modern China, 1919–1925* (Tokyo: The Centre of East Asian Cultural Studies, 1977), pp. 10, 82, *passim*.

35. "Zuola de zuopin ji qi yifan" (Zola's Works and Example), by Ba-bi-sai (Barbusse), translated into Chinese by Mu Mutian, *Beidou* (Big Dipper) 1.2 (1931): 89–96; a translation of a lecture given at a 1919 memorial gathering that is almost unreadable because of its stilted literariness.

36. Ding Ling, "Shui," pp. 29, 32.

37. Ibid., p. 55. C. T. Hsia has criticized this story on the grounds of credibility: famished people cannot shout and march this way. "Ding Ling has appar-

ently forgotten the all too apparent physiological reality of people under famine. This blindness to physical reality, and to psychological and social reality, constitutes the one fundamental weakness of Communist writers, though ideally there is no reason why they should be so unobservant"; see *A History of Modern Chinese Fiction*, 2nd ed., pp. 271–272. The same charge, interestingly enough, can also be leveled against Zola. In spite of his care to observe and document, descending into the mining pits, notebook in hand, for *Germinal*, the novel contains the unlikely episode of the two lovers, Catherine and Étienne, consummating their passion after being trapped in the flooded mine for eight days without food or drink. Yet this "wedding night in their tomb" is appropriate and even necessary for the theme of *Germinal*, which is that death contains the germ of new life. The myth of revolution is reinforced by the myth of resurrection. If we accept that scene, it will not be because it conforms to our notions of "physiological reality," but because the theme has been reiterated in many guises throughout the book, establishing what Sternberg calls the "internal universalization of the theme." Émile Zola, *Germinal* (Paris: Bibliothèque-Charpentier, 1950), II, 248.

38. (He) Danren, "Guanyu xin de xiaoshuo de dansheng—ping Ding Ling de 'Shui'" (Concerning the Birth of a New Fiction: A Criticism of Ding Ling's "Flood"), *Beidou* 2.1 (1932): 236.

39. Liu Shousong, *Zhongguo xinwenxue shi chugao* I, 358; I am quoting from the original version. A 1979 edition of this history, published ten years after its author's death and based on an unpublished revised version which circulated at Wuhan University, substantially retains the account of "Flood," but tones down the extravagant praise. Liu Shousong, *Zhongguo xinwenxue shi chugao* (Peking, 1979), I, 343–344.

40. I have discussed "Mouye" (A Certain Night) and "Cong yewan dao tianliang" (From Night till Daybreak) in an article, "The Changing Relationship Between Literature and Life: Aspects of the Writer's Role in Ding Ling," in *Modern Chinese Literature in the May Fourth Era*, ed. Merle Goldman, pp. 285–287.

41. Ding Ling, "Shiren Ya-luo-fu" (The Poet Alov), in *Yehui*, p. 88.

42. Ding Ling, "Mouye" (A Certain Night), in *Yehui*, p. 2.

43. Harold R. Isaacs discusses the five writers and the *nineteen* others, "always mentioned but never named," in his *Straw Sandals*, pp. xxvii, xli.

44. See Ding Ling's postscript to the story when it was first published in *Wenxue yuebao* (Literature Monthly) 1.1 (1932): 100.

45. Ding Ling, "Mouye," p. 4. I have benefited by consulting the English translation of the story by George A. Kennedy: "One Certain Night," in Harold R. Isaacs, ed., *Straw Sandals*, pp. 254–260.

46. In her *Battle Hymn of China*, Agnes Smedley records the account of a German pilot who saw a dozen Communists beheaded in Hankow as they sang the "Internationale" in "high shrill voices," p. 76.

47. Shen Congwen, *Ji Ding Ling xuji*, pp. 41–109. The account of Ding Ling's and Shen Congwen's visit to the prison (pp. 63–79) is probably one of the most affecting narratives in modern Chinese literature.

48. Ding Ling, "Cong yewan dao tianliang" (From Night till Daybreak) in *Shui* (Hong Kong, 1954), pp. 129–141.

49. "Yigeren de dansheng" (The Birth of a Person), in Ding Ling, *Yigeren de dansheng* (Shanghai, 1931), p. 127. Although published under her name in the collection, this is one of the stories not written by Ding Ling, but "borrowed"; "the name of this dead friend having become taboo now everywhere," p. 1. The other story, "Xisheng" (Sacrifice), was first published by Hu Yepin in *Xiaoshuo yuebao*.

50. Ding Ling, "Yige zhenshiren de yisheng — ji Hu Yepin," p. 19.

51. A connection that Tsi-an Hsia notes in his perceptive discussion of Hu Yepin as one of the Five Martyrs, but Hsia confuses the sexual identity of the aborted fetus, which was female, not male; whereas the child allowed to be born in the other story, and in real life, was of course male. See *The Gate of Darkness*, p. 178.

52. Ding Ling, preface to *Yigeren de dansheng*, in *Ding Ling xuanji*, ed. Ye and Xu, pp. 151–152.

53. Ibid., p. 151.

54. Ibid., pp. 153–154.

55. *Beidou* 2.1 (1932): 168.

56. Raymond Williams discusses the difference between "author" and "writer" in his *Marxism and Literature* (Oxford: Oxford University Press, 1977), p. 192. The English word "author" is closely associated with "authority"; the idea of the individual author is also a "characteristic form of bourgeois thought," p. 193.

57. Ding Ling, "Bianhou" (Editorial Afterword), *Beidou* 2.3 and 4 (1932): 555.

58. Qian Xingcun, "Yijiusanyinian wentan zhi huigu" (Looking Back on the Literary Scene of 1931), *Beidou* 2.1 (1932): 21.

59. Qu Qiubai, "Puluo dazhong wenyi de xianshi wenti" (Practical Problems of Proletarian Popular Literature and Art), in *Zhongguo xiandai wenxueshi cankao ziliao* (Research Materials on Modern Chinese Literary History), ed. Beijing shifan daxue zhongwenxi xiandai wenxue jiaoxue gaige xiaozu (Committee on the Revision of the Teaching of Modern Literature, Department of Chinese Literature, Peking Normal University) (Peking, 1959), I, 310.

60. Qian Xingcun, "Yijiusanyinian wentan zhi huigu," p. 22.

61. He Dabai, "Wenxue de dazhonghua yu dazhong wenxue" (The Popularization of Literature and Popular Literature), *Beidou* 2.3 and 4 (1932): 426.

62. Harold R. Isaacs, *Straw Sandals*, p. xx.

63. Ibid., p. xv. Guo Moruo died in 1978. The outpouring of eulogies and reminiscences in the Chinese press, mingled with attacks on the Gang of Four, strongly suggests that underlying the grief was the recognition that he had been one of the few survivors of modern literature's tragic history.

64. George Steiner, "Marxism and the Literary Critic," in *Language and Silence: Essays on Language, Literature, and the Inhuman* (New York: Atheneum, 1970), p. 323. See also "The Writer and Communism," p. 357. George Steiner is discussing the matter in terms of communism specifically, but the "sinister tribute" to literature is paid also at times by other autocratic systems.

65. Shen Congwen, *Ji Ding Ling xuji*, p. 24.

66. Ibid., p. 184. Mention of most of these activities was edited out of the book. Some are included in *Guowen zhoubao* (Guowen Weekly), in which the text had originally been serialized. Nevertheless, this passage is replete with "x's," each "x" representing one censored character. Some of the risky activities Ding Ling participated in are described in her "Guanyu zuolian de pianduan huiyi" (Fragmentary Reminiscences Concerning the League of Left-Wing Writers), *Xinwenxue shiliao* (Historical Materials of the New Literature) 1 (1980): 30–32.

67. Qian Qianwu, "Guanyu *Muqin*" (About *Mother*), in *Ding Ling pingzhuan*, pp. 128–130.

68. Ibid., p. 131.

69. Ding Ling, *Muqin* (Mother) (Hong Kong, 1973), p. 1.

70. Ibid., pp. 48–49.

71. Wang Shuming, "Muqin," in *Ding Ling pingzhuan*, p. 174.

72. Qian Qianwu, "Guanyu *Muqin*," in *Ding Ling pingzhuan*, pp. 130, 131–132.

73. Ding Ling, "Wo de chuangzuo shenghuo," p. 27.

74. Ding Ling said that in this novel she had consciously tried to use a Chinese technique, to write in the manner of *Hongloumeng* (Dream of the Red Chamber). Dong Xiao, "Zoufang Ding Ling" (Interview with Ding Ling), *Kaijuan* (Book Reviews Monthly) 2.5 (December 1979): 22.

75. Andrew H. Plaks, "Towards a Critical Theory of Chinese Narrative," in *Chinese Narrative: Critical and Theoretical Essays*, ed. A. Plaks (Princeton: Princeton University Press, 1977), p. 336.

76. Ding Ling, *Muqin*, pp. 112, 134.

77. "Bianzhe yan" (Word from the Editor), in *Muqin* (Shanghai, 1933), last page, unnumbered.

78. Qian Xingcun, "Guanyu *Muqin*" (About *Mother*), in *Ding Ling xuanji*, ed. Yao Pengzi, pp. 314–315. Except for this additional last paragraph, this article is identical with Quian Qianwu's "Guanyu *Muqin*" in *Ding Ling pingzhuan*.

79. Ding Ling, "Shafei riji dierbu" (Sophie's Diary, Part Two), in *Yiwaiji* (Unexpected Collection) (Shanghai, 1936), pp. 191–192.

80. Ibid., p. 201.

81. Ding Ling, "Shafei riji dierbu," p. 198.

82. See Zhao Jiabi, "Chongjian Ding Ling hua dangnian – 'Muqin' chubande qianqianhouhou" (Seeing Ding Ling Again and Talking About the Past: The Ins and Outs of the Publication of "Muqin"). *Wenhui zengkan* (Supplement to Wenhui) 4 (1980): 67.

83. Ding Ling, "Yitian" (One Day), *Shui*, p. 115. The story was first published in *Xiaoshuo yuebao* 22.9 (1931): 1133–1138. Subsequent references to this story appear in the text.

84. In the story, Lu Xiang is asked specifically for a report of his work (*gongzuo de baogao*), but the term could be translated as "correspondence," "bulletin," "newsletter," or "communication."

85. D. W. Fokkema and Elrud Kunne-Ibsch, *Theories of Literature in the Twentieth Century* (New York: St. Martin's Press, 1977), p. 111.

86. James Pinckney Harrison, *The Long March to Power: A History of the Chinese Communist Party, 1921–72* (New York: Praeger, 1972), p. 148.

87. Ibid., p. 219.

88. Henry James, "The Vessel of Consciousness," preface to *The Princess Casamassima*, in *The Future of the Novel: Essays on the Art of Fiction*, ed. Leon Edel (New York: Vintage, 1956), pp. 54–55. Hyacinth, the central character in James's novel, is another youth in the throes of initiation into political realities.

89. Guo Moruo, "Geming yu wenxue" (Revolution and Literature), in *Zhongguo xiandai wenxue shi cankao ziliao*, I, 214.

90. Zhu Jing, "Guanyu 'chuangzuo' " (On "Creative Writing"), *Beidou* 1.1 (1931): 75, 84.

91. Lu Xun, "Duiyu zuoyi zuojia lianmeng de yijian – sanyueerri zai zuoyi zuojia lianmeng chengli dahui jiang" (Opinions Concerning the League of Left-Wing Writers; speech given at the founding meeting of the League of Left-Wing Writers on March 2) in *Lu Xun zawen xuan*, I, 1918–1932 (Selected Essays of Lu Xun, I, 1918–1932), ed. Departments of Chinese Literature, Fudan University and Shanghai Normal University (Shanghai, 1973), I, 158, 159.

92. Shen Congwen, *Ji Ding Ling xuji*, p. 12. In a 1980 article Ding Ling condemns Shen Congwen's *Reminiscences of Ding Ling* as an "inferior piece of 'fiction'." She does so specifically to refute this and other statements by Shen concerning Hu Yepin's development as a revolutionary. Ding Ling, "Yepin yu geming" (Yepin and Revolution) in *Shikan* (Poetry Magazine), March 1980, pp. 30–31. Shen Congwen had his own political biases, which led to the break between himself and Ding Ling. Nevertheless at the time he wrote the book he felt deep concern over the fate of his friends, and his point about the then limited nature of their knowledge and experience remains valid.

3. Yanan and the Uses of Literature

1. Ding Ling, preface of *Yiwaiji* (Unexpected Collection) (Shanghai, 1936), p. 4.
2. Ibid., p. 2.
3. Ibid., p. 3.
4. Ibid., p. 4.
5. Ibid., p. 3.
6. Ding Ling, "Songzi" (Songzi), in *Yiwaiji*, p. 30.
7. Ding Ling, preface to *Yiwaiji*, p. 4.
8. Yanan is of course not just the name of a city, but represents "the military, political, social, and economic experiments" that collectively made up the historical experience of the Chinese Communist Party during the period when Yanan was its headquarters, starting in January 1937. This experience becomes the ideal, model, or principle for the subsequent history of the revolution. See, for example, Mark Selden, *The Yenan Way in Revolutionary China* (Cambridge, Mass.: Harvard University Press, 1971), p. vii.
9. James Pinckney Harrison, *The Long March to Power*, p. 270.
10. Ji Feng, "Ding Ling de fuqi shenghuo" (The Conjugal Life of Ding Ling), in *Yanan de nüxing* (The Women of Yanan) (n.p., n.d.), p. 14. See also Zhao Chaogou, *Yanan yiyue* (A Month in Yanan) (Nanking, 1946), p. 135.
11. Ding Ling, "Zuihou yiye" (The Last Page), in *Yike wei chu tang de qiangdan* (A Bullet Not Yet Fired from Its Barrel) (Chungking, 1939), p. 88.
12. Zhao Chaogou, *Yanan yiyue*, p. 129.
13. Ding Ling, "Xuyan" (Preface), in *Suqu de wenyi* (Literature and Art in the Soviet Areas) (Shanghai, 1938), p. 2; first published in *Jiefang zhoukan* (Liberation Weekly) 1.3 (May 11, 1937) as "Wenyi zai Suqu."
14. Ibid., p. 3.
15. Ren Tianma, "Jiti chuangzuo he Ding Ling" (Collective Writing and Ding Ling), in *Ding Ling zai xibei* (Ding Ling in the Northwest), ed. (Shi) Tianxing (Hankow, 1938), p. 10.
16. Dick Wilson, *The Long March, 1935: The Epic of Chinese Communism's Survival* (London: Hamish Hamilton, 1971), p. 284.
17. Zhao Chaogou, *Yanan yiyue*, p. 137. Actually, writing was quite well paid in Yanan. "The monthly salary of the highest leader was ten dollars (*yuan*) a month, but the pay for writing was extremely high: 50 cents (*mao*) for a thousand words. Last month Ding Ling wrote 7,000 words and received three dollars and fifty cents." Ren Tianma, "Jiti chuangzuo he Ding Ling," p. 11.
18. There is a tendency in Merle Goldman's excellent book *Literary Dissent in Communist China*, to whose clear and conscientious account we are all deeply indebted, to emphasize the sheer oppositional nature of the conflicts between dissenting writers and the Communist Party. This emphasis at times obscures the fact

of broad areas of agreement or overlap between the two sides.

19. Qu Qiubai, leader of the League of Left-Wing Writers in the early 1930s, expressed in greater detail "many essential features of Mao's remarks in 1942." See Paul G. Pickowicz, "Ch'u Ch'iu-pai and the Chinese Marxist Conception of Revolutionary Popular Literature and Art," *China Quarterly* 70 (1977): 296–314.

20. Ding Ling's comments on the topic "Chuangzuo buzhen zhi yuanyin ji qi chulu" (Reasons and Solutions for the Depressed State of Creative Writing), *Beidou* 2.1 (1932): 168.

21. Gunther Stein, *The Challenge of Red China*, p. 256; Chen Binyin, *Ding Ling zhuan* (Biography of Ding Ling) (Shanghai, 1938), p. 96; Ding Ling, *Yike wei chu tang de qiangdan*, p. 88.

22. Ding Ling, *Yike wei chu tang de qiangdan*, pp. 87–88.

23. Ding Ling, *Yinian* (One Year) (Chungking, 1939), preface.

24. Ibid., pp. 2–3.

25. Ibid., pp. 6–7.

26. Ibid., p. 11. When the Service Corps was established the news was announced and its program included in the first issue of *Zhandi* (Battleground), a supplement published by the group in *Xin zhonghua bao* (New China), the official newspaper of the Soviet government in Yanan. There are several discrepancies between the program outlined there and the one given in *Yinian*. Most noteworthy is the omission in Ding Ling's book of the special goals of the Corps: the need to improve the livelihood of the people, and the struggle for democratic rights; for the freedom to assemble, publish, and organize in order to arm against Japan. This was the time of the United Front and it appeared advisable to play down the dimension of social reform in both the program of the Service Corps and the policy of the Communist Party in a book that was to be published and circulated in Kuomintang-controlled areas as well. Despite the social goals included in the *Zhandi* announcement, the main focus of the Corps's activities was mobilization for the war against Japan. See "Bentuan xingdong gangling" (Our Corps's Program of Action), *Zhandi* 1 in *Xin zhonghua bao*, August 19, 1937, p. 4.

27. Agnes Smedley, *China Fights Back: An American Woman with the Eighth Route Army* (New York: Vanguard Press, 1938), p. 143.

28. "Xibei zhandi fuwutuan chuwai shiyuelai zhi gongzuo baogao" (A Report on the Work of the Northwest Front Service Corps During its Past Ten Months on the Road) in Xibei zhandi fuwutuan jiti chuangzuo (Collectively Authored by the Northwest Front Service Corps), *Xixian shenghuo* (Life at the Western Front), (Chungking, 1939), pp. 223–226.

29. Ding Ling, *Yinian*, pp. 115–116.

30. Ibid., pp. 113, 114.

31. Ibid., pp. 50–51.

32. Ibid., pp. 18–19, 20.

33. Mao Dun, "Wenyi dazhonghua wenti" (The Problem of the Popularization of Literature and Art), in *Zhongguo xiandai wenxueshi cankao ziliao*, vol. I, part 2, p. 761.

34. Luo Sun, "Kangzhan wenyi yundong niaokan" (A Bird's Eye View of the Literature and Art Movement of the War of Resistance), in ibid., p. 654.

35. Ibid., p. 653.

36. Zhou Yang, "Kangzhan shiqi de wenxue" (Literature during the Period of the War of Resistance), in ibid., p. 643.

37. Ding Ling, *Yinian*, p. 112.

38. For a historical account of Ding Ling's experiences during the rectification campaign, see Merle Goldman, *Literary Dissent in Communist China*, pp. 18–50. The pressure to accentuate the positive can be seen in a note Ding Ling appended to her description of an incident in *One Year*. It was written in response to criticism that the guerilla troops do not come off well in her account. In her defense she argues that 1) the troop was newly formed; 2) it was made up of students and old-style officers; 3) it was in the early days of the war; and 4) "guerilla troops are good, but inevitably at times there may be something bad." See "Jicun zhi ye" (The Night at Ji Village), *Yinian*, p. 63.

39. Mao Zedong, "Zai Yanan wenyi zuotanhuishang de jianghua" (Talks at the Yanan Forum on Literature and Art), *Jiefang ribao*, October 19, 1943, p. 1. This was the seventh anniversary of Lu Xun's death. Thus, Mao's "Yanan Talks" were not published until well over a year after they were delivered at the Forum. All versions of the "Yanan Talks" published after 1953 are based on a revised text that differs in several respects from the original. An official English translation of the post–1953 text was published in 1965. Textual variants are listed in *Mō Taku-tō shū* (Collected Writings of Mao Tse-tung), compiled by Takeuchi Minoru (Tokyo: Hokubōsha, 1971), viii, 111–148. For a detailed discussion of the various editions of the "Yanan Talks," a comparison between the 1943 text and the official 1953 text and translation, and a complete translation of the original version, see Bonnie S. McDougall, "Mao Zedong's 'Talks at the Yan'an Conference on Literature and Art': A Translation of the 1943 Text with Commentary," *Michigan Papers in Chinese Studies*, no. 39 (Ann Arbor, Mich.: Center for Chinese Studies, The University of Michigan, 1980).

40. In a September 1978 interview, Zhou Yang singles out the "bright versus dark side" issue as the outstanding one. "There were two factions in Yanan then. One was represented by 'Luyi' [Lu Xun Art Academy] . . . of which I of course was leader. The other was represented by 'Wenkang' [All China Literature and Art Circles Resist Enemy Federation] with Ding Ling as leader. We of the 'Luyi' faction advocated praising brightness (*gesong guangming*) . . . but the 'Wenkang' faction wanted to expose darkness." See Zhao Haosheng, "Zhou Yang xiaotan lishi gongguo" (Zhou Yang Jokingly Talks about [his] Merits and Faults in History), *Qishi niandai* (The Seventies) 104 (September 1978): 31–32. That the two factions in Yanan were so clearly divided between those "praising brightness" and those "exposing darkness" is not, however, the view of the opposing group. In conversations I had with Ding Ling she repeated that everyone was committed to the "bright side", and furthermore that there was no such thing as a "Wenkang" faction, much less one headed by her. The "bright versus dark side" controversy is therefore in her opinion more a consequence of the evils of "factionalism" perpetrated by the Zhou Yang group than a matter of different approaches to literature. It is indeed true that Ding Ling (and the other writers who were similarly attacked at the time) took a supportive and positive stance toward the party's revolutionary and war policies in Yanan. What caused trouble was her belief that within the overall framework of positive support there should also be room for criticism.

41. Ding Ling, "Fengci" (Satire), in *Yinian*, pp. 136–137.

42. Ding Ling, "Women xuyao zawen" (We Need *zawen*), *Jiefang ribao*, October 23, 1941, p. 4.

43. Ding Ling, "Sanbajie you gan" (Thoughts on March 8), *Jiefang ribao*, March 9, 1942, p. 4. A translation of this article is included in Gregor Benton, "The Yenan Literary Opposition," *New Left Review* 92 (July–August 1975): 93–106.

44. Ding Ling, "Wenyijie dui Wang Shiwei yingyou de taidu ji fanxing" (The Attitude and Self-Introspection That the Literary Circles Should Take toward Wang Shiwei), *Jiefang ribao*, June 16, 1942, p. 4.

45. Ding Ling, "Bianzhe de hua" (Words from the Editor), *Jiefang ribao*, March 12, 1942, p. 4. When the term *zawen* is used later to refer to a category of writings, the connotations of "criticism" have been shed. She refers to her book *Kuadao xin de shidai lai* (Stride into the New Era) as a collection of *zawen*. See "Houji" (Afterwords), p. 265.

46. My translation of a sentence omitted from the post-1953 version of the "Yanan Talks" but included in their first publication in *Jiefang ribao*, October 19, 1943, p. 1. The rest of the quotation is from Mao Zedong, "Talks at the Yenan Forum on Literature and Art" (official English translation), in *Selected Readings from the Works of Mao Tse-tung* (Peking, 1971), pp. 278–279.

47. Ding Ling, "Guanyu lichang wenti wojian" (My Views Concerning the Question of Standpoint), in *Kuadao xin de shidai lai*, pp. 46–47. She included the essay for publication in 1951 but wrote that in looking back she felt it to be "in several respects unsatisfactory, not thorough, and incomplete." See "Houji" (Afterwords), p. 265.

48. Zhou Yang, "Wang Shiwei de wenyiguan yu women de wenyiguan" (Wang Shiwei's Concept of Literature and Art and Our Concept of Literature and Art), in *Zhongguo xiandai wenxueshi cankao ziliao*, II, 209 and 210.

49. Ibid.

50. Jonathan Culler, *Structuralist Poetics*, p. 230.

51. W. J. Harvey, "The Retreat from Character," in *Character and the Novel* (Ithaca: Cornell University Press, 1968), pp. 191–205.

52. Donald J. Munro, *The Concept of Man in Contemporary China* (Ann Arbor: The University of Michigan Press, 1977), p. 138.

53. Such a tendency may appear in some respects to be a reversion to the practice of character portrayal in premodern Chinese fiction and drama. It would not be the only way in which Maoist notions about literature and art represent a continuity with tradition.

54. Ding Ling, "Yike wei chu tang de qiangdan" in *Yike wei chu tang de qiangdan*, pp. 40, 41. Almost twenty years later Ding Ling retold this as a children's story, giving the name of the boy as Xiao Sen, "now over thirty, and a cadre in the People's Liberation Army." *Yige xiaohongjun de gushi* (The Story of a Little Red Soldier) (Shanghai, 1956), p. 1.

55. Ding Ling, "Xin de xinnian" (New Faith), in *Wo zai Xiacun de shihou* (When I Was in Xia Village) (Peking, 1951), pp. 117–148.

56. Ding Ling, "Ye" (Night), in *Wo zai Xiacun de shihou*, p. 6.

57. Ibid., p. 10.

58. Ding Ling, "Zai yiyuan zhong" (In the Hospital), p. 16. Originally published in the Yanan journal *Guyu* (Grain Rain) 1 (1941): 1–7, 18, as "Zai yiyuan zhong shi" (When in the Hospital). It was revised and published in *Wenyi zhendi* (Literary Base) 7.1 (1942). This version was copied and printed in *Wenyi bao* (Literary Gazette) 2 (1958): 11–16.

59. Ibid., pp. 11–12.

60. Ibid., p. 14.

61. Liao Ying, "Ren zai jianku zhong shengzhang—ping Ding Ling tongzhi de 'zai yiyuan zhong shi'" (It is through Hardship That One Grows—A Criticism of Comrade Ding Ling's "When in the Hospital"), *Jiefang ribao*, June 10, 1942, p. 4.

62. Ding Ling, "Jiao hou ji suo gan" (Thoughts after Proofreading), in *Shaanbei fengguang* (Scenes of Northern Shaanxi) (Peking, 1951), p. 91.

63. Ibid., p. 92.

64. Liu Shousong, *Zhongguo xinwenxue shi chugao*, II, 193. This comment as well as all mention of Ding Ling's collection of reportage pieces are omitted from the revised editions of Liu's history published in 1979. Such high praise for someone who had been condemned in 1957 as a rightist would have been inappropriate. It would have been even more awkward to recall Mao Zedong's enthusiastic recommendation of Ding Ling's piece on Tian Baolin.

65. Donald J. Munro, *The Concept of Man in Contemporary China*, p. 156: "Chinese analyses of human motivation often ignore the fact that people's motives are complex and varied."

66. Ding Ling, "Yuan Guangfa" (Yuan Guangfa), in *Shaanbei fengguang*, p. 35.

67. Ibid., p. 34.

68. Ding Ling, "Tian Baolin" (Tian Baolin), in *Shaanbei fengguang*, p. 62.

69. See Wayne C. Booth, *The Rhetoric of Fiction* (Chicago: University of Chicago Press, 1961), pp. 70–76, for a discussion of the important critical concept of "the implied author."

70. Ding Ling, "Wo zai Xiacun de shihou," in *Wo zai Xiacun de shihou*, pp. 13–41. This edition and others printed after 1950 include several additional sentences spoken by Zhenzhen, about the importance of her work and her satisfaction over Japanese defeats because of what she did. The story was first published in the Yanan journal *Zhongguo wenhua* (Chinese Culture) 3.1 (June 1941): 24–31. Early versions of the story can also be found in the more accessible *Beifang wenhua* (Northern Culture) 1.1 (March 1946): 44, 49–56; and in *Ding Ling wenji* (Works of Ding Ling) (Shanghai, 1949), pp. 143–160.

71. I haved discussed the issue of feminism in Ding Ling's work elsewhere: see Yi-tsi M. Feuerwerker, "The Changing Relationship Between Literature and Life: Aspects of the Writer's Role in Ding Ling," in *Modern Chinese Literature in the May Fourth Era*, ed. Merle Goldman, particularly pp. 295–300; and "Ting Ling's 'When I was in Sha Chuan (Cloud Village),'" *Signs: Journal of Women in Culture and Society* 2.1 (Autumn 1976): 255–279.

72. Wang Liaoying, "Kangzhan shiqi Ding Ling xiaoshuo de sixiang qingxiang" (The Trend of Thought in Ding Ling's Wartime Stories), *Wenxue pinglun* (Literary Criticism) 4 (October 1957): 107.

73. Hua Fu, "Ding Ling de 'fuchou de nüshen'—ping 'wo zai Xiacun de shihou'" (The "Vengeful Goddess" of Ding Ling: A Criticism of "When I Was in Xia Village"), *Wenyi bao* 3 (1958): 22–25.

74. Yao Wenyuan, "Shafei nüshimende ziyou wangguo . . ." p. 212.

75. Dong Xiao, "Zoufang Ding Ling," p. 25. When repeating this information to me, Ding Ling added that she had written about one-third of the story in the third person; then seeing that it was not working out, started over again with a first-person narrator.

76. Ding Ling, "Minjian yiren Li Bu" (The People's Artist Li Bu), in *Shaanbei fengguang*. Subsequent references to this edition appear in the text. The piece was first published in *Jiefang ribao*, October 30, 1944, p. 4, ten days after it was written. In its first published form, years are indicated by the Republican calendar; that is, the fourteenth year of *Minguo* instead of 1925.

77. Ding Ling, "Jiao hou ji suo gan," in *Shannbei fengguang*, p. 91.

78. Ibid., p. 91.

79. Tzvetan Todorov, "An Introduction to Verisimilitude," in his *The Poetics of Prose*, tr. Richard Howard (Ithaca: Cornell University Press, 1977), p. 82.

80. Ibid., p. 83.

81. Jonathan Raban, *The Technique of Modern Fiction: Essays in Practical Criticism* (South Bend, Ind.: University of Notre Dame Press, 1969), p. 36.

82. Ding Ling, "Mengke," in *Zai heianzhong*, pp. 41–42.

83. Ding Ling, "Jiao hou ji suo gan," p. 92.

84. Gao Kelin, "Lu Zhongcai changzhengji" (The Long March of Lu Zhongcai), *Jiefang ribao*, September 14, 1941, p. 2.

85. Mao Zedong, "Zai Yanan wenyi zuotanhui shang de jianghua," *Mō Taku-tō shū*, VIII, 128–129.

86. Ding Ling, "Xu 'Cheng zai dafengsha li benzou de gangweimen'" (Preface to The Sentries Who Run about in the Great Wind and Sand,') in *Yinian*, p. 106.

87. According to a note to the story, the term *xinwenji* is used by soldiers at the front to refer to general cultural types (*yiban wenhuaren*) or literary writers (*wenren*) who come and visit but have no specific work.

88. Ding Ling, "Ruwu" (Enlistment), in *Wo zai Xiacun de shihou*, p. 51.

89. Ma Jianling, "Wo duiyu difangju de kanfa" (My View of Regional Theatre), quoted in Wang Yao, *Zhongguo xinwenxue shigao* (Draft History of Modern Chinese Literature) (Hong Kong, 1972), II, 380–381.

90. Ding Ling, "Lüetan gailiang pingju" (A Brief Discussion on Reforming Peking Opera), in *Yinian*, pp. 166–167.

91. Ding Ling, "Shenghuo, sixiang yu renwu," p. 123.

4. *The Sun Shines on the Sanggan River*

1. Ding Ling, "Women yongyuan zai yiqi" (We Shall Always Be Together), in *Kuadao xinde shidai lai*, p. 154. Between the short Yanan works and *The Sun Shines on the Sanggan River*, Ding Ling was co-author with Chen Ming and Lu Fei of a play, *Yaogong* (Tile Workers), dated March 1946 (Peking, 1949). She also wrote, in the space of three days, in July 1944, *Yierjiushi yu jinjiluyu bianqu* (The 129th Division and the Shaanxi, Hebei, Shandong, Henan Border Regions), which "should be seen as a true record (*shilu*) not as a piece of literary or artistic reportage or a piece of literary prose." (Peking, 1950), p. 5.

2. Fredric Jameson, *The Prison–House of Language: A Critical Account of Structuralism and Russian Formalism* (Princeton: Princeton University Press, 1972), p. 73.

3. Ibid., p. 74.

4. L. M. O'Toole, "Analytic and Synthetic Approaches to Narrative Structure: Sherlock Holmes and 'The Sussex Vampire,'" in *Style and Structure in Literature*, p. 151.

5. Claudio Guillen, "Toward a Definition of the Picaresque," in *Actes du IIIᵉ Congrès de l'Association Internationale de Litterature Comparée* (The Hague, 1962), p. 262. A revised form of this essay is included in his *Literature as System: Essays Toward a Theory of Literary History* (Princeton: Princeton University Press, 1971).

6. Ding Ling, *Taiyang zhao zai Sangganheshang* (The Sun Shines on the Sanggan River) (Peking, 1955), p. 176. Subsequent references to this edition appear in the text. I have benefited from consulting the English translation of the novel, *The Sun Shines over the Sanggan River*, tr. by Yang Hsien-yi and Gladys Yang (Peking, 1954).

7. O. E. Brim, Jr., "Personality Development as Role-Learning," quoted in Martin Price, "The Other Self: Thoughts about Character in the Novel," in *So-*

ciology of Literature and Drama, ed. Elizabeth and Tom Burns (London: Penguin, 1973), p. 263.

8. William Hinton, *Fanshen: A Documentary of Revolution in a Chinese Village* (New York: Monthly Review Press, 1966), p. vii.

9. Feng Xuefeng, " 'Taiyang zhao zai Sangganheshang' zai women wenxue fazhanshang de yiyi" (The Significance of *The Sun Shines on the Sanggan River* in the Development of Our Literature), appendix to the 1955 edition of the novel used here, p. 6. In 1949 Ding Ling said in an interview that when she took part in land reform at Zhuolu, she paid particular attention to the people: "whenever I had time I would go and talk to them, to understand their character, situation, psychology, but what should be even more emphasized is their ideological change (*sixiang bianhua*) during this great movement, the psychological change (*xinli bianhua*) as they carried each policy." Fu Dong, *Ding Ling fangwenji* (Visit with Ding Ling) in *Quanguo wenxue yishu gongzuozhe daibiao da hui jinian wenji* (Volume Commemorating the Representative Congress of All–China's Literature and Art Workers) (Peking, 1950), p. 527.

10. Robert Scholes and Robert Kellogg, *The Nature of Narrative,* p. 168.

11. Others suffered the death penalty, as for example Han Laoliu in Zhou Libo's *Baofengzhouyu* (Hurricane) (Peking, 1977, first published in 1948). Zhou Libo "justifies" the lynching of Han by having him commit acts of unspeakable violence in the novel, whereas the crimes of Ding Ling's landlord–tyrant in *Sanggan River* are milder and subtler. Nevertheless, Ding Ling was not insensitive to the moral problems that such a killing would have created. Throughout the novel there are reports of landlords being lynched in neighboring villages. But Zhang Pin, the District Propaganda Head, who arrives toward the end of the novel to tie all the loose ends, specifically asks the local cadres to save the landlord from being beaten to death (p. 256). During the confrontation scene, the moral and physical courage of Zhang Yumin, the local party secretary, is tested when he places himself bodily between the aroused mob and its target to protect Qian Wengui. Still, the question of whether revenge justifies the taking of lives without legal procedure has not been answered. By sparing Qian Wengui but not others in surrounding villages, Ding Ling has to some extent evaded the issue.

12. Eudora Welty, "Place in Fiction," *The South Atlantic Quarterly* LV.1 (January 1956): 57.

13. Suzanne Pepper, *Civil War in China: The Political Struggle, 1945–1949* (Berkeley: University of California Press, 1978), p. 235.

14. Ding Ling said that she began her novel with Gu Yong because she felt that the problem of the prosperous middle peasant was one that had not been solved in her experience of land-reform work. She cited the case of a peasant classified as rich, but who turned out to be wearing unmatched shoes and a belt made of rags. As a result of life-long labor, his back was so bent that he could no longer stand up straight. To the other peasants it seemed excessive (*guofen*) that his land should have been taken away from him. "Shenghuo, sixiang, yu renwu," p. 123.

A translation of *Sanggan River* was published serially in the Soviet magazine *Znamya* (Banner) in 1949. When Ding Ling passed through Moscow that year she visited the magazine's editorial department and was asked whether Gu Yong was a rich peasant or a middle peasant and questioned about her handling of the character. Her answer was that at the time she did not think it was right to classify such people as rich peasants and treat them the way landlords were treated, but the category of "well-to-do middle peasant" was not added by the party until a year later. She had then revised some wording in the book but agreed that she had not adequately dealt with the problem. See *Ouxing sanji* (Random Notes on Travels in Europe) (Peking, 1952), pp. 86–87.

15. Roland Barthes, *S / Z, an Essay*, p. 17.

16. Jurij Lotman, *The Structure of the Artistic Text*, tr. by Donald Vroon (Ann Arbor: The University of Michigan Press, 1977), p. 234.

17. Suzanne Pepper, *Civil War in China*, p. 277.

18. The chapter on land reform (pp. 229–330) in Suzanne Pepper's *Civil War in China* summarizes several party directives and reports that reveal some of the shifts, deviations, and excesses found in several regions during different phases of the movement.

19. Ding Ling, "Yidian jingyan" (A Bit of Experience), in *Zuojia tan chuang-zuo* (Writers Talk about Writing) (Peking, 1955), p. 4.

20. Ibid., p. 4.

21. Ding Ling, "Xie zai qianbian" (Preface), *Taiyang zhao zai Sanggan-heshang*, p. 1.

22. Wang Liaoying, "Taiyang zhao zai Sangganheshang' jiujing shi shenme yang de zuopin" (What Kind of Work is *The Sun Shines on the Sanggan River*?) *Wenxue pinglun* 1 (1959): 72.

23. She describes the effect of a *yangge* drama with the antisuperstition message that medical doctors should be consulted instead of shamans (*wushen*) when children are sick. At the death of a child on the stage (due to the evils of shamanism), several women, whose children had died in similar circumstances, broke into sobs and had to leave the theater. Ding Ling, "Ji zhuanyaowan luoma dahui" (Livestock Fair at Zhuanyaowan), in *Shaanbei fengguang*, pp. 56–58. William Hinton gives an account of emotional audience reaction to a modern opera, *Red Leaf River*, in *Fanshen*, pp. 314–316.

24. Andrew H. Plaks, "Towards a Critical Theory of Chinese Narrative," pp. 312–313. The affinities between history and fiction are discussed by Frank Kermode in "An Approach through History," in *Towards a Poetics of Fiction*, ed. Mark Spilka (Bloomington, Ind.: Indiana University Press, 1977), pp. 23–30. Some "plausible view of the world" is necessary to history as well as fiction. The texts of the historian and the novelist can achieve coherence and *followability* only if there is some "organizing scheme," some "typological basis." His idea that "the novel ought also to be considered a branch of a wider subject," involving history among other things, would be supported by the Chinese tradition.

25. Liu Shousong, *Zhongguo xinwenxue shi chugao*, II, 252.

26. D. C. Twitchett, "Chinese Biographical Writing," in *Historians of China and Japan*, ed. W. G. Beasley and E. G. Pulleyblank (London: Oxford University Press, 1961), pp. 95–114.

27. Ding Ling, "Yidian jingyan," p. 4. *Sanggan River* was to have been the first part of a trilogy but Ding Ling dropped plans for parts II and III. In 1956 she published one part of a projected sequel to the novel, "Zai yanhan de rizili" (During the Coldest Days), *Renmin wenxue* 10 (1956): 60–82. Before long the anti-rightist campaign began and she went into exile. The rest of the manuscript was lost when her home was raided during the Cultural Revolution. She began the sequel again and after her rehabilitation published twenty-four chapters in 1979. As she explains in her prologue, the story begins after the conclusion of land reform in the village when the People's Liberation Army is forced to withdraw because of attacks from the Kuomintang. The name of the village has been changed and there is a different cast of characters. See "Zai yanhan de rizili", *Qingming* 1 (1979): 4–92.

28. Martin Price, "The Other Self: Thoughts about Character in the Novel," p. 268.

29. Shuen-fu Lin, "Ritual and Narrative Structure in *Ju-lin wai-shih*," in *Chinese Narrative*, ed. Andrew H. Plaks, p. 251.

30. The dilemma posed by these contradictory propositions and their implications for realism and the hero in literature are discussed in Rufus W. Mathewson, Jr., *The Positive Hero in Russian Literature*, 2nd ed. (Stanford: Stanford University Press, 1975), pp. 115–135.

31. Jonathan Culler, *Structuralist Poetics*, p. 192.

32. Liu Shousong, *Zhongguo xinwenxue shi chugao* (1957), II, 248.

Conclusion

1. Ding Ling, "Dao qunzhongzhong qu luohu" (Go Make Your Dwelling among the Masses), in *Dao qunzhongzhong qu luohu*, p. 95.

2. Ibid., p. 101.

3. Ibid., p. 102.

4. Ibid., pp. 102–103.

5. Merle Goldman, *Literary Dissent in Communist China*, pp. 106–113.

6. An instance of Ding Ling's arrogance brought up during the antirightist drive was that her picture hung in the classroom of the Central Literary Institute alongside Tolstoy's. Sun Xiaoping, "Ding Ling guanxin guo qingnian zuozhe ma?" (Has Ding Ling Ever Been Concerned with Young Writers?) *Mengya* (Sprouts) 20 (October 1957): 6.

7. Some recent essays can be found in two collections that include mostly pieces written before 1956: *Ding Ling sanwen ji* (Collected Essays by Ding Ling) (Peking, 1980) and *Shenghuo chuangzuo xiuyang* (Life, Creative Writing, and Discipline) (Peking, 1981). Other essays written after 1979 are collected in *Ding Ling jinzuo* (Recent Writings of Ding Ling) (Chengdu, 1980) (there is considerable overlapping of material in the three books) and in *Shenghuo chuangzuo shidai linghun* (Life, Creative Writing, and the Spirit of the Times) (Changsha, 1981).

WORKS CITED

Chinese characters are written in either regular or simplified form, depending on the original source.

Works by Ding Ling 丁玲

"Amao guniang" 阿毛姑娘 (Miss Amao). *Zai heianzhong*, pp. 203–270.

"Bayue shenghuo" 八月生活 (Eight Months). *Yiwaiji*, pp. 105–124.

"Ben" 奔 (Flight). *Yehui*, pp. 189–215.

"Bianhou" 編後 (Editorial Afterword). *Beidou* 北斗 (Big Dipper) 2.3–4 (1932): 555–556.

"Bianzhe de hua" 編者的話 (Words from the Editor). *Jiefang ribao* 解放日報 (Liberation Daily), March 12, 1942, p. 4.

"Chen Boxiang" 陳伯祥 (Chen Boxiang). *Yiwaiji*, pp. 89–102.

"Chuangzuo buzhen zhi yuanyin ji qi chulu" 創作不振之原因及其出路 (Reasons and Solutions for the Depressed State of Creative Writing). *Beidou* 2.1 (1932): 167–168.

"Cong yewan dao tianliang" 從夜晚到天亮 (From Night till Daybreak). *Shui*, pp. 129–141. First published in *Weiyin* 微音 (Subtle Sounds) 1.3 (May 1931): 17–28. Written under the name Binzhi 彬芷

Dao qunzhongzhong qu luohu 到羣衆中去落戶 (Go Make Your Dwelling among the Masses). Peking, 1954.

"Dao qunzhongzhong qu luohu." *Dao qunzhongzhong qu luohu*, pp. 88–103.

Ding Ling duanpian xiaoshuoxuan 丁玲短篇小說选 (Selected Short Stories by Ding Ling). 2 Vols. Peking, 1981.

Ding Ling jinzuo 丁玲近作 (Recent Writings of Ding Ling). Chengdu, 1980.

Ding Ling sanwen ji 丁玲散文集 (Collected Essays by Ding Ling). Peking, 1980.

Ding Ling wenji 丁玲文集 (Collected Works of Ding Ling). 2 vols. Shanghai, 1936; reprinted in Hong Kong, 1972.

Ding Ling xuanji 丁玲選集 (Selected Works of Ding Ling). Edited by Xu Chensi 徐況泗 and Ye Wangyou 葉忘憂. Shanghai, preface dated 1936.

"Du Wanxiang" 杜晚香 (Du Wanxiang). *Renmin wenxue* 人民文学 (People's Literature) 7 (1979): 45–58.

"Duo shi zhi qiu" 多事之秋 (Troubled Times). *Beidou* 2.1 (1932): 25–37; 2.3–4 (1932): 516–529. Written under the name Binzhi 彬芷.

"Fawang" 法網 (The Net of the Law). *Yehui*, pp. 12–71.

"Fengci" 諷刺 (Satire). *Yinian*, pp. 136–137.

"Guanyu lichang wenti wojian" 關於立場問題我見 (My Views Concerning the Question of Standpoint). *Kuadao xin de shidai lai*, pp. 45–52.

"Guanyu zuolian de pianduan huiyi" 关于左联的片断回忆 (Fragmentary Reminiscences Concerning the League of Left-Wing Writers). *Xinwenxue shiliao* 新文学史料 (Historical Materials of the New Literature) 1 (1980): 29–32.

"Guonian" 過年 (New Year's). *Ding Ling wenji*, pp. 500–520.

"Houji" 後記 (Afterwords). *Kuadao xin de shidai lai*, pp. 265–266.

"Ji Zhuanyaowan luoma dahui" 記碻窰灣騾馬大會 (Livestock Fair at Zhuanyaowan). *Shaanbei fengguang*, pp. 47–58.

"Jiao hou ji suo gan" 校後記所感 (Thoughts after Proofreading). *Shaanbei fengguang*, pp. 89–94.

"Jicun zhi ye" 冀村之夜 (The Night at Ji Village). *Yinian*, pp. 53–63.

Kuadao xin de shidai lai 跨到新的時代來 (Stride into the New Era). Peking, 1953.

"Lüetan gailiang pingju" 略談改良平劇 (A Brief Discussion on Reforming Peking Opera). *Yinian*, pp. 166–177.

"Mengke" 夢珂 (Mengke) in *Zai heianzhong*, pp. 1–71.

"Minjian yiren Li Bu" 民間藝人李卜 (The People's Artist Li Bu). *Shaanbei fengguang*, pp. 36–46.

"Mouye" 某夜 (A Certain Night). *Yehui*, pp. 1–11.

Muqin 母親 (Mother). Hong Kong, 1973.

"Nianqian de yitian" 年前的一天 (The Day before New Year's). *Shui*, where the title is given as "Nianqian de yinian" 年前的一年 (The Year before New Year's), pp. 142–157.

" 'Niupeng' xiaopin (san zhang)" '牛棚' 小品 (三章) (Three "Cowshed" Sketches). *Shiyue* 十月 (October) 3 (1979): 196–202.

Ouxing sanji 歐行散記 (Random Notes on Travels in Europe). Peking, 1952.

"Qian laile ke de yueye" 潛來了客的月夜 (A Secret Visitor on a Moonlit Night). *Ding Ling wenji*, pp. 488–499.

"Qingyunli zhong de yijian xiaofangli" 慶雲里中的一間小房裏 (A Small Room in Qingyun Lane). *Ding Ling wenji*, pp. 153–164.

"Ri" 日 (Day). *Ding Ling wenji*, pp. 576–586.

"Ruwu" 入伍 (Enlistment). *Wo zai Xiacun de shihou*, pp. 43–71.

"Sanbajie you gan" 三八節有感 (Thoughts on March 8). *Jiefang ribao*, March 9, 1942, p. 4.

"Sanri zaji" 三日雜記 (Miscellaneous Notes of Three Days). *Shaanbei fengguang*, pp. 1–23.

Shaanbei fengguang 陝北風光 (Scenes of Northern Shaanxi). Peking, 1951.

"Shafei nüshi de riji" 莎菲女士的日記 (The Diary of Miss Sophie). *Xiaoshuo yuebao* 小説月報 (Fiction Monthyl) 19.2 (1928): 202–223.

"Shafei riji dierbu" 莎菲日記第二部 (Sophie's Diary, Part Two). *Yiwaiji*, pp. 191–202.

Shenghuo, chuangzuo, shidai linghun 生活，創作，时代灵魂 (Life, Creative Writing, and the Spirit of the Times). Changsha, 1981.

Shenghuo, chuangzuo, xiuyang 生活，創作，修养 (Life, Creative Writing, and Discipline). Peking, 1981.

"Shenghuo, sixiang yu renwu" 生活，思想與人物 (Life, Thought, and Characters). *Renmin wenxue* 3 (1955): 120–128.

"Shibage" 十八個 (The Eighteen). *Shaanbei fengguang*, pp. 81–88.

"Shiren Ya-luo-fu" 詩人亜洛夫 (The Poet Alov). *Yehui*, pp. 86–109.

Shui 水 (Flood). Hong Kong, 1954.

"Shui" (Flood). *Shui*, pp. 1–55.

"Shujia zhong" 暑假中 (Summer Vacation). *Zai heianzhong*, pp. 137–202.

"Songzi" 松子 (Songzi). *Yiwaiji*, pp. 3–30.

Suqu de wenyi 蘇區的文藝 (Literature and Art of the Soviet Areas). Shanghai, 1938.

The Sun Shines over the Sangkan River. Translated by Yang Hsien-yi and Gladys Yang. Peking, 1954.

Taiyang zhao zai Sangganhe shang 太陽照在桑乾河上 (The Sun Shines on the Sanggan River). Peking, 1955.

"Ta zou hou" 他走後 (After He Left). *Ding Ling wenji*, pp.165–184.

"Tian Baolin" 田保霖 (Tian Baolin). *Shaanbei fengguang*, pp. 59–70.

"Tianjiachong" 田家沖 (Tian Family Village). *Shui*, pp. 56–112.

"Tuanju" 團聚 (Reunion). *Yiwaiji*, pp. 127–185.

(*Wei Hu*) 韋護 (Wei Hu). Hong Kong, 1953.

"Wei tigao women kanwu de sixiangxing, zhandouxing er douzheng" 為提高我們刊物的思想性、戰鬥性而鬥爭 (To Struggle for the Elevation of Consciousness and Fighting Spirit of Our Journals). *Dao qunzhongzhong qu luohu*, pp. 12–24.

"Wenyijie dui Wang Shiwei yingyou de taidu ji fanxing" 文藝界對王實味應有的態度及反省 (The Attitude and Self-Introspection That the Literary Circles Should Take toward Wang Shiwei). *Jiefang ribao*, June 16, 1942, p. 4.

"Wo de chuangzuo jingyan" 我的創作經驗 (My Experience in Creative Writing). *Ding Ling xuanji*, pp. 142–144.

"Wo de changzuo shenghuo" 我的創作生活 (My Life in Creative Writing). *Chuangzuo de jingyan* 創作的經驗 (Experiences in Creative Writing). Shanghai, 1935, pp. 19–28.

"Wo de zibai" 我的自白 (A Personal Statement). *Ding Ling xuanji*, pp. 145–150.

"Wo dui 'duoyu de hua' de lijie" 我对'多余的话'的理解 (My Understanding of "Superfluous Words"). *Guangming ribao* 光明日报 (Guangming Daily), March 21, 1980, p. 3.

"Wo suo renshi de Qu Qiubai tongzhi—huiyi yu suixiang" 我所认识的瞿秋白同志—回忆与隨想 (The Comrade Qu Qiubai I Knew: Memories and Rambling Thoughts). *Xinhua yuebao wenzhaiban* 新华月报文摘版 (Xinhua Monthly, Literary Digests) 5 (1980): 155–163.

Wo zai Xiacun de shihou 我在霞村的時候 (When I Was in Xia Village). Peking, 1951.

"Wo zai Xiacun de shihou." *Wo zai Xiacun de shihou*, pp. 13–41.

"Wo zenyang fei xiang le ziyou de tiandi" 我怎樣飛向了自由的天地 (How I flew toward a Free Heaven and Earth). *Kuadoa xin de shidai lai*, pp. 157–162.

"Women xuyao zawen" 我們需要雜文 (We Need *zawen*). *Jiefang ribao*, October 23, 1941, p. 4.

"Women yongyuan zai yiqi" 我們永遠在一起 (We Shall Always Be Together). *Kuadao xin de shidai lai*, pp. 150–156.

"Xiaohuolun shang" 小火輪上 (On a Small Steamboat). *Zisha riji*, pp. 91–107.

"Xin de xinnian" 新的信念 (New Faith). *Wo zai Xiacun de shihou*, pp. 117–148.

Xu 序 (Preface), *Yepin shixuan* 也頻詩選 (Selected Poems by Yepin). Shanghai, 1929, pp. 1–6. Written under the name Manjia 曼伽.

"Xu 'Cheng zai dafengsha li benzou de gangweimen'" 序'呈在大風砂裏奔走的岡衞們' (Preface to "The Sentries Who Run about in the Great Wind and Sand"). *Yinian*, pp. 106–111.

"Xuyan" 序言 (Preface). *Suqu de wenyi* pp. 1–6. This preface was first published under the title *Wenyi zai suqu* 文藝在蘇區 (Literature and Art in the Soviet Areas) in *Jiefang zhoukan* 解放週刊 (Liberation Weekly) 1.3 (May 11, 1937): 23–24.

"Ye" 夜 (Night). *Wo zai Xiacun de shihou*, pp. 1–11.

"Yecao" 野草 (Yecao). *Ding Ling wenji*, pp. 311–323.

Yehui 夜會 (Night Meeting). Shanghai, 1933.

"Yepin yu geming" 也頻与革命 (Yepin and Revolution). *Shikan* 诗刊 (Poetry Magazine), March 1980, pp. 30–31.

"Yidian jingyan" 一點經驗 (A Bit of Experience). *Zuojia tan chuangzuo* 作家

談創作 (Writers Talk about Writing). Peking, 1955, pp. 1–5.

Yierjiushi yu jinjiluyu bianqu 一二九師与晉冀魯豫邊區 (The 129th Division and the Shanxi, Hebei, Shandong, Henan Border Regions). Peking, 1950.

Yige nüren 一個女人 (A Woman). Shanghai, 1930.

"Yige nüren he yige nanren" 一個女人和一個男人 (A Woman and a Man). *Ding Ling wenji*, pp. 521–558.

Yigeren de dansheng 一個人的誕生 (The Birth of a Person). Shanghai, 1931.

Yige xiaohongjun de gushi 一个小红军的故事 (The Story of a Little Red Soldier). Shanghai, 1956.

"Yige zhenshiren de yisheng—ji Hu Yepin" 一個真實人的一生—記胡也頻 (The Life of an Upright Man: Reminiscences of Hu Yepin). *Hu Yepin xiaoshuo xuanji* 胡也頻小説選集 (Selected Stories of Hu Yepin). Peking, 1955, pp. 1–21.

"Yijiusanlingnian chun Shanghai (zhier)" 一九三〇年春上海 （之二) (Shanghai, Spring 1930, II). *Ding Ling wenji*, pp. 240–310.

"Yijiusanlingnian chun Shanghai (zhiyi)" 一九三〇年春上海 （之一) (Shanghai, Spring 1930, I). *Ding Ling wenji*, pp. 185–239.

Yike wei chu tang de qiangdan 一顆未出鏜的槍彈 (A Bullet Not Yet Fired from Its Barrel). Chungking, 1939.

"Yike wei chu tang de qiangdan." *Yike wei chu tang de qiangdan*, pp. 21–41.

Yinian 一年 (One Year). Chungking, 1939.

"Yitian" 一天 (One Day). *Shui*, pp. 113–127.

Yiwaiji 意外集 (Unexpected Collection). Shanghai, 1936.

"Yiyueershisan ri" 一月二十三日 (January 23rd). *Yiwaiji*, pp. 33–85.

"Yuan Guangfa" 袁廣發 (Yuan Guangfa). *Shaanbei fengguang*, pp. 24–35.

Zai heianzhong 在黑暗中 (In the Darkness). Shanghai, 1933.

"Zai yanhan de rizili" 在严寒的日子里 (During the Coldest Days). *Renmin wenxue* 10 (1956): 60–82; *Qingming* 清明 (Brightness) 1 (1979): 4–92. The second is a longer version.

"Zai yiyuan zhong" 在医院中 (In the Hospital). Originally published in 1941 in the Yanan journal *Guyu* 穀雨 (Grain Rain), under the title "Zai yiyuan zhong shi" 在医院中时 (When in the Hospital), it was revised and published in *Wenyi zhendi* 文藝陣地 (Literary Base) 7.1 (August 1942): 3–10. This version was reprinted in *Wenyi bao* 文艺报 (Literary Gazette) 2 (1958): 11–16.

Zisha riji 自殺日記 (A Suicide's Diary). Shanghai, 1937.

"Zisha riji" (A Suicide's Diary). *Ding Ling wenji*, pp. 138–152.

"Zuihou yiye" 最後一頁 (The Last Page). *Yike wei chu tang de qiangdan*, pp. 87–88.

"Zuowei yizhong qingxiang lai kan—gei Xiao Yemu tongzhi de yifengxin" 作為一種傾向來看—給蕭也牧同志的一封信 (To Be Viewed as a Kind of Tendency: A Letter to Comrade Xiao Yemu). *Dao qunzhongzhong qu luohu*, pp. 1–11.

"Zuozheji—'Yigeren de dansheng' xu" 作者記—'一個人的誕生' 序 (Author's Note: Preface to *The Birth of a Person*). *Ding Ling xuanji*, pp. 151–154.

Ding Ling 丁玲, Chen Ming 陳明, and Lu Fei 逯斐. *Yaogong* 窰工 (Kiln Workers). Peking, 1949.

Other Works

Bai Jieming 白杰明 (Geremie Barmè). "Ding Ling manhua ershinian zaoji" 丁玲漫話二十年遭際 (Ding Ling Talks Informally about Twenty Years of Her Experiences). *Qishi niandai* 七十年代 (The Seventies) 115 (August 1979):

90–92.

————"Ding Ling tan yangji de gushi" 丁玲談養鷄的故事 (Ding Ling Tells Stories about Raising Chickens). *Huaqiao ribao* 華僑日報 (China Daily News), August 8, 1979, p. 6.

Bai Ye 白夜. "Dangguo jizhe de Ding Ling" 当过記者的丁玲 (Ding Ling Has Been a Reporter). *Xinwen zhanxian* 新闻战缐 (News Front) 2 (1979): 57–61.

Barthes, Roland. *S/Z, an Essay*. Translated by Richard Miller. New York: Hill and Wang, 1974.

Benton, Gregor. "The Yenan Literary Opposition." *New Left Review* 92 (July-August 1975): 93–106.

"Bentuan xingdong gangling" 本團行動綱領 (Our Corps's Program of Action). *Zhandi* 戰地 (Battleground) 1, *Xin zhonghua bao* 新中華報 (New China) August 19, 1937, p. 4.

Bjorge, Gary J. "Sophia's Diary: An Introduction." *Tamkang Review* 5.1 (1974): 97–110.

Booth, Wayne C. *The Rhetoric of Fiction*. Chicago: University of Chicago Press, 1961.

Cao Xueqin 曹雪芹. *Hongloumeng* 紅樓夢 (Dream of the Red Chamber). Peking, 1953.

Chang Jun-mei. *Ting Ling, Her Life and Her Work*. Taipei, Taiwan: Institute of International Relations, National Chengchi University, 1978.

Chatman, Seymour. *Story and Discourse: Narrative Structure in Fiction and Film*. Ithaca: Cornell University Press, 1980.

————"The Structure of Narrative Transmission." In *Style and Structure in Literature: Essays in the New Stylistics*, pp. 213–257. Edited by Roger Fowler. Ithaca: Cornell University Press, 1974.

Chen Binyin 陳彬蔭. *Ding Ling zhuan* 丁玲傳 (Biography of Ding Ling). Shanghai, 1938.

Chin, A. L., tr. "The Diary of Miss Sophia." In *Straw Sandals: Chinese Short Stories, 1918–1933*, pp. 129–169. Edited by Harold R. Isaacs.

Culler, Jonathan. *Structuralist Poetics, Structuralism, Linguistics, and the Study of Literature*. Ithaca: Cornell University Press, 1977.

Dong Xiao 冬曉. "Zoufang Ding Ling" 走訪丁玲 (Interview with Ding Ling). *Kaijuan* 開卷 (Book Reviews Monthly) 2.5 (December 1979): 22–26.

Elegant, Robert. *China's Red Masters: Political Biographies of the Chinese Communist Leaders*. New York: Twayne, 1951.

Fang Mao 方矛. "Ding Ling he ta de nüer" 丁玲和她的女兒 (Ding Ling and Her Daughter). *Dagongbao* 大公報, November 4, 1978, p. 3 and November 5, 1978, p. 3.

Feng Xiaxiong. "Ding Ling's Reappearance on the Literary Stage," *Chinese Literature* 1 (1980): 3–16.

"Fensui Ding Ling, Chen Qixia, Feng Xuefeng fandang jituan: baowei dang dui wenxue shiye de lingdao" 粉碎丁玲, 陳企霞, 馮雪峯反党集团: 保衛党对文学事业的領導 (Smash the Antiparty Clique of Ding Ling, Chen Qixia, Feng Xuefeng: Protect the Leadership of the Party in Literary Matters). *Renmin wenxue* editorial, 9 (1957): 1–3.

Feng Xuefeng 馮雪峯. " 'Taiyang zhao zai Sangganheshang' zai women wenxue fazhanshang de yiyi" '太陽照在桑乾河上' 在我們文學發展上的意義 (The Significance of *The Sun Shines on the Sanggan River* in the Development of Our Literature). Appendix to the 1955 edition of the novel, pp. 1–17.

Feuerwerker, Yi-tsi M. "The Changing Relationship between Literature and Life: Aspects of the Writer's Role in Ding Ling." In *Modern Chinese Literature in the May Fourth Era*, pp. 281–307. Edited by Merle Goldman. Cambridge, Mass.: Harvard University Press, 1977.

————"Ting Ling's 'When I was in Sha Chuan' (Cloud Village)." *Signs; Journal of Women in Culture and Society* 2.1 (Autumn 1976): 255–279.

————"Women as Writers in the 1920's and 1930's." In *Women in Chinese Society*, pp. 143–168. Edited by Margery Wolf and Roxanne Witke. Stanford: Stanford University Press, 1975.

Fokkema, D. W. *Literary Doctrine in China and Soviet Influence, 1956–1960*. The Hague: Mouton, 1965.

Fokkema, D. W. and Elrud Kunne-Ibsch. *Theories of Literature in the Twentieth Century*. New York: St. Martin's Press, 1977.

Fu Dong 傅冬. "Ding Ling fangwenji" 丁玲訪問記 (Visit with Ding Ling). In *Quanguo wenxue yishu gongzuozhe daibiao dahui jinian wenji* 全國文學藝術工作者代表大會紀念文集 (Commemoration Volume of the Representative Congress of All China's Literature and Art Workers). Peking, 1950, pp. 525–529.

Gao Kelin 高克林. "Lu Zhongcai changzhengji" 魯忠才長征記 (The Long March of Lu Zhongcai). *Jiefang ribao*, September 14, 1941, p. 2.

Geertz, Clifford. "Ideology as a Cultural System." In his *The Interpretation of Cultures*, pp. 193–233. New York: Basic Books, 1973.

Goldknopf, David. *The Life of the Novel*. Chicago: University of Chicago Press, 1972.

Goldman, Merle. *Literary Dissent in Communist China*. Cambridge, Mass.: Harvard University Press, 1967.

Guillen, Claudio. "Toward a Definition of the Picaresque." *Actes du IIIᵉ Congrés de l'Association Internationale de Litterature Comparée*. The Hague, 1962. A revised version of this essay appears in his *Literature as System: Essays toward a Theory of Literary History*. Princeton: Princeton University Press, 1971.

Guo Moruo 郭沫若. "Geming yu wenxue" 革命与文学 (Revolution and Literature). *Zhongguo xiandai wenxueshi cankao ziliao* I.1: 210–219.

Harrison, James Pinckney. *The Long March to Power: A History of the Chinese Communist Party, 1921–1972*. New York: Praeger, 1972.

Harvey, W. J. "The Retreat from Character." In his *Character and the Novel*, pp. 191–205. Ithaca: Cornell University Press, 1968.

He Dabai 何大白. "Wenxue de dazhonghua yu dazhong wenxue" 文學的大眾化與大眾文學 (The Popularization of Literature and Popular Literature). *Beidou* 2.3 and 2.4 (1932): 426–431.

(He) Danren (何) 丹仁. "Guanyu xin de xiaoshuo de dansheng—ping Ding Ling de 'Shui' " 關於新的小說的誕生—評丁玲的 '水' (Concerning the Birth of a New Fiction: A Criticism of Ding Ling's "Flood"). *Beidou* 2.1 (1932): 235–239.

He Yubo 賀玉波. "Ding Ling nüshi lunping" 丁玲女士論評 (Critical Discussions on Miss Ding Ling). In her *Zhongguo xiandai nüzuojia* 中國現代女作家 (Contemporary Women Writers of China), pp. 89–114. 2nd ed. Shanghai, 1936. (1st ed., 1931).

Hinton, William. *Fanshen: A Documentary of Revolution in a Chinese Village*. New York: Monthly Review Press, 1966.

Hsia, C. T. *A History of Modern Chinese Fiction*. 2nd ed. New Haven: Yale

University Press, 1971.

Hsia, Tsi-an. *The Gate of Darkness: Studies on the Leftist Literary Movement in China*. Seattle: University of Washington Press, 1968.

(Hu Yepin) 胡也頻. "Xisheng" 犧牲 (Sacrifice). In *Yigeren de dansheng* 一個人的誕生 (The Birth of a Person), by Ding Ling, pp. 177–204. Shanghai, 1931. First published as a story by Hu Yiping 胡一平 in *Xiaoshuo yuebao* 21.12 (1930): 1713–1722.

————"Yigeren de dansheng." In *Yigeren de dansheng*, by Ding Ling, pp. 125–176.

Huang Ying 黃英. *Xiandai zhongguo nüzuojia* 現代中國女作家 (Women Writers of Contemporary China). 2nd ed. Shanghai, 1934.

L. Insun. "Ding Ling zai Shaanbei" 丁玲在陝北 (Ding Ling in Northern Shaanxi). In *Nüzhanshi Ding Ling* 女戰士丁玲 (The Woman Warrior Ding Ling), pp. 25–73. Shanghai, 1938.

Isaacs, Harold R., ed. *Straw Sandals: Chinese Short Stories, 1918–1933*. Cambridge, Mass.: The M.I.T. Press, 1974.

James, Henry. "The Vessel of Consciousness," preface to *The Princess Casamassima*. In *The Future of the Novel: Essays on the Art of Fiction*, pp. 54–60. Edited by Leon Edel. New York: Vintage, 1956.

Jameson, Fredric. *The Prison-House of Language: A Critical Account of Structuralism and Russian Formalism*. Princeton: Princeton University Press, 1972.

Ji Feng 濟鳳. "Ding Ling de fuqi shenghuo" 丁玲的夫妻生活 (The Conjugal Life of Ding Ling). In *Yanan de nüxing* 延安的女性 (The Women of Yanan), pp. 12–14. N.p. and n.d.

"Jianchi shehuizhuyide wenyi luxian" 堅持社會主义的文艺路綫 (Hold Fast to the Socialist Line in Literature). Editorial in *Wenyi yuebao* 文艺月报 (Literature Monthly) 10 (1957): 3–5.

Jianru 堅如. "Ding Ling yinxiang" 丁玲印象 (Impressions of Ding Ling). In *Ding Ling pingzhuan*, pp. 183–184. Edited by Zhang Baiyun.

Kermode, Frank. "An Approach through History." In *Towards a Poetics of Fiction*, pp. 23–30. Edited by Mark Spilka. Bloomington: Indiana University Press, 1977.

Lang, Olga. *Pa Chin and His Writings: Chinese Youth Between the Two Revolutions*. Cambridge, Mass.: Harvard University Press, 1967.

Lau, Joseph, tr. "Sophia's Diary," *Tamkang Review* 5.1 (1974): 57–96.

Leaf, E. H. "Ting Ling, Herald of a New China." *T'ien Hsia Monthly* 5 (October 1937): 225–236.

Lee, Leo Ou-fan. *The Romantic Generation of Chinese Writers*. Cambridge, Mass.: Harvard University Press, 1973.

Levin, Harry. "On the Dissemination of Realism." In his *Grounds for Comparison*, pp. 244–261. Cambridge, Mass.: Harvard University Press, 1972.

Liao Ying 燎熒. "Ren zai jianku zhong shengzhang—ping Ding Ling tongzhi de 'zai yiyuan zhong shi'" 人在艱苦中生長—評丁玲同志的 '在医院中時' (It Is through Hardship That One Grows: A Criticism of Comrade Ding Ling's "When in the Hospital"). *Jiefang ribao*, June 10, 1942, p. 4.

Lin, Shuen-fu. "Ritual and Narrative Structure in *Ju-lin Wai-shih*." In *Chinese Narrative: Critical and Theoretical Essays*, pp. 244–265. Edited by Andrew Plaks.

Lin Zhihao 林志浩, chief ed. *Zhongguo xiandai wenxueshi* 中国现代文学史 (History of Modern Chinese Literature). 2 vols. Peking, 1980.

Link, Perry. "Traditional-Style Popular Urban Fiction in the Teens and Twenties." In *Modern Chinese Literature in the May Fourth Era*, pp. 327–349. Edited by Merle Goldman.

Liu Shousong 刘綬松. *Zhongguo xinwenxue shi chugao* 中國新文学史初稿 (Draft History of Modern Chinese Literature). 2 vols. First published in Peking, 1957. Rev. ed. Peking, 1979.

Lotman, Jurij. *The Structure of the Artistic Text*. Translated by Donald Vroon. Ann Arbor: The University of Michigan Press, 1977.

Lu Xun 鲁迅. "Duiyu zuoyi zuojia lianmeng de yijian—sanyueerri zai zuoyi zuojia lianmeng chengli dahui jiang" 对于左翼作家联盟的意見—三月二日在左翼作家联盟成立大会讲 (Opinions Concerning the League of Left-Wing Writers: Speech at the Founding Meeting of the League of Left-Wing Writers on March 2). In *Lu Xun zawen xuan* 鲁迅杂文选 (Selected Essays of Lu Xun), I (1918–1932), 157–164. Fudan daxue shanghai shifan daxue zhongwenxi xuanbian 复旦大学上海师范大学中文系选編 (Edited by the Departments of Chinese Literature, Fudan University and Shanghai Normal University). Shanghai, 1973.

Lukács, Georg. "The Ideology of Modernism." In *Marxism and Human Liberation: Essays on History, Culture and Revolution*, pp. 277–307. Edited by E. San Juan, Jr. New York: Dell Publishing Co., 1973.

Luo Sun 罗蓀. "Kangzhan wenyi yundong niaokan" 抗战文艺运动鸟瞰 (A Bird's Eye View of the Literature and Art Movement of the War of Resistance). In *Zhongguo xiandai wenxueshi cankao ziliao*, I.2, 650–667.

Luo Zhanglong 罗章龙. "Shanghai dongfang fandian huiyi qianhou" 上海东方饭店会议前后 (Events Surrounding the Meeting in the Shanghai Eastern Hotel). Oral account by Luo Zhanglong, recorded by Qiu Quanzheng 丘权政. *Xinwenxue shiliao* 1 (1981): 141–145.

McDougall, Bonnie S. *The Introduction of Western Literary Theories into Modern China, 1919–1925*. Tokyo: The Centre of East Asian Cultural Studies, 1977.

———"Mao Zedong's 'Talks at the Yan'an Conference on Literature and Art': A Translation of the 1943 Text with Commentary," *Michigan Papers in Chinese Studies*, no. 39. Ann Arbor: Center for Chinese Studies, The University of Michigan, 1980.

Ma Jianling 馬健翎. "Wo duiyu difangju de kanfa" 我對於地方劇的看法 (My View of Regional Theatre). Quoted in Wang Yao 王瑶, *Zhongguo xinwenxue shigao* 中國新文學史稿 (Draft History of Modern Chinese Literature). II, 380–381. Hong Kong, 1972.

Mao Dun 茅盾. "Nüzuojia Ding Ling" 女作家丁玲. (The Woman Writer Ding Ling). In *Ding Ling xuanji*, pp. 36–40.

———"Wenyi dazhonghua wenti" 文艺大众化問題 (The Problem of the Popularization of Literature and Art). In *Zhongguo xiandai wenxueshi cankao ziliao*, I.2, 761–764.

Mao Tse-tung. "Talks at the Yenan Forum on Literature and Art." In *Selected Readings from the Works of Mao Tse-tung* (English translation), pp. 250–286. Peking, 1971.

Mao Zedong 毛泽东. "Zai Yanan wenyi zuotanhuishang de jianghua" 在延安文艺座谈会上的讲话 (Talks at the Yanan Forum on Literature and Art). *Jiefang ribao*, October 19, 1943. In *Mō Taku-tō shū* 毛泽东集 (Collected Writings of Mao Tse-tung), VIII, 111–148. Compiled by Takeuchi Minoru 竹內実. Tokyo: Hokubōsha 北望社, 1971.

Mathewson, Rufus W., Jr. *The Positive Hero in Russian Literature*. 2nd ed. Stanford: Stanford University Press, 1975.

Mu Mutian 穆木天, tr. "Zuola de zuopin ji qi yifan" 左拉的作品及其遺範 (Zola's Works and Example), by Ba-bi-sai 巴比塞 (Barbusse). *Beidou* 1.2 (1931): 89–96.

Munro, Donald J. *The Concept of Man in Contemporary China.* Ann Arbor: The University of Michigan Press, 1977.

"Nüzuojia Ding Ling zhengzai zhuanxie xinzuo" 女作家丁玲正在撰写新作 (The Woman Writer Ding Ling Is Now Writing New Works) *Guangming ribao*, June 14, 1979, p. 2.

O'Toole, L. M. "Analytic and Synthetic Approaches to Narrative Structure: Sherlock Holmes and 'The Sussex Vampire.'" In *Style and Structure in Literature: Essays in the New Stylistics*, pp. 143–176. Edited by Roger Fowler.

Payne, Robert. *China Awake.* New York: Dodd, Mead, 1947.

Pepper, Suzanne. *Civil War in China: The Political Struggle, 1945–1949.* Berkeley: University of California Press, 1978.

Pickowicz, Paul. "Ch'u Ch'iu-pai and the Chinese Marxist Conception of Revolutionary Popular Literature and Art." *China Quarterly* 70 (June 1977): 296–314.

Plaks, Andrew H. "Towards a Critical Theory of Chinese Narrative." In *Chinese Narrative: Critical and Theoretical Essays*, pp. 309–352. Edited by A. Plaks. Princeton: Princeton University Press, 1977.

Price, Martin. "The Other Self: Thoughts about Character in the Novel." In *Sociology of Literature and Drama*, pp. 260–279. Edited by Elizabeth and Tom Burns. London: Penguin, 1973.

Průšek, Jaroslav. "Subjectivism and Individualism in Modern Chinese Literature." *Archiv Orientální* 25 (1957): 261–283.

———*Three Sketches of Chinese Literature.* Prague: Oriental Institute in Academia, 1969.

Qian Qianwu 錢謙吾. "Ding Ling" 丁玲. In *Ding Ling pingzhuan*, pp. 39–60. Edited by Zhang Baiyun.

——— "Guanyu *Muqin*" 關於 '母親' (About *Mother*). In *Ding Ling pingzhuan*, pp. 123–141. Edited by Zhang Baiyun.

Qian Xingcun 錢杏邨. "Guanyu *Muqin*" (About *Mother*). In *Ding Ling xuanji* 丁玲選集, pp. 299–315. Edited by (Yao 姚) Pengzi 蓬子. Shanghai, 1939. (Except for an additional last paragraph, this text is identical with Qian Qianwu's article above.)

——— "Yijiusanyinian wentan zhi huigu" 一九三一年文壇之回顧 (Looking back on the Literary Scene of 1931). *Beidou* 2.1 (1932): 1–24.

Qu Qiubai 瞿秋白. "Puluo dazhong wenyi de xianshi wenti" 普洛大众文艺的現实問題 (Practical Problems of Proletarian Popular Literature and Art). In *Zhongguo xiandai wenxueshi cankao ziliao*, I.1, 305–323.

Raban, Jonathan. *The Technique of Modern Fiction: Essays in Practical Criticism.* South Bend, Indiana: University of Notre Dame Press, 1969.

Ren Tianma 任天馬. "Jiti chuangzuo he Ding Ling" 集體創作和丁玲 (Collective Writing and Ding Ling). In *Ding Ling zai xibei* 丁玲在西化 (Ding Ling in the Northwest), pp. 8–11. Edited by (Shi 史) Tianxing 天行. Hankow, 1938.

Scholes, Robert. *Structuralism in Literature: An Introduction.* New Haven: Yale University Press, 1974.

Scholes, Robert and Robert Kellogg. *The Nature of Narrative.* New York: Oxford University Press, 1966.

Selden, Mark. *The Yenan Way in Revolutionary China.* Cambridge, Mass.:

Harvard University Press, 1971.

The Shanghai Evening Post & Mercury, June 15, 1933, pp. 1 and 7.

Shen Congwen 沈從文. *Ji Ding Ling* 記丁玲, *Ji Ding Ling xuji* 記丁玲續集 (Reminiscences of Ding Ling, Further Reminiscences of Ding Ling). Shanghai, 1940. These texts are much revised and censored versions of Congwen, *Ji Ding Ling nüshi* 記丁玲女士 (Reminiscences of Miss Ding Ling), serialized in *Guowen zhoubao* 國聞週報 (Guowen Weekly) 10. 29 to 51, from July 20 to December 18, 1933.

—— *Ji Hu Yepin* 記胡也頻 (Reminiscences of Hu Yepin). 3rd ed. Shanghai, 1935.

Shen Mo 沈墨, "Ding Ling ersan shi" 丁玲二三事 (Two or Three Things about Ding Ling), *Dagongbao*, May 19, 1979, p. 3.

Shroder, Maurice Z. "The Novel as a Genre." In *The Theory of the Novel*, pp. 13–29. Edited by Philip Stevick. New York: The Free Press, 1967.

Smedley, Agnes. *Battle Hymn of China*. New York: Knopf, 1943.

—— *China Fights Back: An American Woman with the Eighth Route Army*. New York: Vanguard Press, 1938.

Snow, Helen Foster. *The Chinese Communists: Sketches and Autobiographies of the Old Guard*. Westport, Conn.: Greenwood, 1972.

—— *Women in Modern China*. The Hague: Mouton, 1967.

Sontag, Susan. *Illness as Metaphor*. New York: Farrar, Straus, and Giroux, 1978.

Stein, Gunther. *The Challenge of Red China*. New York: McGraw Hill, 1945.

Steiner, George, "Marxism and the Literary Critic," and "The Writer and Communism." In his *Language and Silence: Essays on Language, Literature and the Inhuman*, pp. 305–324, 356–364. New York: Atheneum, 1970.

Sternberg, Meir. *Expositional Modes and Temporal Ordering in Fiction*. Baltimore: The Johns Hopkins University Press, 1978.

Sun Xiaoping 孫肖平. "Ding Ling guanxin guo qingnian zuozhe ma?" 丁玲关心过青年作者嗎? (Has Ding Ling Ever Been Concerned with Young Writers?) *Mengya* 萌芽 (Sprouts) 20 (October 1957): 6–7.

Todorov, Tzvetan. "An Introduction to Verisimilitude." In his *The Poetics of Prose*, pp. 80–88. Translated by Richard Howard. Ithaca: Cornell University Press, 1977.

Twitchett, D. C. "Chinese Biographical Writing." In *Historians of China and Japan*, pp. 95–114. Edited by W. G. Beasley and E. G. Pulleyblank. London: Oxford University Press, 1961.

Uspensky, Boris. *A Poetics of Composition: The Structure of the Artistic Text and Typology of a Compositional Form*. Translated by Valentina Zavarin and Susan Wittig. Berkeley: University of California Press, 1973.

Vogel, Ezra F. "The Unlikely Heroes: The Social Role of the May Fourth Writers." In *Modern Chinese Literature in the May Fourth Era*, pp. 145–159. Edited by Merle Goldman.

Wang Liaoying 王燎熒. "Kangzhan shiqi Ding Ling xiaoshuo de sixiang qingxiang" 抗战時期丁玲小説的思想傾向 (The Trend of Thought in Ding Ling's Wartime Stories). *Wenxue pinglun* 文学評論 (Literary Criticism) 4 (1957): 95–110.

—— " 'Taiyang zhao zai Sangganheshang' jiujing shi shenme yang de zuopin" '太陽照在桑乾河上' 究竟是什么樣的作品? (What Kind of Work is *The Sun Shines on the Sanggan River*?). *Wenxue pinglun* 1 (1959): 67–84.

Wang Shuming 王淑明. "Muqin" '母親' (Mother). In *Ding Ling pingzhuan*, pp. 169–178. Edited by Zhang Baiyun.

Wang Ziye 王子野. "Fengming xiezuo" 奉命寫作 (Writing to Order). *Renmin wenxue* 10 (1957): 8–9.

Watt, Ian. *The Rise of the Novel: Studies in Defoe, Richardson, and Fielding.* London: Chatto and Windus, 1957.

Welty, Eudora. "Place in Fiction." *The South Atlantic Quarterly* LV.1 (January 1956): 57–72.

Williams, Raymond. *Culture and Society, 1780–1950.* New York: Harper & Row, 1966.

———— *Marxism and Literature.* Oxford: Oxford University Press, 1977.

Wilson, Dick. *The Long March, 1935: The Epic of Chinese Communism's Survival.* London: Hamish Hamilton, 1971.

Wright, Mary Clabaugh. *China in Revolution: The First Phase, 1900–1913.* New Haven: Yale University Press, 1968.

Xibei zhandi fuwutuan jiti chuangzuo 西北戰地服務團集體創作 (Collectively Authored by the Northwest Front Service Corps). "Xibei zhandi fuwutuan chuwai shiyuelai zhi gongzuo baogao" 西北戰地服務團出外十月來之工作報告 (A Report on the Work of the Northwest Front Service Corps During its Past Ten Months on the Road) in *Xixian shenghuo* 西線生活 (Life at the Western Front), pp. 223–250. Chungking, 1939.

(Yao 姚) Pengzi 蓬子. "Bianwan zhihou" 編完之後 (After Editing). In *Ding Ling xuanji*, pp. 317–318. Edited by (Yao) Pengzi.

———— "Women de pengyou Ding Ling" 我們的朋友丁玲 (Our Friend Ding Ling). In *Ding Ling xuanji*, pp. 7–35. Edited by Xu and Ye.

Yao Wenyuan 姚文元. "Shafei nüshimen de ziyou wangguo—Ding Ling bufen zaoqi zuopin pipan, bing lun Ding Ling chuangzuo sixiang he chuangzuo qingxiang fazhan de yige xiansuo" 莎菲女士们的自由王国—丁玲部分早期作品批判，并论丁玲创作思想和创作倾向发展的一个缐索 (The Free Kingdom of the Miss Sophies: A Criticism of Some of Ding Ling's Early Works, and a Discussion of a Clue to the Thought and Direction of Development in Ding Ling's Creative Writing). In *Wenyi sixiang lunzheng ji* 文艺思想论争集 (Polemics in Literary Thought), pp. 206–248. Edited by Yao Wenyuan. Shanghai, 1965.

Ye Xiaoshen 叶孝慎. "Ding Ling de biming" 丁玲的笔名 (The Pen Names of Ding Ling). *Gansu shida xuebao* 甘肃师大学报 (Journal of Gansu Normal University) 1 (1981): 56–58.

Yizhen 毅真. "Ding Ling nüshi" 丁玲女士 (Miss Ding Ling). In *Ding Ling pingzhuan*, pp. 107–114. Edited by Zhang Baiyun.

Zhang Baiyun 張白雲, ed. *Ding Ling pingzhuan* 丁玲評傳 (Critical Biography of Ding Ling). Shanghai, 1934.

———— "Ding Ling zhuan" 丁玲傳 (Biography of Ding Ling). In *Ding Ling pingzhuan*, pp. 1–3.

Zhang Guangnian 張光年. "Shafei nüshi zai Yanan—tan Ding Ling de xiaoshuo 'Zai yiyuanzhong'" 莎菲女士在延安—談丁玲的小説'在医院中' (Miss Sophie in Yanan: A Discussion of Ding Ling's Story "In the Hospital"). *Wenyi bao* 文艺报 (Literary Gazette) 2 (1958): 9–11.

Zhao Chaogou 趙超構. *Yanan yiyue* 延安一月 (A Month in Yanan). Nanking. 1946.

Zhao Haosheng 趙浩生. "Zhou Yang xiaotan lishi gongguo" 周揚笑談歷史功过 (Zhou Yang Jokingly Talks about [his] Merits and Faults in History). *Qishi niandai* 104 (September 1978): 26–33.

Zhao Jiabi 赵家璧. "Chongjian Ding Ling hua dangnian—'Muqin' chubande qianqianhouhou" 重见丁玲话当年—'母亲' 出版的前前后后 (Seeing Ding Ling Again and Talking about the Past: The Ins and Outs of the Publication of 'Muqin'). *Wenhui zengkan* 文汇增刊 (Supplement to Wenhui) 4 (1980): 64–68.

Zhong Chen and Ling Yuan 中忱 凌源 eds. *Ding Ling zuopin xinian* 丁玲作品系年 (Chronology of Ding Ling's Works), *Jilin shida xuebao* 吉林师大学报 (Journal of Jilin Normal University), supplementary issue, 1980.

Zhongguo xiandai wenxueshi cankao ziliao 中国现代文学史参考资料 (Research Materials on Modern Chinese Literary History). Edited by Beijing shifan daxue zhongwenxi xiandai wenxue jiaoxue gaige xiaozu 北京师范大学中文系现代文学教学改革小組 (Committee on the Revision of the Teaching of Modern Literature, Department of Chinese Literature, Peking Normal University). 2 vols. Peking, 1959.

Zhou Libo 周立波. *Baofengzhouyu* 暴风骤雨 (Hurricane). Peking, 1977.

Zhou Yang 周揚. "Kangzhan shiqi de wenxue" 抗战时期的文学 (Literature during the Period of the War of Resistance). In *Zhongguo xiandai wenxueshi cankao ziliao*, I.2, 636–644.

———"Wang Shiwei de wenyiguan yu women de wenyiguan" 王实味的文艺观与我們的文艺观 (Wang Shiwei's Concept of Literature and Art and Our Concept of Literature and Art). In *Zhongguo xiandai wenxueshi cankao ziliao*, II, 191–212.

Zhou Yang, *et al. Wenyi zhanxianshang de yichang dabianlun* 文艺战綫上的一場大辯論 (A great debate on the literary front). Peking, 1960.

Zhu Jing 朱璟. "Guanyu 'chuangzuo' " 關於 '創作' (On "Creative Writing"). *Beidou* 1.1 (1931): 75–87.

Zola, Émile. *Germinal*. Paris: Bibliothèque-Charpentier, 1950.

CHRONOLOGICAL LIST OF DING LING'S FICTION

This list of Ding Ling's fiction does not claim to be exhaustive; first, some of her works, particularly those of the Yanan period, were originally published in ephemeral and hard to locate newspapers or journals; second, the line between fiction and descriptive or journalistic essays is difficult to draw and the inclusion or exclusion of a particular title may often be a matter of judgment.

As I was completing this list, two chronologies of Ding Ling's works, both aiming to include her writings in all categories, and both indicating access to some sources not available to me, appeared within a short time of each other. Although I have benefited greatly from these efforts, the near-impossibility of compiling a definitive list becomes even more evident in view of their omissions and the many discrepancies between them. See Yuan Liangjun 袁良駿 "Ding Ling zhuzuo nianbiao (yijiuerqinian qiu—yijiusijiunian shiyue)" 丁玲著作年表 (一九二七年秋——一九四九年十月) (Chronological Table of Ding Ling's Writings, Fall 1927—October 1949), *Xinwenxue shiliao* 新文学史料 (Historical Materials of the New Literature) 3 (1980): 263–279; and Zhong Chen and Ling Yuan, 中忱 凌源, eds., *Ding Ling zuopin xinian* 丁玲作品系年 (Chronology of Ding Ling's Works), *Jilin shida xuebao* 吉林师大学报 (Journal of Jilin Normal University), supplementary issue, 1980.

The list that follows provides page numbers for all items that I have seen. Dates of composition, when supplied by the author at the end of a work, appear in brackets. The next item provides as much information as is available about the first publication of the work: by year, month, day, and page number if in a newspaper; by volume and number if in a periodical, with the year and month following in parentheses and page numbers last of all. Items constituting the entire issue of a journal or pamphlet are identified by date and full pagination. I have occasionally deviated from a strict chronological order so that works can be grouped by their first appearance in a collection or in book form. The collection titles that head the listings of individual stories, for which full citations can be found in the bibliography, are followed by dates of their first editions.

Zai heianzhong (1928)

"Mengke" 夢珂 (Mengke) [fall 1927]. *Xiaoshuo yuebao* 小説月報 (Fiction Monthly) 18.12 (Dec. 1927): 11–35.

"Shafei nüshi de riji" 莎菲女士的日記 (The Diary of Miss Sophie). *Xiaoshuo yuebao* 19.2 (Feb. 1928): 202–223.

"Shujia zhong" 暑假中 (Summer Vacation). *Xiaoshuo yuebao* 19.5 (May 1928): 564–587.

"Amao guniang" 阿毛姑娘 (Miss Amao). *Xiaoshuo yuebao* 19.7 (July 1928): 792–815.

Zisha riji (1929)

"Qian laile ke de yueye" 潛來了客的月夜 (A Secret Visitor on a Moonlit Night). *Zhongyang ribao* 中央日報 (The Central Daily News) 1928.8.14, p. 12.

"Zisha riji" 自殺日記 (A Suicide's Diary). *Ronglu* 熔爐 (Crucible) 1 (Dec. 1928).

"Qingyunli zhong de yijian xiaofangli" 慶雲里中的一間小房裏 (A Small Room in Qingyun Lane). *Honghei* 紅黑 (Red and Black) 1 (Jan. 1929): 51–59.

"Guonian" 過年 (New Year's) [1929.1.11]. *Honghei* 2 (Feb. 1929): 67–80.

"Xiaohuolun shang" 小火輪上 (On a Small Steamboat). *Honghei* 3 (Mar. 1929) 155–164.

"Suimu" 歲暮 (The End of the Year). *Renjian yuekan* 人間月刊 (Human World Monthly) 2 (Feb. 1929): 63–70.

Yige nüren (1930)

"Yige nüren he yige nanren" 一个女人和一个男人 (A Woman and a Man). *Xiaoshuo yuebao* 19.12 (Dec. 1928): 1362–1375.

"Ta zou hou" 他走後 (After He Left). *Xiaoshuo yuebao* 20.3 (Mar. 1929): 549–556.

"Ri" 日 (Day). *Honghei* 5 (May 1929): 217–224.

"Yecao" 野草 (Yecao). *Honghei* 6 (June 1929): 285–293.

> This collection contains two stories by Hu Yepin: "Shaonian Mengde de shimian" and "Zai yige wanshang."

Wei Hu (1930)

Wei Hu 韋護 (Wei Hu). *Xiaoshuo yuebao* 21.1–5 (Jan.-May 1930): 85–100; 373–391; 565–580; 691–700; 851–858.

Yigeren de dansheng (1931)

"Yijiusanlingnian chun Shanghai (zhiyi)" 一九三〇年春上海 (之一) (Shanghai, Spring 1930, I). *Xiaoshuo yuebao* 21.9 (Sept. 1930): 1297–1316.

"Yijiusanlingnian chun Shanghai (zhier)" 一九三〇年春上海 (之二) (Shanghai, Spring 1930, II). *Xiaoshuo yuebao* 21.11 (Nov. 1930): 1603–1615; 21.12 (Dec. 1930): 1723–1734.

> This collection contains two stories by Hu Yepin: "Xisheng" and "Yigeren de dansheng."

Shui (1932)

"Nianqian de yitian" 年前的一天 (The Day before New Year's). *Xiaoshuo yuebao* 21.6 (June 1930): 933–938.

"Tianjiachong" 田家冲 (Tian Family Village). *Xiaoshuo yuebao* 22.7 (July 1931): 861–882.

"Yitian" 一天 (One Day) [5.8; finished in one night]. *Xiaoshuo yuebao* 22.9 (Sept. 1931): 1133–1138.

"Shui" 水 (Flood). *Beidou* 北斗 (Big Dipper) 1.1 (Sept. 1931): 27–36; 1.2 (Oct. 1931): 33–38; 1.3 (Nov. 1931): 59–71.

"Cong yewan dao tianliang" 從夜晚到天亮 (From Night till Daybreak) [.23].

Weiyin 微音 (Subtle Sounds) 1.3 (May 1931): 17–28.

"Duo shi zhi qiu" 多事之秋 (Troubled Times) [Unfinished and uncollected]. *Beidou* 2.1 (Jan 1932): 25–37; 2.3–4 (July 1932): 516–529.

Yehui (1933)

"Mouye" 某夜 (A Certain Night) [1932.5]. *Wenxue yuebao* 文學月報 (Literature Monthly) 1.1 (June 1932): 93–100.

Fawang 法網 (The Net of the Law) [1932.6]. First published as no. 34 in the "Yijiao congshu" 一角叢書 (Ten-Cents Series) of the Liangyou Publishing Company (April 1932) 71 pp.

"Xiaoxi" 消息 (News) [1932.6]. *Wenxue yuebao* 1.2 (July 1932): 33–38.

"Yehui" 夜會 (Night Meeting) [1932.9]. *Wenxue yuebao* 1.3 (Sept. 1932): 9–14.

"Shiren Ya-luo-fu" 詩人亞洛夫 (The Poet Alov) [1932.9.3]. *Dongfang zazhi* 東方雜誌 ("Eastern Miscellany") 29.5 (Nov. 1932): 2–8, under the title "Shiren" 詩人 (Poet), by Ding Ning 丁寧.

"Gei haizimen" 給孩子們 (For the Children). *Dongfang zazhi* 30.1 (Jan. 1933): 40–53; 30.2 (Feb. 1933): 21–27.

"Ben" 奔 (Flight) [1933, end of March]. *Xiandai* 現代 (Contemporary Times) 3.1 (May 1933): 23–34.

Muqin (1933)

Muqin 母親 (Mother). *Dalu xinwen* 大陸新聞 (Mainland News) 1932.6.15–1932.7.3 (serialization incomplete).

Yiwaiji (1936)

"Yangma de riji" 楊媽的日記 (Auntie Yang's Diary). *Liangyou tuhua zazhi* 良友圖畫雜誌 (The Young Companion Pictorial Magazine) 79 (Aug. 1933): 9.

"Busuan qingshu" 不算情書 (Not Considered a Love Letter). *Wenxue* 文學 (Literature) 1.3 (Sept. 1933): 367–370.

"Shafei riji dierbu" 莎菲日記第二部 (Sophie's Diary, Part 2). *Wenxue* 1.4 (Oct. 1933): 530–532.

"Songzi" 松子 (Songzi). *Dagongbao* 大公報 ("Ta-Kung-Pao") (Tianjin) 1936. 4.19, p. 11.

"Yiyueershisan ri" 一月二十三日 (January Twenty-Third). First published in *Shinian* 十年 (Ten Years), a volume commemorating the tenth anniversary of the Kaiming Publishing Company (July 1936) pp. 251–274.

"Chen Boxiang" 陳伯祥 (Chen Boxiang). *Guowen zhoubao* 國聞周報 (Guowen Weekly) 13.22 (1936.6.8): (1–4).

"Bayue shenghuo" 八月生活 (Eight Months). *Jindai wenyi* 今代文藝 (Contemporary Literature) 1.2 (Aug. 1936): 302–309.

"Tuanju" 團聚 (Reunion) [8.13]. *Wenji yuekan* 文季月刊 (Literary Season Monthly) 1.4 (Sept. 1936): 737–749.

Suqu de wenyi (1938)

"Yike wei chu tang de qiangdan" 一顆未出鏜的槍彈 (A Bullet Not Yet Fired from Its Barrel) [1937.4.14]. *Jiefang zhoukan* 解放週刊 (Liberation Weekly) 1.1 (1937.4.24): 20–24, under the title "Yike meiyou chu tang de qiangdan" 一顆沒有出鏜的槍彈.

"Dongcun shijian" 東村事件 (Incident at East Village) [1937.6]. *Jiefang zhoukan*

1.5 (1937.5.31): 26–28; 1.6 (6.14): 25–26; 1.7 (6.22): 25–26; 1.8 (6.28): 27–28; 1.9 (7.5): 28–30.

This collection also includes the play "Chongfeng" 重逢 (Meeting Again). The two stories above were also published with other pieces describing Ding Ling's experiences with the Red Army and as deputy director of the political department of its Guard Unit in the collection *Yike wei chu tang de qiangdan* (1938).

Yinian (1939)

"Jicun zhi ye" 冀村之夜 (The Night at Ji Village). *Wenyi zhendi* 文藝陣地 (Literary Base) 2.7 (Jan. 1939): 599–600, 616.
"Yasui de xin" 壓碎的心 (A Crushed Heart). [1939].

Beginning with this Yanan collection the line between fictional narrative and journalistic essay becomes increasingly difficult to draw. Several works from this list are included in *Ding Ling sanwenji* (Collected Essays by Ding Ling) (Peking, 1980). Ding Ling herself acknowledges the difficulty of making the distinction in a postface to a collection of short stories that contains most of the stories she has written during the past fifty-two years: *Ding Ling duanpian xiaoshuoxuan* (Selected Short Stories by Ding Ling) (Peking, 1981), 2 vols. It also contains two essays, because "from the point of view of their literary form, some comrades consider them to be stories" (II, 651).

Wo zai Xiacun de shihou (1943)

"Xin de xinnian" 新的信念 (New Faith) [spring 1939]. *Wenyi zhanxian* 文藝 戰綫 (Literary Front) 1.4 (Sept. 1939): 1–9, under the title "Leiyan mohu zhong zhi xinnian" 淚眼模糊中之信念 (Faith through Eyes Dimmed by Tears).
"Xianzhang jiating" 縣長家庭 (The Magistrate's Family) [1939.9]. *Qiyue* 七月 (July) 6.12 (Dec. 1940): 28–32.
"Qiushou de yitian" 秋收的一天 (Harvest Day) [fall 1939]. *Zhongguo funü* 中國婦女 (Chinese Women) 1.5–6 (Nov. 1939): 21–24.
"Ruwu" 入伍 (Enlistment) [1940]. *Zhongguo wenhua* 中國文化 (Chinese Culture) 1.3 (May 1940): 38–45.
"Wo zai Xiacun de shihou" 我在霞村的時候 (When I Was in Xia Village) [1941.1.2]. *Zhongguo wenhua* 3.1 (June 1941): 24–31.
"Ye" 夜 (Night) [1941.6]. *Jiefang ribao* 解放日報 (Liberation Daily) 1941. 6.10, p. 2; 6.11, p. 2.

This collection also includes "Yasui de xin."

"Zai yiyuan zhong" 在醫院中 (In the Hospital). *Gu yu* 穀雨 (Grain Rain) 1 (Nov. 1941): 1–7, 18, under the title "Zai yiyuan zhong shi" 在醫院中時 (When in the Hospital). Not included in a collection until 1981, in *Ding Ling duanpian xiaoshuoxuan*.

Shaanbei fengguang (1948)

"Shibage" 十八個 (The Eighteen) [1942.7.3]. *Jiefang ribao* 1942.7.9, p. 4.

"Ershiba banfu" 二十把板斧 (Twenty Broad Axes). *Jiefang ribao* 1944.6.13, p. 4.

"Sanri zaji" 三日雜記 (Miscellaneous Notes of Three Days) [1944.6]. *Jiefang ribao* 1945.5.19, p. 4.

"Tian Baolin" 田保霖 (Tian Baolin). *Jiefang ribao* 1944.6.30, p. 4.

"Ji Zhuanyaowan luoma dahui" 記磚窰灣騾馬大會 (Livestock Fair at Zhuanyaowan) [1944.8]. *Jiefang ribao* 1944.9.17, p. 4.

"Minjian yiren Li Bu" 民間藝人李卜 (The People's Artist Li Bu) [1944.10.20 night]. *Jiefang ribao* 1944.10.30, p. 4.

"Yuan Guangfa" 袁廣發 (Yuan Guangfa). *Jiefang ribao* 1945.1.12, p. 4.

Taiyang zhao zai Sangganhe shang 太陽照在桑乾河上 (The Sun Shines on the Sanggan River) [preface 1948.6.15]. Sept. 1948. Selections appeared in various journals before and after publication.

"Liangmo zhuren" 粮秣主任 (The Provisions Director) [1953.11.9]. *Renmin ribao* 人民日报 (People's Daily) 1953.11.20, p. 3. Collected for the first time in 1981, in *Ding Ling duanpian xiaoshuoxuan*.

Yige xiaohongjun de gushi 一个小紅軍的故事 (The Story of a Little Red Soldier). Mar. 1956. 18 pp.

"Zai yanhan de rizili" 在严寒的日子里 (During the Coldest Days). *Renmin wenxue* 人民文学 (People's Literature) 10 (Oct. 1956): 60–82; revised and expanded in *Qingming* 清明 (Brightness) 1 (Sept. 1979): 4–92 (unfinished).

"Du Wanxiang" 杜晚香 (Du Wanxiang) [spring 1966, rewritten 1978.8]. *Renmin wenxue* 7 (July 1979): 45–58. Collected in *Ding Ling jinzuo* (Recent Writings of Ding Ling) in 1980, and in *Ding Ling duanpian xiaoshuoxuan*, 1981.

INDEX

Ai Qing, 12, 100
And Quiet Flows the Don (Mikhail Sholokov), 122
Anna Karenina (Leo Tolstoy), 122
Antirightist campaign, 11–12, 14–15, 21, 35, 113–114, 143, 144
Artist as model hero, 117–118
"Autobiographical attitude" in narrative, 29–31

Ba Jin, 21
Baimaonü (White-Haired Girl), 121
Baodao (or *baogao*) *wenxue* (reportage literature), 89, 105, 107, 111 and verisimilitude, 115–116
Barthes, Roland: on the "hermeneutic code," 136; on the "cultural code," 154n42
Beethoven, 54, 96
Beidou (Big Dipper, 8, 67, 73, 75, 93
Bing Xin, 37
The Birth of a Person (Yigeren de dansheng), Ding Ling's preface to, 72–73
"The Birth of a Person" (Hu Yepin), 72
"Bright versus dark side" debate, 9, 17, 91, 99–104; Ding Ling on, 166n40

Cao Xueqin, 144
Central Literary Institute, Ding Ling and, 11, 12, 172n6
Character(s), 105–115; women characters in Ding Ling's early fiction, 19, 20, 24–25, 28, 33–36, 52; "autobiographical attitude" in characterization, 29–30; range expanded, 30, 60, 106–107; defined by milieu, 60, 62–64; as totalizing force in fiction and world, 105–106; as member of collective, 107; treatment in response to political orientation, 106–107; and real-life models, 106–107, 111; children and child-like characters, 107–108; and community, 111–112, 114–115, 117–118, 125–126; in land-reform novel, 124–126, 127, 129, 142; community as "character," 126–127; developmental characters, 127–129; in traditional historiography, 140–141; and Marxian concept of man, 142. *See also* "Mentor" figure
Character in Western fiction: emphasis on, 106; "retreat from character," 106: as autonomous individual, 125; "illusion of freedom" of, 142
Character-author identification: in "romantic generation," 19, 21; applied to Ding Ling, 21–22, 35, 113–114; in Marxist criticism, 105–106
Chen Ming, 9, 13, 14
Chen Qixia, 12, 15
Culler, Jonathan, 64, 105

La Dame aux Camélias (Alexandre Dumas fils), 25, 43; *Camille* (film), 26
Dazhonghua (popularization), 73–74, 92, 93, 98–99
Detective story as genre, 123
Dewey, John, 4
Dialogue, 118
Diary form, 28, 30, 38; embedded in narrative in "A Suicide's Diary," 38–39; in "The Diary of Miss Sophie," 45, 46–47, 48–49, 50; as self-reflexive medium, 48, 50

191

HARVARD EAST ASIAN SERIES

79. *Russia and the Roots of the Chinese Revolution, 1896–1911*. Don C. Price.
80. *Toward Industrial Democracy: Management and Workers in Modern Japan.* Kunio Odaka.
81. *China's Republican Revolution: The Case of Kwangtung, 1895–1913*. Edward J. M. Rhoads.
82. *Politics and Policy in Traditional Korea*. James B. Palais.
83. *Folk Buddhist Religion: Dissenting Sects in Late Traditional China*. Daniel L. Overmyer.
84. *The Limits of Change: Essays on Conservative Alternatives in Republican China*. Ed. Charlotte Furth.
85. *Yenching University and Sino-Western Relations, 1916–1952*. Philip West.
86. *Japanese Marxist: A Portrait of Kawakami Hajime, 1876–1946*. Gail Lee Bernstein.
87. *China's Forty Millions: Minority Nationalities and National Integration in the People's Republic of China*. June Teufel Dreyer.
88. *Japanese Colonial Education in Taiwan, 1895–1945*. E. Patricia Tsurumi.
89. *Modern Chinese Literature in the May Fourth Era*. Ed. Merle Goldman.
90. *The Broken Wave: The Chinese Communist Peasant Movement, 1922–1928.* Roy Hofheinz, Jr.
91. *Passage to Power: K'ang-hsi and His Heir Apparent, 1661–1722*. Silas H. L. Wu.
92. *Chinese Communism and the Rise of Mao*. Benjamin I. Schwartz.
93. *China's Development Experience in Comparative Perspective*. Ed. Robert F. Dernberger.
94. *The Chinese Vernacular Story*. Patrick Hanan.
95. *Chinese Village Politics in the Malaysian State*. Judith Strauch.
96. *Chinese Elites and Political Change: Zhejiang Province in the Early Twentieth Century*. R. Keith Schoppa.
97. *Hideyoshi*. Mary Elizabeth Berry.
98. *Ding Ling's Fiction: Ideology and Narrative in Modern Chinese Literature.* Yi-tsi Mei Feuerwerker.

(Some of these titles may be out of print in a given year. Write to Harvard University Press for information and ordering.)